A Real Emotional Girl

A REAL EMOTIONAL GIRL

A Memoir of Love and Loss

TANYA CHERNOV

Skyhorse Publishing, Inc.

Disclaimer: This work is a memoir. It reflects the author's current recollection of her experiences over a period of years. Dialogue and events have been re-created from both written sources and the author's memory. In some cases, names have been changed to protect the innocent.

Skyhorse Publishing books may be purchased in bulk at special discounts for sales promotion, corporate gifts, fund-raising, or educational purposes. Special editions can also be created to specifications. For details, contact the Special Sales Department, Skyhorse Publishing, 307 West 36th Street, 11th Floor, New York, NY 10018 or info@skyhorsepublishing.com.

Skyhorse® and Skyhorse Publishing® are registered trademarks of Skyhorse Publishing, Inc.®, a Delaware corporation.

Visit our website at www.skyhorsepublishing.com.

10 9 8 7 6 5 4 3 2 1

Library of Congress Cataloging-in-Publication Data

Chernov, Tanya.
 A real emotional girl : a memoir about cancer, death, grief, and moving forward / Tanya Chernov.
    p. cm.
 ISBN 978-1-61608-869-9 (hardcover : alk. paper)
1. Chernov, Tanya. 2. Chernov, Tanya--Family. 3. Colon (Anatomy)--Cancer--Patients--United States--Family relationships. 4. Fathers--Death--Case studies. 5. Fathers and daughters--Case studies. 6. Grief--Case studies. 7. Adjustment (Psychology)--Case studies. I. Title.
 RC280.C6C475 2012
 616.99'4347--dc23
                        2012018659

Printed in the United States of America

For Dad, who saw the writer in me before I did.
And for my family, who remind me of him every day.

CONTENTS

"Dead has a smile like the nicest man you've never met . . ."

—E. E. CUMMINGS

Chapter 1

I WATCHED

I remember myself at sixteen, a thief. I'd taken my parents' house keys and given them to friends so they could party while my family was away for the summer. Even though I was living the kind of life— the kind of happy ignorance—that made being a teenager my only problem, I found rebellion an insatiably contagious endeavor. Of course I'd been caught and promptly banished to work at the all-girls' summer camp my parents owned in a blink-and-you'll-miss-it town in Northwestern Wisconsin. The camp provided an ideal backdrop for a picturesque life—the sun, the lake, the moon, and the stars— but it held no appeal to me. I couldn't resist throwing rocks into the calm family waters.

Not that long ago, I'd been a scrawny little ham who could not possibly get enough of the spotlight. With 300 kid-loving staff members and campers telling me how adorable I was and carrying me all over the place like some overgrown infant, it's a miracle I retained the ability to walk or perform simple tasks without the benefit of an audience. And at sixteen, stuck in the camp office, I found that I still craved the attention of spectators.

Through the tiny black squares of the window screen beside my desk, I watched a half-dozen campers gathering around the end of a Slip 'n Slide, unrolling it flat atop the grass before turning on the sprinklers and flooding the shiny plastic with the sun-warmed first bursts of hose water. Hand in hand, the girls flailed and squealed as they jettisoned themselves onto the bright, yellow strip before sliding onto the grass on either side of the sprinklers and coming back to the end of the line for more. Like everyone else on staff, I watched the campers closely, shifting my eyes over to the woods behind the tennis courts. We'd had a bear in camp the last few days and though it wasn't unusual to hear of bears in the area, we were all on alert.

Behind the Slip 'n Slide, a group of older campers rehearsed a dance for the upcoming evening program, constantly stopping and restarting the Backstreet Boys' "Quit Playin' Games (With My Heart)." I thought to myself, *I'm either going to burn every single copy of that damn song or pray to be struck by lightning.* I pulled the cap off my pen and began drawing a Seussian tree on the side of my shin, licking my thumb and smudging it against my skin to erase the parts I didn't like. Looking outside every few minutes to scan the tree line, I drank in the same halcyon scenes I'd witnessed all my life: smiling children shouting hellos to me through the windows as they passed and, in the distance, campers writing letters in the sun and tying string bracelets while rocking back and forth on swinging wooden benches.

Our camp was exactly what people expected—lots of land, a picturesque little lake, oxford-brown log cabins, silly games and activities, campfires. In my teenage mind, though, it was simply my summer home's backyard, overrun with a few hundred extra guests who wouldn't be leaving for another four or eight weeks. Camp was our own little city: food, transportation, sanitation, health care, entertainment, safety, and the welfare of about 300 people all rested on my family's shoulders for four months out of the year.

It was the summer before my senior year of high school, and all of my friends were 2,000 miles away in Arizona, where my family now lived during the off-season. August seemed an interminable expanse of time—every day unfolding just the same as the one before, with me cooped up in the office answering phones, sorting mail. Feeling and acting put-upon.

Pen gripped at an angle against the bony part of my ankle, I was working on the ink-spread of the roots down into the curve of my inner heel when the phone rang. Though I was sure I was alone in the building, I cleared my throat loudly enough for people in the upstairs office to hear me, just in case someone was up there. I answered on the third ring, immediately setting the phone on my shoulder and cocking my ear down to hold it in place so I could keep doodling.

"G'afternoon, this is Tanya," I answered in my sweetest phone voice, reaching for the spiral-bound message book on the other side of the L-shaped desk.

"Oh, hi there. This is Lucy Brenner's mom, Sheila. Is Richard in?" the woman on the other end asked sharply.

"No, I'm sorry, he's out on the water this afternoon, but I'd be happy to give him a message at dinner," I answered, knowing I likely wouldn't even get to talk to my father at dinner because he was always busy at mealtime. "Or is there anything I can help you with? I just saw Lucy this morning when she came in for a few envelopes, and I have to tell you, Mrs. Brenner—your daughter has excellent manners."

"Really?"

"Oh, yes," I said enthusiastically, finishing the well-rehearsed icebreaker I often liked to use with campers' parents. "She always remembers to say please and thank you—she's just really very sweet."

This wasn't untrue—Lucy *was* polite, especially compared to most kids. But I found that simple compliments like this one usually made a parent loosen up and get to the point of the call a little faster. Outside, I could see my own parents walking toward the office from the waterfront, each with a clipboard at the hip and overflowing key ring attached to either belt or shorts. Mom and Dad looked as if they were filling one another in on the details of whatever minor crisis they'd each just come from.

"Oh, well, thanks—I'm so glad to hear it!" Mrs. Brenner blurted in lightning-fast staccato beats. "Maybe I can ask you then—is Lucy having fun? Because I haven't seen a clear picture of her on the parents' private website for about a day and a half, and I just wanted to make sure that everything is okay."

"Hmmm. How about this—I can drop by Lucy's cabin after dinner and check in with her. And I'll make sure our videographer gets a few new pictures of her on the site today or tomorrow."

"Thanks, Tanya—that would be great. That would be a big help."

"It's really no trouble at all. You have a good day now. Thanks, mm-hmm. Take care." I hung up the phone, still scribbling out Mrs. Brenner's message about Lucy's picture on the message pad, before tearing off the thin white top sheet and sticking it in the mail tray near the stairs, knowing I'd just successfully saved my father from at least one tiny bit of the everyday needs he was expected to meet. Minimizing any unnecessary phone time for Dad was good, especially when it was something I knew I could easily handle. I leaned back against my chair and realized the phone call had probably been the first productive thing I'd done all day. Surveying the landscape outside my window, the frame encasing the outside world seemed to grow and stretch, closing me in. I was determined to hate everything around me, as teenagers are wont to do. And I was good at it.

With about an hour left before the dinner bell rang, the older campers—only a year or two younger than I—would soon be coming in to hang out. This was my favorite part of the day, interacting with the campers like my parents did, listening to their stories and songs, handing out Band-Aids, and answering silly questions. As the kids shuffled in, quickly crowding the office, I thought I saw a shadow move in the bushes behind the dining lodge, but when I stood to get a better look I saw nothing at all.

Kicking my heels back up onto the pine-green laminate surface of the desk, I wondered if my dad felt the same way around the campers—buoyed by their energy, constantly amused by their shenanigans, and awed by their tenderness. To those who didn't know him well, I'm sure it looked like all my father did was goof around with the campers every day, like some kind of real-life Peter Pan. But there was a strategy behind his play—a precise method and effort that went into the role my dad played for the kids, the staff, the entire camp community. My father *was* camp. His was the face on the brochures and in each year's reunion videos, and when camp was in session he was omnipresent—the object of so many people's sheer and complete adoration.

It was hard to remember how we'd ever managed to run the place in the days before walkie-talkies and golf carts, but Dad always made sure that no matter how it got done, everyone's needs were met. And somehow, the campers loved him more and more fiercely each year they returned to spend the summers with us.

* * *

After dinner, I went down to the council fire ring for the evening program with my two older brothers, Gabe and Dylan, who also worked for the family business during their college summer breaks. Though they'd already had several days' worth of time to tease me about the bold, foolish stunt I'd just gotten busted for, they still hadn't had enough fun taunting me the way only big brothers can. They closed in on either side of me and exchanged a few menacing smirks.

"So I heard it was Aunt Mickey who busted your boyfriend at the house with the keys, Tan," Dylan chided, glancing over at Gabe for a nod of approval. "I don't think I've ever seen Dad this pissed off." I kept my head down and walked faster, thinking they'd give up if I stayed quiet. But staying quiet to avoid conflict was never my best or most practiced skill.

"I'm sorry, but correct me if I'm wrong here. Weren't you grounded your entire senior year, Dylan? Because you got drunk and barfed in your own bed ten feet from Mom and Dad's room?" I snapped.

"Re-lax! Jeez," Dylan laughed. "We're just kidding. You still get away with murder and you know it. Quit being such a baby."

I stalked off to sit with some counselors, seething over how pleased they were with themselves for getting a reaction out of me. I knew I was only making an easy target of myself but couldn't, and didn't, care to do anything to counteract it.

The evening program ended about an hour later, after the entire camp had exhausted the traditional council fire itinerary of songs and skits they'd come to love so fiercely over the years. As the campers began dispersing in all directions to their cabins for the night, my father started walking back up to the lodge and I stayed behind to gather the tattered green songbooks strewn haphazardly around the small, grassy amphitheater.

"How's your day going, Tanya?" Dad shouted at me from the other side of the slope, hands in his pockets as he walked backward up the hill.

"Great!" I yelled back, sure that he'd caught the thick layer of sarcasm in my voice and instantly regretting it. I watched as he lumbered slowly along the gravel road, campers with dirty feet hanging off his arms and begging him to let them raid the soda machine before bed.

But halfway around the curve, I noticed Dad's gaze falling on a camper running toward the water in tears. My father stopped in his tracks, turned, and jogged down to the waterfront. Dylan's dog, a rambunctious but lovable mutt named Jimmy, had stolen a camper's teddy bear right out of her hands. He was trotting through the sandy beach with the stuffed toy in his mouth, heading for the lake. Sure enough, Jimmy strutted right into the water until he was chest-deep, then promptly dropped the bear neatly onto the surface of the water and turned around, leaving it in the middle of the swimming area. By the time Dad arrived on the scene, Jimmy was already sauntering off someplace else in search of his next adventure, leaving wet paw prints in the sandy road. The distraught little camper, probably just a

Lower Maple at seven or eight years old, was standing at the water's edge in a fit of tears, watching her beloved bear float farther out into the lake, slowly sinking as it drifted away.

I watched as my father walked straight into the lake without even removing his shoes, the water soon reaching his torso, and retrieved the soggy animal. The little girl ran to my father and threw her arms around him, clutching the dripping bear at her side. Together they walked up the road to my parents' house, his arm around her shoulders, so that he could wash and dry her stuffed animal before bedtime.

I caught up with my father and the little girl on the road. "Chocolate, vanilla, or mud-flavored ice cream?" Dad asked her as the three of us rounded the meander leading one way into Maple Village and the other way to my family's house.

"Um, just vanilla, please," she answered bashfully. I walked behind them, counting the seconds before my father would find a way to dissolve the camper's shyness into laughter.

"Do you like hot fudge or caramel sauce?" he asked once inside, while closing the fridge door so that it purposely caught on his shirt and pulled him forward with it to get another laugh out of the camper.

"Can I have both?"

"Of course you can! But don't tell Barbara—it's already nine o'clock."

"Don't tell me what?" my mother asked as she walked into the kitchen. "Do I see ice cream in those bowls so late at night, you two?" With a joking wag of her finger, my mom cracked a wide smile and stooped to kiss my father on the forehead before throwing a fleece jacket over one arm and walking out the back door.

My dad and the camper talked over their sundaes and laughed at Jimmy for being such a bully while I changed into a sweatshirt and long pants in the other room. It was still warm outside, but I hated getting attacked by mosquitoes—I hated it enough to sweat under long clothes if I had to. By the end of the night, my dad and the camper made an agreement to hold no ill will toward the dog but decided that the girl would leave her bear tucked safely inside her cabin for the rest of the summer—just in case. Dad and I walked her back to her cabin, each of us listening for the rustle of branches or the padding of paws in the trees around us.

* * *

As I drove down the long, dusty driveway into camp the following afternoon with the day's mail filling all three backseats in Mom's old white minivan, everything seemed disturbingly quiet. Though it was still Rest Hour, the after-lunch time when it was normal for most of the campers to be lounging in their cabins or getting dressed for their activities, I didn't see a single person outside, and that most certainly was not normal. I pulled up to the office and got out of the car, feeling uneasy in the silence. As I walked across the deck to the office, dragging a heavy canvas bag filled with letters, Dylan called to me from behind the lodge.

"That bear is back," he said when I got close enough for him to avoid shouting. He lifted his arm to his face and wiped his forehead with the sleeve of his T-shirt. "It went after Greg, but we scared it off with the Jeep. It's somewhere in the woods behind the dumpsters, we think."

Rounding the corner where my parents stood with a few staff members, I saw a man in faded jeans and a flannel sitting in one of our dining room chairs, eating a peanut butter and jelly sandwich. A very clean-looking shotgun leaned against his side, with its strap draped over the white plastic of the chair.

"'Course you know I would've rushed over here for you folks no matter where I was, but believe it or not," the man said to my father, "I was actually fishing a few lakes over and heard you guys on my CB radio. I wasn't even planning on coming into the office today, so it was lucky I could get over here right quick like this." He went back to eating his sandwich, as if it were all part of a day's work. As if things just worked this way in small towns.

I set the mailbag and keys down on a table in the back of the kitchen, the industrial ovens and fans humming behind me. We couldn't do anything but wait until the bear decided to come out of the woods again. My brothers chatted with the game warden, now sweating beneath the mid-afternoon sun, while my mother filled me in on what I'd missed.

While I was in town at the post office, Greg, one of camp's long-time staff members, radioed my father, sounding short of breath and somewhat annoyed.

"Richard, what's your twenty?" Greg asked, using the semi-serious mix of radio language we used at camp to communicate over our walkie-talkies. Greg was working on the ropes course forty-five feet up in the pine trees, tightening some knots and seeing to other routine maintenance.

"Office," Dad replied.

"I think you should get down here if you've got a minute," Greg said anxiously. "Our friend is back." There was a rustling kind of static after Greg finished speaking, as if he'd shoved his walkie-talkie in his pocket and started walking. However, Dad became sidetracked and, five minutes after the call, was still sitting at his desk when Greg radioed again.

"Uh, Richard. You *really* need to make your way over here." Hearing the strong note of worry in Greg's voice, Dad grabbed his keys and walked down the stairs toward the Trip House parking lot. Again, Greg's voice came over the radio hanging at my father's waist.

"*Now*, Richard! I need you here *now!*"

With Dylan in the passenger seat of his open-air CJ-5 Jeep, Dad hurried down the road leading to the water-ski point, sliding into the clearing of tall red pine trees where Greg was suspended on a small wooden platform forty-five feet up in the air. Inches below the platform, a female black bear swatted angrily at Greg while gripping the tree with her claws. At the edge of the clearing, two springtime cubs brayed and whined. Greg was shouting now, wildly swinging large, heavy steel cables down at the bear, trying to scare her back down the tree trunk. But she only inched farther toward him, snapping her jaws and growling—a sound more like a lion's roar than a bear's growl. Dad and Dylan yelled and banged on the metal hood of the car, sounding the horn and revving the Jeep's Mustang engine before ramming it up against the tree, all in an effort to scare her off—or at least distract her. The Jeep's horn eventually gave out during the chaos, fading and choking with the suspended pressure of Dad's hands. Finally, after what seemed to them like hours, the bear scooted down, then clumsily dropped to the ground and ran to place herself between the Jeep and her cubs.

When he had enough distance to make a run for it, Greg lowered himself down onto the hood of the Jeep, climbed into the car, and the three men sped off, sending radio orders to get all campers and staff indoors immediately. Though we'd placed calls to the department of natural resources, the sheriff's department, and the game warden's office, we were lucky that it had been Warden Swanson who'd arrived first to help. He was one of those through-and-through rural men who carried a gun like he was born with it in his hands and, if nothing else, knew how to aim and shoot to protect us. We were in good care because, like most of the local businesses and citizens, Warden Swanson often gave us special treatment and attention due to our long-standing congenial relationship with the community around us. But now, sitting with Swanson, there was nothing to do but wait. It was the bear that would have to make the next move.

I pulled a chair outside and sat next to Warden Swanson, resigned to kill time with everyone else. Only a few minutes later, though, my father took a couple quiet steps out toward the dumpsters and signaled for Swanson to follow him. I stood, too, but stayed right where I was, my feet frozen. With a great tumbling of noise—claws scraping against metal and that metal buckling and bending beneath her great weight—I saw the bear climb onto the large blue container and sniff her way up onto her hind legs, swaying side to side to scan our scents. When she reached her full height, she let out a snarling sort of cry and swatted at the air, looking like she might leap toward us at any second. In my periphery, I saw Warden Swanson raise the shotgun to his shoulder and aim. Before I could even shift my eyes from the bear to the gun, the warden pulled the trigger and the shotgun lurched into his arm with a snapping sound, thrusting his upper body backward against the weight of his back leg. The shot hit the bear in her shoulder, sending her back to one side as if she were being pulled down to the earth by some invisible force. Then another shot exploded into the bear, this one hitting her hard in the center of her woolly chest, throwing her to the ground.

I didn't breathe. No one said a word. The sound of the shot hung in the air around the buildings, eclipsing the hum of the kitchen behind me. Big gulps of tears rushed to my eyes and dropped on either side of my face as I moved my gaze to the ground, away from whatever was going to come next. I heard the bear lumber off into the bushes and tried to get my mom's attention, but she, too, was looking away.

"You boys got some work gloves nearby?" Warden Swanson broke the quiet. "And some rope?"

Twenty minutes passed, though, before my brothers followed the warden into the trees, holding their leather gloves and nylon climbing rope. Following smears of blood on leaves and branches, the bear's body was easy to find. Splayed out on her belly, limbs spread on either side of her, the bear had not traveled far before lying down to die. The men rolled her over and tied the rope around her neck, pulling her through the woods and onto a wide set of trails leading to the main road. My parents and I joined them there, helping to transport the dead bear up to the warden's truck parked on top of the hill near the highway.

Dad used a surgeon's knot to secure the bear carcass to the Jeep: one end around the lilting, limp neck and the other around the bumper.

"I need you to hop in the passenger seat, Tanya," Dad said. I looked up at him, horrified, not wanting to do anything of the sort after what I'd just witnessed. The image of the bear falling to the ground kept replaying in my mind, the sharpness of the sounds as the bullet left the gun still skipping over and over in my ears. "Can't one of the boys—"

"I'm sorry, honey. They need to help Warden Swanson fill out his report before he loads the bear into his truck. You have to turn around and make sure the bear stays tied on while I'm driving. I'm also going to need your help letting the kids know they can get back to their projects too."

I dropped my head down, feeling my nose start to burn and my eyes tear up again. Dad wrapped one arm around my shoulder and pulled me close to him, then kissed the top of my head. "You'll be fine—just keep your eyes on the bear."

My mouth shut and pressed against the clean leather of the passenger seat, I turned around. I shook with each bump up the rough and grassy road, cupping the seat's shoulder with my hands. I moved with the quick, small movements of a child leaning to see out the back. There were no windows, no roof, or even doors to dirty my view of this unnamable thing.

An older bear, we could see that her pair of springtime cubs had thinned her out, and she was now made porous by the warden's bullets. There was no breath, no blood, no food for the ticks left inside her as we all moved up the hill. She was limp in the gravel and grass as I shut my eyes against the sight of her behind us, as we made our way back up to the main road.

Just minutes earlier she was massive and bold, a beast straight out of a nightmare. The echo of her guttural cries still filled my ears. Now dead, the bear seemed vulnerable, as delicate as a hallelujah whispered across a field of summer grass. The rope was still tied tightly around her throat when we reached the top of the hill and climbed out of the Jeep. I studied the whole body of the bear: the claws, the fur, the teeth, the teats. I could think only of how small she seemed now—the size of a large dog, perhaps. I couldn't let myself look at the gunshot holes anymore; I'd seen enough. Gathered around the dead bear in a funereal circle, the men still talked, waiting to lift the body into the warden's truck as he backed it up into place. Finally letting my shoulders bounce in sobs, the panic I'd felt when the bear was shot brought itself up to the surface and overflowed. Mom held me against her and walked me off to the side of the road near the trees, where I could cry into her arms, away from the men and the bear. My mom and I, shedding our tears, tried to give the bear the only honor she'd received that day. That was my last day spent as a little girl; death punctured my view and leeched itself to my eyes.

Chapter 2

UPON WISHING FOR ROCKY MOUNTAIN SPOTTED FEVER

> *There are days we live*
> *as if death were nowhere*
> *in the background; from joy*
> *to joy to joy, from wing to wing,*
> *from blossom to blossom to*
> *impossible blossom, to sweet impossible blossom.*
> —LI-YOUNG LEE

The memory of the dead bear faded for everyone else within a week's worth of camp activities, and life resumed its normally harried summertime pace. But the bear wove herself into my dreams every night, and I couldn't keep myself from wondering how things might have turned out differently. The two cubs she'd been protecting had been safely trapped and relocated, and Warden Swanson told me they'd be fine, old enough to fend for themselves even though they seemed so tiny inside their metal cages. Every time the image of the bear, bouncing and rolling up the hill behind the Jeep, came into my mind, I pushed it back down and replaced it with whatever was in reach, most often trivial plans for my senior year. I let my brain fill completely with my desire for camp to hurry up and finish for the season so I could get back to my normal life at home. I repeated this process enough that I soon found it easier to forget the traumatic memories of that day.

While Dad and I unloaded the dishwasher together one afternoon, he paused our conversation about the prank he pulled at the previous night's staff meeting, cleared his throat, and told me that he would be driving into town the next day to have some tests done to check his colon.

"They're going to give me something called barium to drink tonight, to prep me for the procedure." He sounded nervous but kept stacking plates in the cupboard as if to distract me from being alarmed by the strange timing of these tests. "I have to drink all of it in order for—"

"I see," I butted in. "And do you have rashes accompanying the pain?"

"No, honey. No rashes. Not really any pain, either." Still, I knew exactly how to proceed.

"So how's your liver feeling?"

"Uh, it's good. Far as I can tell." He handed me two glasses, still wet from the rinse cycle. I dried them with a tea towel and ran through the list of diseases I had learned about in school. In my self-perceived expert opinion, even though he apparently had none of the typical symptoms, Rocky Mountain Spotted Fever seemed to fit the lab work prescribed. And despite being far from the areas where Rocky Mountain Spotted Fever usually occurred, I stood by my diagnosis.

"Dad, I wouldn't even bother going in to see Dr. Harrison tomorrow. I'm pretty sure I could just treat you myself." My dad magnanimously listened and intently nodded his head along with my observations, humoring my incredibly high opinion of my own worth as a "medical expert."

The way I saw it, my dad was healthier than he had ever been in his life—full of energy, eating well, working out, and keeping his weight down. But some age-appropriate, routine tests had come back a little suspicious after his last checkup and so now there were more tests to be had.

"We'll just check it out," he said. "Make sure everything is all right."

* * *

I'd been sentenced to working off my punishment just before the start of camp's second four-week session, and the morning the campers started rolling in I was put on duffel-duty, hating every minute of it. I stood off to the side of the giant circular lawn in the Trip House parking lot, watching the new campers as they stepped off the buses amid the chaos and excitement of their first day, and looked on in petty judgment of the girls who walked onto the dirt and grass in clean shoes, perfectly arranged hair, and makeup, still afraid of getting dirty. Already sweating from the effort of moving around so many overstuffed duffel bags, I rolled up the sleeves of my staff T-shirt and tucked them into the straps of my sports bra.

I watched the youngest ones as they spilled out onto the grass, wide-eyed and shy, and thought back to when I was that small. But, raucous little monster that I was, I had never been shy by any definition. Though camp was always my home, it had never been an easy life for me, and I had a hard time adjusting when we first started out. I didn't like having babysitters who watched over me when I was too young to be placed in a cabin, and I had never truly managed to be a "regular" camper as I got older—it simply wasn't possible for a director's kid to be considered normal, after all. And for a few years, I did have a nasty habit of strutting around camp, enthusiastically yet impotently "firing" anyone who looked at me the wrong way. Or so I've been told.

Even now—especially now—I struggled with how fiercely I both loved and hated our camp, my feelings often alternating back and forth in the space of a single day. I was roasting in the humid afternoon heat, dragging a large black duffel through the dusty lot and trying my best to ignore all the laughter and cheering all around me. Checking the large luggage tag against the cabin list, I drew a big blue "7" on the bag's flap before hoisting it up and throwing it on top of all the other "7" bags and trunks. I walked back to the luggage-filled U-Haul and grabbed another bag, pulling it across the floor of the truck by the long shoulder strap, letting it fall to rest on my back. Standing at just five-foot-one, I was so weighted down by the bag that it sagged nearly to the ground as I clamped my jaw together and clumsily speed-walked over to the sorted piles, finally stopping, out of breath, the muscles in my shoulders screaming with the strain. Right now it was pretty clear which way I was leaning in my feelings toward camp, and it definitely wasn't love.

More than anything, I just wanted the summer to be over so I could go back to our house in Tucson. When camp wasn't in session, I never had to do manual labor as punishment—why couldn't my parents just ground me like normal people, like they did at home? Things were always different here, when we were working, keeping the business going. I knew my parents didn't have the extra time or energy to deal with my defiant teenage behavior the way they did during the off-season, but that didn't stop me from testing the limits, and their patience, at camp.

Because the summer months were so demanding, we'd always compartmentalized and shifted our lives between our two seasons: Camp and Winter. When I was younger and still adjusting to the unique camp director's lifestyle, I often felt tossed around between our two homes with two sets of dishes, pots and pans, furniture, vehicles, bedrooms, toasters, and friends to keep track of. As soon as school let out each spring, we'd pack up a summer's worth of tube socks and shorts, sleeping bags, ratty sneakers, and the office equipment we'd transfer back and forth from our respective homes.

My brothers were old enough at the time to have long since stopped vying for the attention of our parents, but I didn't yet have a handle on the difference between when my mom and dad were parenting me and when they were parenting the other little girls; I loathed it. Through the years, our house was constantly open to everyone, our family and our privacy on display for public consumption. Even my current punishment was taking place in front of the camp audience, and I felt everyone's eyes on me as I hauled, dragged, pouted, and sulked my way through the day.

Imagine life inside a fishbowl. Now turn that picture over in your mind and amplify it by the power of a child's wild imagination until you can picture a lonely little goldfish swimming behind the glass of an ocean-size aquarium. Directing a summer camp is much the same: Everyone watches you feed, exercise, and emote while you can neither escape nor hide. Privacy takes the backseat, allowing the emotional security and trust of the campers to move ahead and ride shotgun during the summer months.

Even now, as a teenager—nearly an adult—I still railed against the community atmosphere my parents worked so hard to create and that so often spilled over into our nuclear family life. Just a few days before, I woke up in the morning and headed to the bathroom in my parents' house, only to find a minefield of campers in sleeping bags on the floor between the toilet and me. I had to navigate around their padded little bodies, strewn willy-nilly across the carpet, and nearly peed my pants with the dance-like effort.

Physically sharing my parents' attention with so many other children each summer was one thing, but sharing them emotionally was something else altogether. All I wanted was attention from my mother and father—there were times I wanted to talk to them without having 200 little girls at my heels, waiting for their turn to get the emotional support and unconditional love I so badly wanted all to myself.

Though I knew I could be a huge help on days like this when my parents would likely be working well past midnight to make sure everyone was comfortable in their new cabins, I fixed my mind on maintaining the sourest face I could muster. They could make me work, but they couldn't make me put a smile on my face while I did it.

Long after all the bags had been sorted, hauled, and delivered, I was free for the rest of the night, as long as I helped my mom by folding the huge piles of laundry she hadn't had time to attend to in our house. I folded for hours in front of the TV, folding my own clothes, my mother's and my father's, mixed in with random camper clothing—shorts that had fallen in the lake, a T-shirt splattered with French dressing, a sweatshirt or two. I organized the piles and set them on the dining room table for my mom to distribute in the morning and stretched out on the couch. As I lay there watching boring summer TV, I knew if I let myself admit it, that I was too old to be so jealous of the campers. And I was resentful—resentful that whatever cry for help my recent bad behavior had tried to convey, I didn't think I'd been heard at all.

Chapter 3

His Real Home

I quickly pushed my father's tests to the back of my mind, successfully convincing myself that he'd be fine—even hoping that he'd be distracted enough to forget some of the mistakes I'd made that summer. Wrapped up in my own teenage drama, I could think only of my own discomfort as I struggled to regain his trust, desperately hoping that he would forgive me for so recklessly giving away our house keys to my friends so they'd have somewhere to hang out. And to my parents' credit, they had forgiven me in a small part enough to let my three best girlfriends visit me at camp for a week. My friends' presence was a welcome distraction from my punishment, the bear, and the uncertainty of my father's health.

Not wanting to be at camp any more than I had to, I took my friends down to Milwaukee, about five hours from camp, to show them around my hometown. My family and I lived in Milwaukee until I was fourteen, and I loved visiting whenever I could. While the four of us idly shopped and gossiped around the city, my father's doctors discovered a malignant tumor in his colon.

Because I wasn't with my father when he received the news of his diagnosis, I don't know how he reacted. I don't know if he felt like crying or screaming; if he was hopeful in those first few moments; or if he already felt his life pulling away from him. I do remember the confusion and cold, hard shock I experienced upon hearing the news. I remember my mom driving all the way down to Milwaukee unplanned and unannounced, pulling me into a tucked-away bedroom at a family friend's house, and sitting me down to talk: the California King-size bed supporting our weight, carpet beige and bumpy, closet-door mirrors mocking our reflections as we watched ourselves shrink beneath the weight of the conversation. As my mom spoke, I took in the logistics of when the surgery was scheduled and to whom I could or could not talk about it. We'd be driving back up to camp that evening, sending my friends home, and making arrangements for Dad's surgery within the day.

I didn't cry out or ask any questions at the time. I didn't show any emotion at all. I was not hopeful or scared. I waited for the tears to come, waited for the reflection of my own face in the mirror to scrunch and frown before exploding in the kind of dramatic display I felt the occasion deserved. But, like my steely exterior inside, I also felt still, quiet. I just assumed he would be fine. It would all work out, and in the end, we'd have a story to tell—all of us together.

I refused to let myself consider the cancer. In those days that blurred together in the usual miasma of monotony and responsibility, I hadn't even thought or spoken the word aloud until the diagnosis prevented my family and me from thinking about anything else. As we marched blindly through the following days, unobservant and numb, my dad saw the clouds thundering in; he saw reality flashing in blaring strobe lights every time he closed his eyes. But he never let it show.

* * *

My dad's initial diagnosis took place precisely in the middle of our busiest months, and it quickly became a critical time both for my family and for the camp. Our primary concern was, of course, for my father's health, but we also had an obligation to protect the well-being of the campers, who were expecting to spend several more weeks with us. Knowing this, we decided not to share my father's diagnosis with our extended camp family. We didn't want the kids—or their parents—to be troubled by the news. But we knew it was going to be hard to keep something like this a secret and so, one evening, my father sat the whole family down to discuss the dilemma.

"People entrust their kids to me personally, and I relish that role and responsibility," he said. "The last thing in the world I'd want to do is bring sadness to their lives at a time when they should be carefree and blissful. So what I've decided is to protect the kids— who are *my* kids in the summer—in the best way I know how."

Camp had always been Dad's sanctuary, and the thought of tainting it with his illness was impossible for him to even consider. When my father was a little boy, he used to count down the days till his departure for camp each summer. He even used to tell my grandma that camp was his *real* home, but that he would let her keep him for a few months out of the year. But this was not just his home now; it was home for the campers and staff. And anticipating that as soon as the camp community at large heard the word "cancer" they would surely assume the worst, he ultimately made the choice to keep his illness private.

When these young girls stepped away from their schools, families, lessons, and the stresses that accompanied those factions of life, my parents tried to take the opportunity to teach them the fine arts of getting dirty, acting goofy, and eating with no hands just for the sake of having a little fun. Along the way, the daily projects, evening programs, camp rules, and Sunday-morning services worked to instill in them camp's crucial core values. My parents worked endlessly to create a fun atmosphere, and by most measures they succeeded, but this wasn't enough for my father. He worried about the children and wanted to make sure we could do more at camp than just have fun.

My father's dream was to build this sanctuary into the kind of place where shy and awkward young girls could become strong, healthy, emotionally intelligent women. It made him so happy to help children through some of the most challenging, most vulnerable times of their young lives; it was his gift. And what made Dad happy had the effect of giving him a certain glow—one that radiated outward from him and made the rest of us feel like the world was nearly flawless because of it.

The moment he'd had the opportunity to buy his own camp and live out his dream of working with kids in the outdoors, my father left his successful law practice to begin creating the home he'd envisioned: where each camper learned to appreciate the beauty of nature, the bonds of lifelong friendships, and the value in a good game of mud football. And since the age of three, this dream camp had been my home too. I was as bound to the responsibilities of keeping that dream alive as my parents were, whatever might come down the road in our personal lives.

Naturally, keeping the cancer a secret was difficult, and it felt incredibly awkward to hide something this life-altering from the people around us whom I'd grown to love over the years. But it wasn't just about me anymore, and it wasn't even just about Dad. Whatever my own feelings, I realized how heavy the responsibilities were that came with being a camp director; no matter how hard it was for us, my dad was acting in the best interest of the campers. I respected him for this and found it strangely comforting.

* * *

In the weeks that followed, I tried to be more helpful, not wanting my parents to carry so much of the load alone. Amid the usual chaos of camp's everyday activities, my parents hurried to locate gastrointestinal surgeons and handle insurance paperwork. All the planning and research, however, needed to be accomplished quickly and quietly so as not to interrupt the well-balanced flow of the daily routine. Our longtime assistant director, Michelle, stepped up to fill in the gaps once we informed her of the diagnosis, allowing my parents some small corner of space in which to put all the hurried plans in place. With Michelle, the rest of camp's administrative team—a core group of staff members who had worked in the industry for many years—often endured seventeen-hour workdays without taking more than one or two days off all summer. For the three months of the season, everyone needed to be prepared for all the major and minor emergencies that could pop up at any time. Turning away a homesick camper or exhausted counselor simply wasn't an option, no matter how we felt or what we were going through as a family.

Chapter 4

IT'S FINE

On the day we planned to make the five-hour drive down to Milwaukee for the tumor resection, my dad went down to the waterskiing dock and put on a life jacket before slipping his right foot into the wet rubber sleeve of a slalom water ski. He yelled, "Hit it!" to Caleb, camp's longtime waterfront director, who sat in a speedboat with his torso twisted to see my father behind the boat. With the *rurr* of the boat's motor and its subsequent forward momentum, my dad threw out a coil of slack in the rope, pulled the ski rope's handle into his chest, and slid his left foot into the pocket behind his right, performing a perfectly executed shallow-water start one final time.

I watched Dad carve artful, tidy slalom turns across the glassy surface of the lake—our lake—and pictured a million other days just like this one. I remembered the day Dad drove the boat for me, instructing me on how to get up on one ski. I tried over and over again, failing each time, until the sun set. Dad never lost his patience, though, and just when there was almost no light left, I managed to stay upright on the slalom ski for a few hundred feet—enough to say I'd done it, but just barely. On the way home, Dad wrapped me in a giant towel and listed all the other things I was good at, making me forget all about the frustration of not having inherited my father's undeniable skill with water sports the way my brothers had.

* * *

A few hours after his final shallow-water start, Dad held the attention of the entire camp at afternoon announcements. He let the girls who wished to make an announcement line up first, grabbing the microphone with tie-dyed hands, bracelets made in the craft shop dangling around the metal mesh of the mouthpiece.

"I lost a white sock with my name on it. If you find it, can you please bring it to cabin M-2?"

"I found a boom box by the archery shed—if it's yours, come to L-5."

"Big applause for my sister, Emily, who made it to the top of the climbing wall today."

When everyone went back to their seats and the usual chatter filled the room, my father stood before his audience, just as he had done so many thousands of times. He looked into the crowd of eager faces, each one expecting the usual slew of horseback riding instructions told with dragging syllables and high-pitched, radio-personality intonations. So many of the sacred camp traditions still upheld today originated in this way: My father's grandiose personality could not help but seep out through his dialects, sillier-than-silly jokes, and exaggerated mannerisms. Just as he held my attention during bedtime stories and long family road trips, so too did he captivate the campers after every meal in the lodge.

But there were no reminders to "slip, slap, and slop" sunscreen that day. Instead, he used his own sturdy, deep voice to succinctly explain that he would be having a minor, routine procedure, which we later explained away as a case of diverticulitis (a digestive disease commonly found in the large intestine). He stood in his shorts and T-shirt, ubiquitous metal clipboard held at his side. He told the kids that it was no big deal and that he would be back in a week. My mom put her arm around my side as we watched from the back of the cavernous and crowded dining hall. Not knowing if she did this more for her own comfort or for mine, I hugged her back, snuggling into her arm. As the faces of those sitting near us turned in our direction for signs of how to take this news, we did as we needed to do. We smiled and nodded, mouthing the words, *It's fine.*

Camp was more than my father's livelihood; it was his lifeblood, and he had never left the property when camp was in session for even one day. I could see from where I stood with my mom, even with my unlearned teenage eyes, that the possibility of being away for a week—or two weeks, or forever—was draining him of energy and confidence as he continued to speak. The moment his announcements were finished and the campers ran off to open the letters and care packages that were delivered after lunch, my dad headed back to the office. There, we had a car packed and waiting, the engine left running. He stood on the deck of the office and hugged a few close friends and staff members, people who by now were confused by my father's splotchy cheeks and glassy eyes, especially since he was only going for what was supposedly a routine procedure.

We'll never know for sure how many people at camp figured out that something was actually wrong—I'm sure rumors and assumptions were passed around among the adults, and perhaps some insightful people were able to guess on their own that things were, in fact, not fine with my father. Thankfully, those who did pick up on the subtle emotive clues my family could not help but emit were respectful enough to keep it to themselves. Regardless of who may or may not have known the truth, camp made things infinitely more complicated for our family, and deep down I knew it would most likely only get worse.

I watched from inside the minivan, not wanting to join in on any of the hugging or crying. It was the first time I'd seen Dad cry since his diagnosis, and I was confused by his choice to do it in front of Caleb, Greg, Tim, and Michelle—the people who would now be the stewards of the camp in his absence. I couldn't understand why Dad was so upset if everything was going to be okay. Everyone kept telling me that Dad would be fine—fine enough for us to keep the whole thing to ourselves. So what was all the fuss about? Even though I was nervous about the surgery, I had convinced myself that Dad's tears and nerves were more in reaction to having to leave camp than to having a major operation the next day. I was good at talking myself into focusing only on what was more pleasant to think about and allowing myself to feel excited about spending some time together as a family away from camp, pushing aside the painful knowledge of the circumstances under which we were leaving.

My parents walked slowly, arm in arm, toward the car where my brothers and I were waiting, anxious to get on the road without too much more upheaval. The pace at which my father moved should have been a signal to me that he was not fine—that he was not fearless. But I didn't get it yet. I could feel only my impatience to get out of there. And with that, off we drove up the long, dusty driveway toward the county highway.

Chapter 5

INTO THE JAWS OF
THE WHALE

Already sheathed in shiny coils of plastic IV tubes and layers of thick, white medical tape in the pre-dawn moments before his surgery, Dad struggled to sit up on the gurney. Every time he moved, the tape pulled at the hair on his arms and he winced, silently trying to loosen its grip on his skin. The five of us passed through the doorway of his room and out into the hallway, escorting him with the two nurses who would be assisting in the operating room. He lifted the IV tubes and rubber monitor cords over his head, and then back again, trying to untangle himself enough to turn or move on the stretcher. Finally managing to prop himself up on one elbow, he waved at the nurses and doctors who moved around us in uniformed flocks: clumps of white lab coats and clipboards, floral-pattern scrubs, blank expressions. Dad knew they would ignore him and shifted his attention to smiling at the patients looking back from their rooms, curious about the booming voice moving through the hallway.

"Well, hello there," my dad said jovially to a woman smiling at him from her room. "You look marvelous!"

"Do you know that lady?" I asked embarrassed, already knowing the answer.

"Nope," my father replied. "She just seemed like a nice gal in need of a compliment." Now inside the patient elevator, Dad stretched a smile across his lips, but I could see a tremble at the corners of his mouth, a slight jitter in his eyes that I wondered if my mom also noticed. The elevator doors opened before us in retracting folds like the jaws of a whale. I'd never seen my father frightened before and wondered if this was what it looked like.

The surgical floor expanded in front of us. I had to speed-walk to keep up with the orderly who wheeled Dad down the long hospital corridors, wondering if he'd get in trouble should we take too long to get there; the walk seemed to last forever. Mom held Dad's hand and jogged every other step to keep up, while my two older brothers and I followed behind. Then Dad turned his attention to the young orderly who walked behind his gurney, carefully pushing and steering him through the long hallways.

"Now, you look like you've had a long day," Dad said. I looked over, expecting the orderly's face to immediately soften, but he wasn't going to be won over easily. My dad persisted: "How about we trade places and I'll give you a ride on the stretcher for a while?" I'd seen that smile on my dad's face before—it was the one that he used when he was still testing out someone's sense of humor. We all looked at the young man, who hadn't yet cracked even a half-smile. Instead, the orderly exhaled a quiet groan and blinked heavily a few times. We rounded the final corner.

"I'm gonna need you to remain on the gurney, sir. It's hospital policy. Please."

We walked the rest of the way in silence. Not even Dad's nervous humor could break the tension and fear floating in the air around us.

When we reached the double doors leading to the operating room, my brothers and I wished our father luck, choking down a bitter cocktail of hope and ignorance, fear lining the rim of the glass. I began haunting myself with an imagined version of my father's thoughts as he lay on that stiff metal bed, being wheeled into a surgery that would determine his fate.

We kissed our father one more time and stepped away. My mom moved forward and climbed up onto the stretcher beside him. Dad's face brightened and then relaxed as he looked at her, the corners of his mouth now relaxing as they talked. She cupped his face in her hands, the fuzz of his beard poking through her fingers. They snuggled into each other on the rough, white hospital sheets and moved their faces forward until they pressed closely together. They whispered for a few minutes and soon they were crying, giving each other small, tender kisses over and over, quietly giggling while the three of us looked on. I stood back between my brothers and watched our parents as they lingered in a moment no one else could ever touch. In that instant, I began to see beyond my personal realm, realizing for the first time as an adult that my parents were still completely in love after almost thirty years of marriage. And I wasn't grossed out or even surprised.

I felt as if I were watching the scene from far away, the three of us kids standing off to the side while my parents huddled together in the hallway. All the kisses, hugs, and inside jokes they had shared throughout my life came rushing to the forefront of my mind as something more important than a mere background to my own experiences. For the first time, I found myself seeing my parents as two people, two adults who were more than just the woman and man who filled the roles of "Mom" and "Dad." They were their own personalities, with individual histories of their own and a history together, and they were still obviously smitten with each other.

I stepped back against the white hospital wall and smiled at them—smiled to combat the fear and the uncertainty of the day, letting it all blow through me. There, in the place where my dad was wheeled in one direction while the rest of us were forced to walk in another, existed the exceptional dynamic of my parents' marriage: the love that would carry us all through the upcoming years.

Though the hallway still teemed with activity after my father was taken into surgery, the blank whiteness of the walls and floor made everything seem empty. Some patients left the doors to their rooms open, so that as I walked past I could peek inside, eager to see how other daughters looked and behaved as they cared for their ill parents. But no one ever looked back at me, as if the doorways created some impermeable seal of invisible privacy. Or maybe they'd been in there long enough that they stopped caring who could see in. Walking back to the waiting room with the omnipresent whiteness of the walls filling my eyes, I felt bits of myself dragging behind, staying with Dad, staying in the hallways, not wanting to move forward with the rest of my body. My brothers walked briskly on ahead, and I eventually ran to catch up, forgetting the pieces of myself I'd left behind.

* * *

"Dad was in rare form just now, wasn't he?" I asked my mom, looking down but still smiling.

"Isn't it just like him to joke around until the last possible minute?" she asked back. My father rarely encountered a situation that couldn't be improved by some of his trademark humor. Making the long walk back to the waiting room, I comforted myself with memories of his best routines. It made me feel better to block out the image of him in a hospital gown, covered with plastic tubes, by digging up my best memories of him being a complete and excellent dork.

Rounding the corner to the waiting room, I remembered one of Dad's classic stories. We often hosted a special "family camp" week after the regular season ended. The family members of a few campers, as well as many of our own family and friends, would join us for a few days of biking, water-skiing, climbing, campfires, and happy-hour lounging. Each family stayed in one of the bathroom-less cabins and used whichever of the three washhouses was nearest to them. To accommodate the coed environment, we used signs to indicate whether the toilets and showers were currently being used by men or by women.

At family camp one August many years ago, my dad's good friend Rory walked into the washhouse just as my dad was walking out. They said hello, chatted a moment, and then Rory made sure the sign had been flipped to the MEN side before proceeding to take a shower. Seeing a camper's mom approach the washhouse wrapped in a towel and holding a bucket filled with toiletries, my dad took the opportunity to quickly flip the sign back over so that it read WOMEN. He snickered from a distance as he watched the hilarity that was about to ensue. Sure enough, the woman walked right in, saw Rory fully naked, and let out a yell so loud that Dad insisted people heard her all the way down the road to the other end of camp. Tickled by his own good-natured trickery, my dad walked away laughing and went about his business.

Even into his fifties, my dad got a kick out of the most juvenile and ridiculous pranks. Perhaps his most commonly used practical joke was the classic "short-sheeted bed." To accomplish this, my dad would tuck the top end of a flat sheet into the head of the bed so that it appeared to be the fitted sheet. Then, picking up the bottom corners of the flat sheet, he folded it up and over itself, so that the bottom edge gave the illusion of a perfectly made bed. Dad loved this one and used it on us every chance he got. When my brothers and I were teenagers, arriving back home just in time for curfew and crawling into bed, our feet would stop short, blocked halfway down the bed by the crease of the folded sheet. We'd roll our eyes, get up, remake the bed, and go to sleep grumbling.

Even halfway around the world during a trip to Fiji with a girlfriend, Gabe could not escape our father's mischievous reach. Dad called the hotel where he knew my brother was staying and spent a hell of a long time and an exorbitant amount of money on long-distance fees trying to convince the hotel staff to help him carry out a short-sheet situation. After a long, arduous span of time trying to get through the language barrier, my dad eventually got the hotel staff to understand not only how a person could short-sheet a bed, but *why*. Dad didn't even need to witness the effects of his tomfoolery; he was satisfied simply knowing he'd brought some silliness into our days, no matter how far away we were.

* * *

Everyone was hopeful while we waited in Dad's hospital room as three, four, then five hours passed, knowing that the nurses would soon be bringing him in from recovery. Friends and family members shuffled in and out with food and flowers; I smiled back and thanked them, but inside I felt no attachment at all. I was surprised at how often I'd felt the absence of emotion in the last few weeks—even though I knew my life was going to be very different from now on, even when I found out that my father's test results had proved what my family feared, what we denied, what Dad knew might be coming.

All the doctors reassured us that the cancer was detected early enough and that all signs pointed to the likelihood of a full recovery. They knew only that the cancer had metastasized to one of five lymph nodes but that treatment options looked good, and we had plenty of reasons to be hopeful. In the surgical waiting room, they repeated the same encouraging platitudes and then moved on to their next cases.

I trusted the doctors, letting their well-rehearsed smiles tuck my anxiety away from the surface while we waited for Dad to be brought in from recovery. Moments later, when they brought Dad through the double doors and down the hall, and I saw him lying so still and so pale, I felt my stomach clench up into a tight fist, lodging itself below my ribs like a rock stuck in the fork of a tree trunk. My hands shook more violently the closer Dad came, and I shrunk back into a corner of the room to wait. As a trio of nurses navigated the portable bed into the room, I could see that Dad's skin was moist and had paled into a greenish-gray. His beard looked oily and flat. He was still unconscious, mouth hanging open, his body laced in tubes and gauze.

I dropped into a chair, my body sinking down as if all my bones had instantaneously disappeared, leaving me limp and formless. I stared at the gleaming silver rails on the gurney to keep my eyes from moving up to Dad's face. He'd left us at the double doors as my strong, funny, confident father and had come back a cancer patient. I wanted to say his name, loud enough to wake him up, but was afraid what would happen if I tried. Mom immediately reached for his hand and bent down to kiss him. She had tracks of tears on her cheeks, but she seemed happy—pleased, almost.

I looked at Gabe, sitting hunched over himself in the corner with his arms crossed and one leg tucked under the other. He, too, was staring at Dad on the stretcher, but he didn't appear as upset as I felt. He cracked his knuckles and looked out the window as the nurses settled Dad into the room. I wanted to say something to break the overbearing silence in the room, but when I opened my mouth to speak, I couldn't think of anything to say that didn't seem stupid. I kept opening my lips to try again, and finally whispered "I . . ." with the uncertainty of voice one has trying to speak for the first time after waking from a too-long nap. But no one heard my inaudible attempt, and I gave up trying.

I looked at Dylan, now standing in the doorway so that his body blocked most of the light coming in from the hall. When he met my gaze, he stepped forward and shut the door behind him. Tears welled up in my eyes and poured down while I stood in the blank hospital room, the fluorescent lighting's artificial brightness glistening on the sterile, squeaky floors. Trying to keep myself together only made it harder to push the sobs back in. I'd never seen Dad sick before, never seen him with his eyes closed in anything other than sleep.

Usually Dad had more energy than all of us combined; just three days earlier, I'd wanted to sit down and relax but Dad had forced me to go sailing with him. I hated sailing with Dad because I almost never stayed in the boat for the duration of the trip. On one of our dinky little Sunfish sailboats, I started to panic when we actually got a gust of wind and moved quickly across the water, yelling at him to give the sail some slack and slow us down. Dad loved the speed but slowed our pace enough to calm me down so we could start moving again.

"See?" he shouted, the wind whipping in our ears. "This isn't so bad, right?"

"Yeah, okay," I shouted back, still gripping the sides of the boat with my fingers as if someone were trying to pull me overboard. "I mean, I know the lake is only like fourteen feet deep and it's not like I've never tipped before—" And just when I actually did start to feel comfortable enough to lift my head up and look around, Dad got an idea.

"Oh, good. Then you won't mind . . . if I do this!" In a flash, Dad put both his hands on my shoulders and pushed me right over the edge of the little boat, with his mouth open in laughter as he did it. My legs popped up over my head and before I could process what had happened, I was flipped upside down and into the water, tumbling to the surface, wiping my eyes, and moving aside my wet hair, now plastered to my bewildered face. He came about, ducking gracefully under the boom in one fluid motion, then circled back around to pick me up, laughing and slapping his knee. As I waited in the water, bobbing up and down, I planned an angry speech in my head and was ready to deliver it with great gusto as soon as I was back in the boat. But when Dad turned about and lifted me into the little Sunfish with ease, though I was now a fully grown teenager, I felt my resolve dripping off me and into the bottom of the boat at the sight of his mischievous smile. He kissed my forehead and handed me the mainsheet line. I couldn't remember the powerful opening line of my rant and before I could begin, he said, "All right now, take us on home." He handed me the rudder handle, and then leaned back and let the sun soak his face, confident in my ability to sail us to shore.

And now, in the dimness cast by the bar of light above his hospital bed, Dad could barely open his eyes when we called his name. I wasn't used to seeing him lie still for so long, and after the nurses left us alone I kept waiting for him to pop open his eyes and make a joke. Hours passed before he woke up fully enough to smile at us and mumble a few groggy words.

After a few days, Dad was able to sit up and walk around a little, his incision healing well. Even though he was given full meals with meat and veggies, Dad couldn't tolerate these foods after such major gastrointestinal surgery and preferred to stick to Popsicles. With him joking around and constantly asking for a new Popsicle, we comforted ourselves in the confidence that his cancer was gone and things would slowly return to normal.

During the afternoon rounds when Dad's doctor, our old family friend, Dr. Ansfield, was checking Dad's charts, I could tell my father was getting too anxious in the stuffy hospital room to keep quiet much longer. He fidgeted with his IV tubes and crossed and uncrossed his ankles several times. While the rest of us read our books or flipped through the public access channels on TV, it seemed as if each passing second became more unbearable for my father. It was challenging to keep Dad entertained enough to stay put and rest, and we were each starting to feel worn out by the effort. Finally, Dad couldn't resist speaking up.

"So, Jim, how about springing me outta here this afternoon?"

Dr. Ansfield didn't even honor the request by looking up from his paperwork, but my father kept trying anyhow. "Come on now, old man. Wouldn't it be fun to put me on a stretcher and sneak me out through the back door?"

Dylan and I glared at our father, angry at him for even suggesting getting back on the stretcher. It had only been a few days since he'd had no choice but to be laid out on a gurney; the joke hit just a little too close to home.

"Dad, cut it out," Dylan said with a crooked half-smile.

"Yeah, Dad. I'm sure he has other patients to see today," I added, wanting my father to stay put to make sure he was actually going to be all right. Mom and Gabe had returned to camp already and, with Dylan and me watching over him, Dad could finally relax knowing that things were well on all fronts. Besides, it was nice spending time together, even if we were cooped up in a hospital room.

"You know, Richard," Dr. Ansfield finally took off his glasses and rubbed his brow before crossing his arms on his chest and looking straight into my father's eyes. "I'm awfully tempted to let you leave ahead of schedule just to get you out of my hair—"

"All right, then it's settled. Saddle up, kids!" Dad interrupted.

"—but it's still a little too soon." Dr. Ansfield fought back a smile, walked over to my father, and rested both hands on his shoulders. "We do need to wait until all your systems return to normal. I promise—a few more days and you'll be right as rain."

And the doctor was right. Soon enough, we were helping Dad into the minivan, the taillights glinting in the late-afternoon sunlight. We were on our way home.

Chapter 6

BY ALL RIGHTS

After Dad's surgery and the rare mid-camp dose of city life, we headed back to Minong. In the car, my father seemed normal—like my daddy again. The worst was behind us. We were sure of it.

His incisions were healing well; he had a ton of energy and even more eagerness to get back to his duties at camp. He'd missed enough of the crucial mid-season days and wasn't going to let his doctors keep him away from the kids any longer. But apparently whatever lesson was meant for him, for all of us, hadn't been learned yet.

Just a few days after returning to camp, Dad started to feel as if something was wrong. Instead of gradually working toward eating and holding down normal foods, he was still unable to eat anything other than his grape Popsicles. When he did try to eat soup or oatmeal, he would almost immediately throw up, hunching over from the pain in his abdomen. Too ill to hug the campers one last time as the buses took them away for the off-season, he was forced to say his goodbyes from inside our house. Not wanting the girls to see the reality of his condition, he gave them his love and well wishes through the bathroom window at the front of the house. I watched him lean his pale face over the top of the window lock, slide it over, and try to push the glass up. Weak and exhausted, he needed my mom's help to get it all the way open so he could hear the campers crying, asking him to please come out onto the lawn and give them the great bear hugs for which he was so well-known. I wanted the girls to hurry up and leave and forced Gabe to help some counselors gently guide each camper back up toward the buses. I didn't care that they were sad, didn't care that they felt like they were being cheated out of a hug or an "I love you" from my dad. Whatever he had left to give was mine, not theirs.

"Dad, this is crazy," Dylan said. "Let's just go now. We can put sheets up in the van windows, and they'll never even know what's going on."

"It can wait another hour if I just rest a minute. I don't want the kids to know that I'm going back to the hospital—not as their last memory from the summer."

"Are you serious?" I asked, growing angrier with each passing minute. "What if something is really wrong and waiting here makes it worse?"

"No, honey." Dad lowered himself back onto the couch by holding onto Dylan's arms, wincing when his weight shifted backward into the cushions. "Better to wait until they're all gone. Gabe can finish getting them on the buses and then we'll go."

I couldn't understand his decision, but neither could I carry him into the car against his will. We'd have to wait until he was ready. The minute the last camper left, we half-carried Dad to the van waiting in the driveway. We turned onto highway 53 North and headed toward Duluth, Minnesota, the closest city to camp at about an hour's drive. Although he was packed tightly into the minivan with pillows and blankets cushioning his body, each bump and shake of the road seemed to tear his belly apart. He winced and heaved, no longer joking around or talking about the campers who had just left. Dylan chewed on his fingernails at the wheel, something I hadn't seen him do in years. He kept looking back in the rearview mirror, apologizing after each pothole.

At St. Luke's Hospital in Duluth, we learned that Dad had a bowel obstruction caused by adhesions that had formed post-op.

My father's doctors first recommended using a special instrument called a nasogastric tube to clear the adhesions. This tube was passed through his nose, down through the esophagus, and finally reached the stomach. While the doctors tried to remedy the problem, my brothers and I shuttled back and forth between the camp and Duluth each day, the routine of navigating hospital corridors already becoming second nature for us. After a week in the hospital with the NG tube in him, the adhesions still hadn't cleared and the doctors decided that it would be necessary to perform a second surgery. Dad was in the operating room for six hours that day, which was also my seventeenth birthday. Again, he came through the procedure well and seemed to be recovering quickly.

"The procedure went as well as could be expected," the surgeon explained. "He'll do just fine now." They kept telling us he'd be *just fine*, A-OK, and they'd always give us some superfluous hand gesture to seal the deal as they moved on to the next patient. After Dad came out of the recovery area, the five of us sat together in his room, doing what had become and would continue to be a newfound family tradition. We played hearts on the bed near my dad's feet and joked about his self-service morphine drip. He kept pushing the button over and over again, not caring that the system would only produce a safe, preset amount of the medication per hour.

"Dad," we said as if scolding, "it's not going to give you any more even if you hold the button down all day. It's got a limit."

"I know, but I *neeeeeeeed* it."

"Why? Are you in a lot of pain?"

"Ah, yeah. I just got my period and I've got real bad cramps. Tell the nurse I need more morphine." Barely able to speak or move, his primary focus was still to keep the rest of us laughing.

Gabe and I had to leave Duluth the next day and head back to Arizona, where senior year was about to start for me. Leaving my father, surprisingly, wasn't as difficult as I'd anticipated; I allowed myself to be lulled by the doctors' many urges for us to relax.

"He's out of the woods now," they kept saying. "He'll be home before you know it."

* * *

Shortly after my brothers and I left the hospital, my mom helped my father sit up at the edge of his bed, a feat seeing as he'd been lying down for so many hours post-surgery. Sitting up felt good, but when Dad moved to a nearby chair, he couldn't catch his breath, gulping and gasping to get enough air into his lungs. My mother put her hands on his arms and crouched down to look at his face. She told him to slow down his breaths and relax, to do as he always instructed the homesick campers to do when they couldn't stop crying. But he wasn't able to get enough breath and as soon as my mom realized that he could not control this erratic breathing, she called for the nurse. Both the respiratory physician and the surgeon arrived within moments and agreed that the pain and shortness of breath were very likely the initial symptoms of a pulmonary embolism. He was rushed into further testing. The blood clots they feared had formed could possibly shoot up into his brain, killing my father on the spot.

At the same time that my father was about to be wheeled down for treatment, Dylan returned from dropping us off at the airport, not yet knowing that anything was wrong at the hospital. As he rounded the corner of the nurses' station outside my dad's room, he heard one of the nurses say, "I know, and he's only fifty-three." Dread welled up in his chest as he rounded the corner, fearing the worst.

Sure enough, the nurses were anxiously discussing my father's fate, having already become attached to his warmth and bold sense of humor in the few days they had cared for him. As Dylan entered the room, he saw Dad sitting in a chair, his face dotted in sweat and his eyes blinking rapidly, then releasing as wide as they would open in his panicked search for oxygen. Doctors and nurses were scurrying to transport my father to a nearby procedure room and in the chaos

Dylan froze, only following my father out of the room when my mom grabbed his arm and pulled him along. After the specialized X-ray, the doctors discovered that Dad had suffered one big embolism and several "showers" of clots in his lungs. The doctors were very clear that the force of these embolisms by all rights should have killed him. They told my mother that he had literally been a single heartbeat away from death. Freshly sprung from the brink of death, he was sedated, treated with blood-thinning medications, and put on a ventilator to help him breathe.

* * *

Saying hello to my Tucson friends whom I hadn't seen all summer and picking up my class schedule at orientation, I was relieved to be back in the real world. I'd had fun getting up early and picking out my first-day-of-school outfit. The hurried transition between camp and dad's cancer back to my home life in Arizona was alarmingly quick, but I was happy to finally be there, starting another school year. In less than twenty-four hours, I had gone from hospital to airport to home to school. The last thing I expected was more bad news, but as things turned out, I would have been better served to have kept an open mind. Comparing schedules with my best friend in the auditorium, I felt someone tap my shoulder. A school secretary, probably another student's mom, handed me a small piece of paper that read: *Your brother called. Your father is dying. Flight out of Phoenix in two hours.*

Chapter 7

HEMINGWAY'S GHOST

I had no idea what had happened since we'd left Dad cracking jokes at the hospital in Duluth, and I rushed past the crowd of students with surprising calm, not sure if I was ready to hear the details of my father's condition. I didn't have time to think about how I felt—I just knew I needed to get home as soon as possible. As I headed for the glass double doors, the woman who brought me the note nonchalantly told me to have a good day.

I threw my book bag into the passenger seat of my car and sped past the guard at the school's entrance. I took a shortcut through a residential neighborhood and, rushing to catch my flight, slammed into a stopped car blocking the road in front of me. Immediately afterward, the car behind me hit my bumper and shoved me forward into the steering wheel. The five-car fender bender originated several yards ahead of me and wasn't my fault, but I panicked. I'd never been in a car accident before and certainly not while I was behind the wheel. I only had a few minutes to get home in time to pack and head for the airport—and I was trapped, wedged like a spring between two cars. Not knowing the process of establishing the cause of the accident and estimating damages, I couldn't understand why everyone tried to keep me at the scene for so long.

"Can I just go?" I kept asking, not understanding why no one understood my haste. Even when I offered pieces of paper with my phone number and insurance information, all the adults who stood around fingering their scrunched bumpers urged me to stay. I didn't feel like telling them why I needed to leave but nevertheless resented them for not knowing about my situation—as if they should have known by the look on my face what was happening several thousands of miles away in Minnesota. Finally an ambulance and several police cars arrived. I refused to be taken to the hospital and was forced to sign the AMA (Against Medical Advice) release so I could get out of there. The protocol seemed so silly to me; images of Dad lying unconscious in a hospital bed kept appearing in my mind every time someone asked me a question, so that my answers were delayed and disjointed. The only words I could properly form came out in a shout:

"My dad is dying in Minnesota, without me, while I'm standing around signing forms. I don't have time for this!" Everyone in the crowd turned to look at the girl shouting at the police officers and stood frozen, silent, then finally parted in two halves so I could leave.

Hours later, Gabe and I pulled back up to the side entrance of the hospital in Duluth, anxious to see Dad and know more about what had happened since we last stood by his bedside just a day earlier. We made it up the stairs, around the hall, in the elevator to the fifth floor, past the waiting room, and directly to the ICU nurses' desk. There, Dylan positioned himself in front of me and held me at the door of my dad's room so both he and Gabe could try to prepare me for what I was about to see.

"Now, Tanya, he's going to look really bad."

"Yeah, I know." I figured, though, that because I had seen him post-surgery twice before, I would be okay with however he looked.

"No, you don't understand. He's really going to look different than even the last two times, okay?"

"Yeah," I said again, trying to move past them down the hall. "I *know*."

"And Mom is having a hard time, so just try not to say anything when you get in there."

"Like what? What could I say that would possibly make this worse? Can't I just go in now?" After looking at each other for a moment, they stepped aside, Dylan shrugging and sheepishly putting his hands up in the air, palms outward, as if I were holding him at gunpoint in the waiting room.

But when I saw my father lying in the ICU, I realized that nothing could have prepared me for the scene. I saw my dad's body, but I couldn't find *him* anywhere; there were so many tubes and monitors running in, out, and through him; there wasn't any untouched skin left to hold, to let him know that we were there beside him. He was pale and bloated from the blood thinners that were saving his life, and he was completely unresponsive. Death had crawled all over him and sat on his chest, breathing its darkness onto his face.

I took my place in a squeaky, light-blue vinyl armchair next to the bed and held onto Dad's pinky finger. As a child, I used to hold his pinky while we walked together and I still have several pictures of us strolling this way. I held on with both hands now and watched the monitors next to Dad's bed for a few hours.

We stayed there all night and by the next afternoon, I realized I would need to find some way to start passing the time more quickly. I took a worn copy of *The Complete Short Stories of Ernest Hemingway* from the book bag I'd packed as a carry-on the day before. This weathered copy was a hand-me-down from Dad, and I'd read through it several times already that summer. I flipped to my favorite story, "The Snows of Kilimanjaro," and started reading, eager to picture some scenery that would oppose Dad's ICU room, which I'd already grown to hate. The idea of this sterile, white room melting into the beauty and danger of the African plains seemed comforting; I thought the landscape of the story would provide some much-needed escape. But when the story again opened with vultures flying overhead, I wasn't so sure I should keep reading.

I'd already analyzed and come to appreciate the story's potent, haunting themes, knew well by then its unflinching, fatalistic perspective on death that only Ernest Hemingway could have written, but as my eyes rolled over each word, the story's full meaning came into view in a new way. I read on: "Because, just then, death had come and rested its head on the foot of the cot and he could smell its breath. . . . It had moved up on him now, but it had no shape any more. It simply occupied space. 'Tell it to go away.' It did not go away but moved a little closer."[1]

I looked up from the page every few sentences to glance at Dad's face, checking the oxygen levels on the monitor above him. A nurse had told us that as long as his oxygen saturation level stayed above 90 percent, he'd be okay, causing me to rely on these numbers for every minute's reassurance. As my eyes moved back and forth between the tattered pages and Dad's tired, swollen face, I could see that just as his beloved Hemingway had written in the story, Death had raised its beastly body on top of my father. And Death was staring him down right in front of me. I wanted to jump on the bed and guard him, wanted to protect his body with my own and fight off what I imagined to be the beast Hemingway described on paper. The presence I sensed in my father's ICU room those long, awful days was so palpable, so relentless, that I felt it cling to me, tugging my shirt tighter against my skin for a moment each time I left the room. Sometimes I'd leave to get lunch or dinner and walk back into the room to find that it suddenly felt empty again, the pressure and unease lifting just a bit, as if Death had released its grip on my father. But I kept the feel of it in my mind, wanting to stay sharp and alert against it.

It would be too soon before I felt Death's presence that way again.

* * *

My grandparents drove the six hours up from Milwaukee as soon as they got the news of Dad's embolism, arriving in Duluth around

---

[1] Hemingway, Ernest. "The Snows of Kilimanjaro." *The Complete Short Stories of Ernest Hemingway.* New York: Simon & Schuster, 1987: p. 39.

the same time as Gabe and I. At that time, my father's chances of survival were grievously slim. A spray of blood clots had entered his system, and we understood that even just one of those clots could kill him at any moment. Though each day that passed with his condition stabilizing increased his chances of recovery, until he was taken off the ventilator we wouldn't know exactly what his prognosis would be. It was possible—likely, even—that the embolism had also caused a stroke. For four days, we sat quietly with my unconscious father, so exhausted and scared we ourselves were barely conscious. We waited and waited some more, the hours passing in terrible silence and the days blending into one another, simultaneously praying for and bracing ourselves against what would come next.

I found that it was almost enough just to hold my dad's hand as he lay motionless and expressionless on the tall hospital bed beside me, though I wondered painfully, persistently, if he could even sense it or if he truly knew I was there with him. While I was thankful for each of those days, I was desperate for the arrival of nighttime and its reminder that the day was over; one more day behind us with my father still in the world. Most of all I welcomed those few fitful hours of sleep I'd manage every night, not even for my physical exhaustion but for the mental shut-off it provided, however temporary. No one else seemed to have much of an appetite and though I always did, I made an effort not to show it, wanting desperately to fit in and fall in line with what my brothers and mother did and felt. I shuttled back and forth between Dad's room and our growing crowd of family members in the waiting area, crying and feeling awful, then feeling awful in those moments when I wasn't crying.

Because they had left in such a hurry, my Nana Mimi had neglected to pack enough clothing. Since we were all holed up at the nearest Holiday Inn without a convenient way to do laundry, she asked me if I would go buy her some new underwear. I scratched my brow, looked at her quizzically, and said, "Sure." I headed out to the nearest shopping center, the small, outdated, and decidedly

Duluthian Miller Hill Mall, and engaged in the unusual endeavor of picking out underpants for my grandmother, wondering what on earth was going to come next.

Dylan also had an unexpected experience with our grandparents. While picking up burgers for dinner from a nearby restaurant named Pickwick with Papa Ben, Dylan was surprised to hear Papa order two drinks while they waited for the food. Though Papa Ben regularly drank a cocktail after work, he had never before poured one for Dylan and had certainly never done so without saying something about it first. After sharing their drink, the two of them returned to the hospital and checked in on Dad together. Dylan watched Papa Ben as he reached for his unconscious fifty-three-year-old son's hand, patted it roughly a few times, and then headed toward the door. Dylan always pictured himself standing with Dad at Papa's bedside in the hospital and still found it disorienting to be instead looking at our father hooked up to tubes and monitors in Papa's place. Dylan told me afterward that at that moment, his vision of the future had unequivocally changed. Everything had changed.

Chapter 8

A NORMAL DAD

My mother never left the hospital, never left my dad's room, never left his side. She kept us all filled with hope but also prepared us for what the doctors thought was probably imminent. For the first time since Dad's initial diagnosis, the doctors discussed his case in quiet, low tones and with carefully selected words. Up until the embolism, they had led us to believe that the cancer would merely be a blip on our otherwise Rockwellian family timeline. But there was nothing they could say to ease our fears now, while Dad lay fully sedated and possibly brain damaged day after day.

Slowly, though, he began to stabilize enough that his physicians felt comfortable taking him off the ventilator. The doctors set up their probes and tests to determine whether or not my father had had a stroke while under sedation. I listened outside his door as the doctors removed the respirator tube. Hearing him cough up that apparatus made me shiver and gag just from the sound—the first that had come from him in so long. I waited with my family in the hallway, and though my brothers stood beside me, I felt devastatingly alone, paralyzed.

Nothing else penetrated that moment; it was just my fear and me. All week I kept thinking I'd become pretty tough, but with the sound of my dad coming back to us from whatever land had held him during his week of sedation, the full reality of our situation hit me like a lightning-quick slap in the face. Beyond fearing the death of my father, I now feared the pain he felt, and would feel, and the emotions he'd experience as he regained consciousness.

After a few minutes of fighting to wake up and once we were allowed back into his room, Dad reached for a pen and paper and, still unable to speak because of the tubes in his throat, he wrote first, "Am I dying?" and below it, "Gabe, Dylan, Tanya?" My mother told him that he was going to be okay and that we were all there with him holding his hands. I was stunned: He was only awake a few moments before thinking of his children. Of us. Of me. The rest of my life, come what may, I will never lose that feeling—the security of knowing how fiercely I was loved.

* * *

As my dad healed and started to regain some strength, his personality came back as well. We'd find an episode of MTV's *Jackass* on the hospital room TV and laugh at the then-fresh comedy of extreme-sports-influenced self-abuse. Watching Steve-O swallow a goldfish and then promptly regurgitate the poor creature back up, Dad yelled out, "Yes! That is disgusting!" He'd laugh so hard that he needed to hold his torso steady with both arms as his body shook, trying to keep his stitches, tubes, and wires all in place. He always loved a good fall-down sketch, but this new, reckless brand of humor simply cracked him up to pieces—perhaps in large part because of how much my brothers and I liked it. One night while he was still in the ICU, my brothers, my cousin Jeff, and I were asked by the head nurse to return to the waiting room. Apparently, she and the rest of the nursing staff didn't appreciate the inappropriately loud ruckus we were creating.

Dad spent another three weeks at the hospital in Duluth, and then another week recovering at camp. When my parents left the hospital and returned to Minong, Dad was so thin that my mom was afraid to bring him home, but she tried to take solace in the weak belief that the doctors wouldn't have released him if he weren't ready.

Though my father was anxious to get home and into the fresh air, Mom couldn't help but question if the doctors were right in sending him home in what was still such a severely diminished state.

Though it was hard to leave Dad again, my brothers and I couldn't miss any more school without forfeiting the entire semester. With our parents at camp and Dylan headed back to college in Alaska, it made sense for Gabe to stay with me at our house in the suburban foothills of Tucson while commuting to his last semester of classes at the University of Arizona across town. Once they settled in at camp without us, Mom busied herself making broth for Dad—toiling for days to get fresh, organic produce only to have him sip two or three teaspoons before filling up. He was exhausted and had little stamina to even talk by phone, but Gabe and I did our best to keep him up to date on the progress of my school year.

* * *

Without my parents there to oversee my first month of school, Gabe did his best to keep me in line and taken care of. My first week back at school after Dad's embolism, I learned that I only needed to take six classes each semester that year in order to graduate. This meant that if I dropped my non-essential courses, I could have several hour-long free periods throughout the day. Knowing this, I promptly quit my choir class in exchange for the extra time off. My parents were, predictably, less than thrilled when they heard about my decision.

"Oh, honey. I just can't believe you'd quit in your last year like that, after making so many friends in choir," my mom moaned into the phone. "After all these years, and you loved it so much. Why would you decide to do this so impulsively? I just don't understand . . ."

"And without our permission?" Dad chimed in from the second phone in their bedroom. And then he rolled out his "lawyer voice" and spoke the words I most dreaded and that unfailingly turned my stomach over whenever he voiced them: "Tanya, I am very disappointed in you."

I bucked against their concerns, though, snottily countering, "I don't see why you guys even care this much. I mean, there's a new choir director this year and everyone says he's a total ass."

"Hey—watch it," Mom said firmly.

"And even so, Won-Ton, you should have stuck it out until we got back, and you know it," Dad added, quietly and calmly, which made me feel even more ashamed. "This just isn't like you."

Gabe picked up the cordless phone in the living room and, looking right at me with a mischievous wink, said, "Yeah, you guys don't even know the half of it. She's completely out of control." A smile snuck into the right corner of his mouth and I rolled my eyes, already irritated that my parents had ordered Gabe to babysit me in their absence. I was a senior in high school after all and didn't think I needed around-the-clock supervision. Stretching the kitchen phone cord as far as its coiled wire could reach, I covered the mouthpiece with one hand and tried to kick Gabe in the legs while keeping my ear against the phone. He dodged me easily, snickering as I tried again, in vain, leaning my lower half one way as the phone cord kept me tethered in place.

"What do you mean?" my mom answered quickly.

"Nothing—I'm just messing with her. Everything's fine," Gabe said, playfully throwing a balled-up napkin at me from across the kitchen island.

"Well, Gabe, you're the one who signed the form so you're just as much to blame here," Dad said, breathing heavily between sentences. "Listen, it's too late to do anything about this now, but your mother is very upset."

"Yes, I am," Mom added, trying to sound stern but as she continued, her voice began to soften. "It's just that now there are no more choir concerts to go to—we've been going to choir concerts for a long time between the three of you and I thought I had at least one more year."

"Ah, Mom, don't make this into something more than what it really is." But as I said this, I did start to feel truly guilty; I'd never meant to make her sad when she was already so preoccupied with taking care of Dad. It simply felt good to make my own decision without their influence, and I didn't think Gabe would care enough to tell on me. But Gabe was already beginning to take his babysitting duties more seriously, doing his best to act in our parents' stead, and after we hung up the phone, he cheered me up with takeout Chinese food. I could never stay mad at Gabe, and we seamlessly transitioned back to our normal role on the way to pick up our food, already enjoying one another's company more now that we'd been through so much together. Spending time together away from the rest of our family was new, but we made quick studies and managed to emerge unscathed, remarkable as it is for a seventeen- and twenty-two-year-old set of siblings to accomplish.

*   *   *

When my parents finally did come back to Tucson, I was startled to see how much my father had changed. Dad was incredibly weak and underweight, and it was clear that it would be a slow and difficult climb back to his previous state of good health. He was still on blood thinners to prevent any more clots and was advised to treat his body with the care its fragility demanded. As soon as he grew strong enough, he then started an extremely aggressive routine of chemo and radiation therapies to try to rid his body of all the remaining cancer.

Though his outward appearance was the most noticeable difference, I could see something else shifting beneath the surface. Dad had always been overly concerned with car care and maintenance, even forbidding anyone from eating or drinking in our cars under any circumstance and often becoming upset over the tiniest scratch or dent. He was known to park in the farthest corners of a parking lot if it meant he could avoid door-dings in exchange for a hearty walk. But now, he was often too tired to drive, much less worry about the condition of the car's interior.

On an early December afternoon a few months after his near-death embolisms, Dad and Gabe took a trip to the grocery store in Dad's fancy red sports car. As they pulled into a parking space, a woman driving next to them ran her car into the rear bumper of my dad's car. Having seen our father's rage in the past over a lost French fry between the seats, Gabe prepared for a blowout of Dad's rarely seen but legendary temper at this poor, unsuspecting woman.

Although he rarely raised his voice, my father could be incredibly intimidating. All the years of using his tone of voice and impressive vocabulary in order to manipulate information in the courtroom as a trial lawyer proved difficult to shut off once he quit his practice and became a camp director. There were many occasions when he used what we referred to as the "lawyer voice," when he would instantaneously and distinctly drop his tone and shift vernacular, calmly and slowly drawing out each syllable in perfect enunciation. All he had to do was say my name using the lawyer voice and I'd tremble.

Pulled over in the parking lot, my Dad opened his door and walked briskly over to the woman, now standing behind Dad's car to assess the damage she'd caused. Gabe threw open his door and rushed around to the rear of the car too, in case he might need to mediate the discussion. But as soon as my dad made his way over to the stranger, he opened his arms as wide as they would go and said, "Oh, you didn't mean to do that, did you?" And he wrapped her up in a great big hug.

The embolisms had, in fact, changed him. There was no more need to get angry over a dent in the car door or even over a totaled vehicle. I can only imagine how my father's kindness might have affected the woman who caused the accident, but I hope she was as inspired by it as I have been all these years. And though it took the experience of nearly dying to teach my father the importance of a little compassion, he made every minute of life after his near-death experience an opportunity to practice it.

* * *

Halfway through Dad's radiation treatments, with continuous, health-diminishing infusions of chemotherapy throughout, he was forced to stop the treatments and take a break to recover because he was in so much pain. He was raw from the radiation and could barely walk due to exhaustion brought on by the chemo; the treatments had, in essence, utterly depleted him. He suffered terrible abdominal pain and spasms, and although we urged him to go to the hospital for treatment and rest, he only wanted to stay at home.

At one point, Dad was given too much radiation by an inexperienced technician, causing a terrible burn in a very compromising place—his penis. Since they had to aim the radiation at his colon, he would lie on his stomach and the waves were angled down through his torso. Unfortunately, the inexperienced technician aimed a little too low that one time. Naturally, this resulted in some seriously unbearable pain. Eventually my mom called the nurse to tell her what happened and to ask what to do. When the nurse asked where the burn was located exactly, my dad grabbed the phone and said, "Well, ma'am, it's about twelve inches up from the base."

No, I suppose he wasn't quite a "normal" dad, but he sure kept himself, and all of us, from feeling sorry for ourselves, even as sick as he was.

Using the original story of a case of diverticulitis, we were able to tell our extended community about the embolisms. It was too monumental to keep hidden. And though he made it through his various rounds of treatment without anyone discovering the severity of his illness, it was a stressful secret for us all to keep. No longer able to travel the way he was accustomed, my mom and our assistant director, Michelle, picked up the slack in the travel schedule. They reassured the camp families that everything was fine and that they were just busier than usual this year, accounting for my father's absence from his annual tour of camper-filled cities.

The day of my senior prom, all my friends gathered together with our parents for the stereotypical prom picture-taking extravaganza. I was elated that, having just completed his last round of chemotherapy, Dad found the energy to stand in a line with all the other parents while my friends and I stood together and posed.

Dad was a gifted photographer and had spent much of my adolescence teaching me about the nuances of aperture, perspective, contrast, and the composition rule of thirds. When I took an interest in the more alternative, hands-on photographic development processes during high school art classes, I knew he was proud that I'd follow in his artistic footsteps. He even gave me the camera he had used all through college to have as my own. Sometimes when I tagged along on camp travels, we'd pull over in the heart of the French Quarter or in the cornfields of Illinois and take pictures, comparing f-stops and lens filters and ideas for building do-it-yourself darkrooms.

As I laughed with my friends in our prom dresses and rented tuxes, I watched my dad struggle to lift the weight of his new Olympus ED/35-180 camera, and my smile straightened, my heart sinking. After the chemo and radiation, Dad's beard had grown in gray and thin. Worrying that he was beginning to look a lot like Papa Ben and not wanting to look so old, he shaved it all off. Without his trademark facial hair, I saw facial features that were not his own; he did look shockingly similar to my grandpa this way, and it was scary to see him grow so unnaturally old, so unnaturally fast.

As my father snapped away—shot after posed shot—with the other parents, he knelt down on the grass. He camouflaged his exhaustion well that day—knowing how to bend and make it look as if he just needed a different angle for the pictures. But I knew. I knew that he would go home after us young folk piled into limos, would be helped to bed by my mother, and fall asleep exhausted, afraid, and hurting.

Chapter 9

ON THE RISERS

I slept in a bed
in a room with paintings
on the walls, and
planned another day
just like this day.
But one day, I know
it will be otherwise.
— JANE KENYON

The summer after I graduated high school, I took a wilderness adventure course from NOLS, the National Outdoor Leadership School. Too old to be a camper and not ready or eager to work at camp full-time quite yet, my family thought a few months spent sea kayaking off the Southeastern coast of Alaska would give me some much-needed time away from the stress of Dad's illness. When Dylan was sixteen, he went on a backpacking trip through Alaska with NOLS, so I dutifully followed in his example and signed up for my own expedition, even though I had never before even considered taking on that kind of physical challenge. I told myself it would be fine—I knew so much about camping that surely I would have no problem excelling throughout the course.

Dad helped me prepare for the trip with the enthusiasm he always had for anything to do with the outdoors. He packed all my camping gear and made endless, alphabetized lists to ensure that I didn't forget any necessary items. I could see by the grin on his face as we checked our lists that I was making him proud by attempting something so adventurous. His illness had affected each of us differently throughout the past year, and he thought the extreme experience of life in the woods for six weeks was just what I needed to get back to the business of being a young person again. But I wasn't so sure.

The day after graduation, I flew to camp, where I'd spend a few days in Minong with my family before making my way to Alaska. The night before I left, everyone could tell how nervous I was at dinner, trying to enjoy my last meal of fresh fruits and vegetables for the better part of two months.

"Are you gonna be okay, Tan?" my brothers asked through their semi-condescending chuckles.

"Yes. I'll be fine. I mean, I don't *really* want to go . . . but I'll be fine."

"What do you mean you don't want to go?" Gabe and Dylan looked at each other, their voices quickly turning serious.

"The only reason I'm even doing this is to prove myself as a Chernov," I blurted out. Though none of my family members ever said it outright, I felt pressured to achieve goals that were equal to or greater than the ones my brothers had attained before me. No one spoke for a moment, taking in my startling declaration. Apparently, they had no idea that I felt the need to live up to such standards.

Horrified, my mother finally said, "Tanya—you don't have to go if you don't want to. It doesn't *matter* to us whether you go or not. We're proud of you either way."

"No, it's too late," I said, defiantly. "I'm obviously going."

And go I did.

Just a few days into the trip, I started making friends and enjoying myself, even though the physical demands of the kayaking, portaging, and hiking far exceeded every one of the unrealistic expectations

I'd had. I was entirely out of contact with the civilized world for the duration of my trip and could only be notified of an emergency at home by helicopter evacuation, which made me nervous. I'd try to envision how a helicopter would even reach us in the obscured, remote places we set up our tents, every night finding myself in a location more isolated than the last. I was terrified that in the interest of letting me have my pre-college adventure in peace, my family would ultimately keep me in the dark if something happened to Dad.

On the waters of Frederick Sound and Chatham Straight, I paddled against the wind, rain, and current, measuring my days by the tides. As the rest of my group spread out against the rocky beaches of Southeastern Alaska, I found myself isolated for a few hundred feet on all sides most days. If the weather hid me from the group enough, I'd sometimes cry for hours as I paddled, the muscles of my shoulders and biceps searing in painful fatigue with each forward rotation.

When it was my turn to lead a small group for the day, I navigated our "pod" of five kayaks through a narrow channel, up into the calm and shallow waters of Keku Straight. As we paddled in exhausted search of a good spot to set up camp for the night, we climbed in and out of our boats several times, defeated at each landing by lack of potable drainage water. With the sunlight dimming behind us, the water flashing its final show of the day, I felt desperate and weak, disappointed in myself for being unable to complete my mission as the group's leader.

Back in my kayak, I brushed beads of ocean water and its serpentine salt dust off my map, and scanned the shorelines ahead. For a moment, it seemed as if all the birds had quieted and all our paddles ceased to make sound as they pierced the water. Another girl in a solo boat behind me pointed to the waves one island over, where it looked like a pod of seven Humpback whales were breaching and playing. We watched from a distance, not even bothering to take pictures now that we'd already seen so many whales in the weeks prior.

Soon though, a black slick—wet and rubbery and the size of a semi-truck—hurled itself out of the water and breached on its side only fifty feet in front of us, bringing gasps and shouts from everyone around me, as we paddled in closer together as a group. Then the humpbacks disappeared from sight, and we paddled on, shrouding ourselves in an even heavier silence than before. This pod of whales had been too close, making me think that they were either playfully curious or extremely pissed off at our presence in the freezing waters.

Though the water was cold and dark, I could now see the mammoth silhouettes of the whales speeding beneath our comparatively Lilliputian pod of kayaks. The mass of their bodies was everywhere—inescapable. It was indeed a potentially dangerous situation; if a whale surfaced underneath one of our boats, it could mean hypothermia within two minutes and a likely helicopter evacuation. Since the whales were unable to see small boats on the surface, we were trained to bang our fists on the sides of our kayaks so they could detect our presence by sonar. But from where we sat in the water, this method seemed only to aggravate the whales, bringing them nearer and nearer to our precarious position. Then without warning, and as quickly as they had moved in on us, they were gone again. We bobbed up and down in the waves, our mouths flung open and eyes blinking quickly, looking like a nest full of dumbstruck newborn baby birds. I knew that I should say something to reassure everyone, or think of a way to get us to safety, but it took all the focus I possessed just to keep myself upright in my boat.

About fifty feet away, I watched my friend, Jen, point at the water in front of her boat's bow with her mouth open but silent, and as I turned my head to see what she was so afraid of, I watched a spike of water rush toward her.

"Backpaddle, backpaddle!" I yelled, soon joined by the rest of the group.

"Move, Jen—haul ass! Paddle, paddle, paddle!" we screamed. Though we couldn't understand why, one of the whales appeared to be charging her little yellow kayak. I was certain the angry whale would soon capsize poor Jen and eat her whole, not that gentle humpbacks have ever been known to do this. But just as we all started to fully panic, with the wave only a few feet from Jen's boat, the whale changed direction once more and headed back out into the Sound. The whales were gone once again, leaving only the rocking of slightly larger than normal waves to remind us of their visit.

For the rest of the trip, I kept checking the waters beneath my boat, untrusting and overly cautious. I was terrified of the whales coming back for us, and the images of the breaching whales returned each night to my dreams in an unending déjà vu—not so unlike the dreams I used to have about the bear we shot at camp. Even as we moved miles and miles farther past the Keku Straight, I felt the whales pulling me back there in my thoughts. I'd expected that such a natural encounter with whales would be beautiful and peaceful, maybe even spiritual, but in reality it had been a rather horrifying experience; I couldn't keep myself from wondering what other life expectations would prove to be so false.

Throughout the rest of the trip, I alternated between struggling and thriving, simultaneously loving and hating life and my role in it. But as the weeks marched on, the muscles in my arms stretching my T-shirt sleeves, my paddling technique progressed and soon even the tallest swells ceased to frighten me. I was gaining strength physically, but emotionally, all I wanted to do was run to the nearest phone, call my dad, and hear his voice as I relayed my adventure—an adventure that, in many ways, had forced me to confront my father's mortality, as well as my own.

* * *

The summer came and went with my father feeling healthy again, more like himself. My parents seemed to grow toward each other more and more as my father continued to regain his strength. My mom cooked special, healthy meals for him even when she was busy taking care of the campers. And they continued to keep the illness from their employees, to save them any worry and concern.

Throughout that summer, Mom and Dad also seemed to experience camp in a different way. Though they had always *acted* as "Mom" and "Dad" to campers and staff alike, they were now feeling the enormity of these important roles. When I returned to camp for the last few weeks of the season, I watched them together, awestruck at how they'd mastered the many challenges and nuances of working side by side for so many years. My mom liked to insist that she and my father deserved extra anniversary presents since they spent double the time together. It couldn't have been an easy time for them, but they seemed to truly enjoy their lifestyle, taking the bad with the good.

* * *

The following September, I began my freshman year at the University of Puget Sound—a small private university in the Pacific Northwest. Obviously still shaken form his stare-down with death the year before, I noticed a change in my father as he and my mom helped me get settled into my dorm room. Dad sat on the floor with two oddly shaped wooden pieces in his lap and a wordless set of IKEA instructions in his hand. I watched his face wrinkle as he looked frantically at the small baggie of fasteners, finally tearing through the plastic.

"Goddamn these Swedes!" he shouted, a hint of reluctant amusement in his voice. He persisted, though, and I was happy to see that he could still find the energy to assemble my bookshelf the way other fathers were for their daughters in rooms all through the dorm. But there were other activities that were now out of his reach and this made me depressed. Walking around downtown Seattle, my parents and I had to take a lengthy detour to avoid a large set of stone steps leading down to the city's waterfront—Dad was forced to admit that he wouldn't be able to walk back up them. *Things will be different from now on,* I told myself as we navigated the city streets. *We've all been changed in one way or another—Dad most of all.*

During the welcome speech the first day of my orientation, the president of the university spoke of how much she looked forward to seeing this group of people sitting before her back in the same spot in four years for graduation. Years later, my mom confessed that this welcome speech had made my dad suddenly unsure about the future. She recalled the conversation they had, sitting a few rows away from me during the ceremony.

"Do you think I'll be here in four years?" my dad asked in a whisper as he turned to face my mom.

"Of course you will," she answered tenderly. "Of course."

My dad told me that when he was first diagnosed with cancer, he had a premonition that he would die at the age of fifty-six—three years from that afternoon on the risers.

Before helping to settle me in for my orientation and first week of classes, my father had gone in for a routine colonoscopy to learn if the chemo and radiation treatments had helped to clear out the cancer and if, in that aim, they had actually done additional harm to his colon. Three weeks after the orientation speech, I was busy establishing a life on my own, making new friends and already thinking about declaring a major in English. While I became comfortable in Tacoma with my roommate, new boyfriend, and coursework, my father's doctor called to inform him that they'd found another tumor on the opposite side of his colon. It's possible that this newly discovered carcinoma could have been inside him all along, blocked by the more visible tumors, or, perhaps it was a new, fast-growing cancer that had formed during—or despite—his treatments the previous year. So just a few weeks into my new life at college, I flew back to Milwaukee, where my parents had decided to stay for the fall, to go through the whole process of surgery and recovery with my family for a third time. Again, we woke early and drove to the hospital in the dark, pre-dawn hours. Again, we walked Dad down to the operating room. Again, we waited for him to be wheeled down the long hallway back to us. Again, we watched him wake up, asking about his status. We even had the very same hospital room we'd had the year before. Again, we waited. Again, we faced our mounting fears.

*　*　*

This surgery removed the newfound tumor, revealing that the cancer had traveled up to the liver and metastasized there. The surgeon removed a thin slice of my father's liver and reported that he felt he had removed all of the cancer. Since Dad had been experiencing pain in his gallbladder, where the surgeon found gallstones, they also removed that organ during the surgery. Dad made it through the operation, and we convinced ourselves to be hopeful, which was more and more challenging. Two weeks after his third surgery, Dad developed another bowel obstruction due to a buildup of scar tissue. The brutal repetition of events seemed cruel and eerily familiar.

This time, Dad went back into the hospital after only being home for two days to have an NG tube put back in. After waiting several days for the obstruction to clear, the doctors next tried an old technique of putting in a Cantor tube, which had to be forced through his nose and down his throat, in hopes that the little balloon on the end would make its way down through the bowel and clear the obstruction. Once this was accomplished, the surgeon informed us that he didn't know if the obstruction was caused by post-surgical adhesions or from damage caused by the radiation Dad had endured the previous year. At every turn, there was something new to scare us, something new to wear my father down.

This part of his treatment—the long, green NG tube coming out of his nose—reminded me of an old friend of ours: the green snake. Dad and I joked about the green snake, thinking back to when I was fifteen years old and starting to get migraines with sudden frequency and in rapid succession. I had always been remarkably healthy and had never even been on antibiotics before, so the cluster migraines I suffered from took my entire family by surprise. The headaches worsened, so that I sometimes endured two or three full migraine cycles per day. I'd never experienced such debilitating pain before; the hypersensitivity to light and sound, nausea, and vomiting completely defeated me. I couldn't go to school and depended on my parents to help me with even the most basic daily functions. Even though I knew it made the pain worse, I sobbed and cried through the duration of each headache while my parents looked on in despair, unable to help.

While we waited for MRI results and a revolving door of new prescriptions, I had no choice but to tough out the migraines as best I could. My parents hung blankets and towels to cover the floor-to-ceiling windows in my room and sat with me until each migraine subsided. After a few weeks, many tests, and fourteen different medications, my neurologist still hadn't figured out the cause. I was exhausted and scared. I had missed nearly a month of school and lost a lot of weight. During one particularly vicious bout of migraines, my dad sat on the floor next to my bed and held my hand while I cried and winced against the thunderous pulsing at my left temple and eye.

I started to feel my father's arms shaking, and then I heard him sniffling and crying beside me. He placed his hands on my head and kissed my cheek.

"Well, what's wrong with *you*?" I asked, trying to be funny.

"I'm so sorry you hurt, honey," my dad said softly through his tears. "I wish I could take it all away. I wish I could."

"Good. Then do it," I whined. "I don't want to be sick anymore." In my narcotic haze, I actually believed that he had the power to heal me. Now that both of us were in tears, Dad decided to turn the mood around in his signature style.

"Okay, here I go. I'm just going to pull the green snake that's peeking out of your nose."

"What snake? What are you talking about? Dad . . ."

"Oh yeah, there's this little green snake coming out. It's kinda cute actually. I think if I just pull slowly—"

"Da-ad. You're being weird."

"No, no. I'm totally serious. Let me just get the tail now and I bet you'll feel much better." I don't know if it was the pain meds finally kicking in or the power of mind-over-very-painful-matter, but after I stopped crying enough to laugh at his silliness, my head hurt a little less.

And now it was my turn, with Dad lying in the bed and me sitting next to him, wishing I could take it all away. Dad lifted the green tube up so he could examine it, then set it back down where it draped across his belly before emptying its contents into a plastic container hanging behind the hospital bed.

"Yup," he said, "the green snake has returned, uglier than ever."

I couldn't stop wondering if this routine of surgeries and hospital visits would become a permanent pattern, constantly throwing my family back into a panic just when things started to feel normal again. I hadn't known my new friends at UPS long enough to miss them, but I did miss being around people my own age. They were all busy situating themselves in their new schools, just as I would otherwise have been doing, and I felt completely isolated in the hospital room all day. Because we had long since sold the house in Milwaukee where my brothers and I grew up, we stayed with Cheryl, my mom's good friend, and her family. Having grown up next door to the Silberman family, I felt comfortable enough in their house and was glad for their company. But I felt displaced nonetheless—suspended in the tenuous strands of hope I kept trying to pull from my mind. I was starting to understand that even if Dad made it through this, there wouldn't be anything easy about it—it seemed like life was going to be challenging and dangerous for a long time until it got better again. *If* it ever got better again.

Chapter 10

THESE DIFFERENT KINDS OF WINTER

When I finally returned to my dorm room in Tacoma, I was completely exhausted and frightened, not sure if I should be returning to school at all. I'd cried like a child when I said goodbye to my father, who was still recovering in the hospital; I clung to him with my arms grasped tightly around his neck and my cheek pressed against his chest, wanting to stay.

Heading into the red-brick-lined stairwell of Schiff Hall, all I wanted was to crawl in bed and watch *General Hospital* on my twelve-inch TV. I much preferred the ridiculous premise of its pretend hospital to the real-life ones in which I'd recently spent so much time. But as I climbed the stairs to my room with duffel bags thrown over each shoulder, I saw that everyone on my floor—my new friends, new boyfriend, all still so unfamiliar and uncomforting—had thrown a big welcome-home party for me. They had balloons and cake, and were smiling huge, unknowing smiles. The last things I wanted in the entire world were balloons, cake, and smiles. They were being good friends to me and to this day I appreciate the sentiment, but they didn't have a clue about what I needed the most and what I didn't feel I could ask for: breathing room.

I did my best to shake off the things that were happening with my father and to enjoy the college life, which suited me just fine. I loved being on my own and easily built a strong community of friends around me. As autumn tumbled into soggy winter, I reluctantly started to fall in love with Washington. I didn't mind waking to the darkness of endlessly clouded skies, but instead reveled in the act of simply wrapping myself into the bed even deeper, sometimes even dragging my clothes under the covers and dressing inside the warmth I'd saved up in there throughout the night.

Walking to classes in the soft mist and rain suited me too—made me feel somehow tougher, more authentic. I took my cue from the locals and got rid of the umbrella my parents had bought me, opting for just a rain jacket or hoodie. I would walk with my hands tucked into my pockets, head shrouded under a hood, and observe how everything seemed to dance in the rain; the leaves shuddered under the weight of the drizzle, and grass on the fields outside my dorm room swayed in the wind, looking more like waves on the ocean's surface than a plot of grass. I could see Mount Rainier from my dorm room when it was clear, which occurred just often enough to lead me to take the sight as a good omen.

Even as I longed for the landscapes of all the places I'd lived—Tucson, camp, Milwaukee—I knew I had found my own hard-won home here. There were nights, sitting with friends under a Madrona tree in the breezeway between our dorms, when the smell of the desert managed to find me, 2,000 miles from the parched landscape of my recent youth. The rain would slap down around us and saturate the asphalt, the grass, the tree wells. The whole neighborhood would sigh during the rain—people, houses, cars, and dogs remembering how good a storm feels, how the quenched air fills with a sudden coolness. And all around me I would smell—or imagine I smelled—a specific kind of creosote scent, like the desert after a furious monsoon shower.

Leaning back in an ancient, cracking plastic deck chair under the porch surrounded by friends being noisy and smoking cigarettes, I'd close my eyes, take in another sip of the blacktop air, and remember the wind in my desert yard, the way it licked my cheeks and lifted my hair. I imagined myself as a mound of sand, a collection of tiny pebbles slowly growing with each gust along the bottom of my empty riverbed. Building and building upon myself, each grain lengthening the silhouette of my shadow beside me.

* * *

That winter my parents traveled to the Simonton Cancer Center and then to the University of Texas M. D. Anderson Cancer Center, spending the rest of their time alternating between Tucson and Wisconsin. Their week at Simonton was paramount to my father's positive outlook on his illness. There, my parents were taught how to deal with the cancer on a psychological level and to achieve a healthy balance of handling Dad's illness, while still attending to the many important things going on in all the other areas of their lives. It was through these teachings that Dad made the decision to separate himself from any toxic people and situations in his life, surrounding himself only with those who were able to love him fully and help him obtain a high quality of life. He needed people around him who could be positive, supportive, and loving no matter how scared they were of losing him. And luckily for him, Dad had a vast network of friends and family who fulfilled such criteria. Ever graceful in his social demeanor, my dad simply and quietly phased out any people or things that made him feel worse. There was no need to be dramatic or drastic; he just let himself follow what felt good and right, using his instincts as his most primary guide. My father truly believed in the power of positive energy, thinking that the cancer could not and would not continue to grow so quickly once all the toxic ingredients had been removed from his body and life.

During his stay at the Simonton Center, my father also came to learn that there is very often a difference between being healed and being cured. With a life-threatening illness, you don't always find a physical cure but you *can* always receive emotional and spiritual healing. As the months passed, my parents continued working with a therapist they'd met at the Simonton Center, who helped guide them through his illness and continue strengthening their marriage.

Spending the entirety of their time together might have put a strain on another marriage, but for my parents the extra alone time they had together was precious. They used the toughest challenge of their lives as a springboard to cultivating a closer, more loving relationship, for whatever time they had left together. As in love as they had been in the beginning of their marriage, they seemed even more romantically fulfilled now.

My mom told me during one of our weekly phone calls what a goof she thought Dad was when they first met. Having attended rival high schools in Milwaukee, my mother and father met each other at parties and social gatherings a few times and eventually planned to go out on a date.

"Of course Dad wanted to go horseback riding," she said, "but since I had my period and obviously had no desire to ride a horse, I cancelled the date. And we never rescheduled."

"And then you went to Madison for college and he went to Bradley—" I repeated wearily. "I know this story, Mom." I thought I knew the details of their entire courtship and wasn't really listening; instead I painted my toenails in front of the TV, the phone held between my ear and shoulder.

"Yes, but do you know how we met the second time?"

"Yeah, you met through camp friends, right?" I asked, only half-interested.

"Well, no. You remember Fred Silver—he lived down the street from Aunt Mickey and Uncle Gary?"

"Mmm, big gray beard, right? Uh-huh, I remember him."

"Well, he brought your father over to my house before a party." I twisted the nail polish cap back on the bottle, sat up, and waited for her to continue.

"When they came into the room, Uncle Wooby and Dad immediately started giving each other a hard time, and I had no idea what was going on."

"Because you didn't know that they already knew each other from camp?"

"No idea." Protective of her little brother, my mom was horrified by this strange guy's rude behavior. Just when she was ready to storm out of the room, Dad and my Uncle Mikey, whom we'd nicknamed "Wooby," let her in on their joke. "After all that, Dad asked me if I'd like to go on a date the next Thursday, so that he could decide if I was worthy of going to a party with him the following Saturday."

The rest of the story was familiar to me, but I let Mom continue, knowing that it made her feel good to relive the good old days when she and Dad were just starting out on their journey together. Indeed, she was more than worthy of a second date and before long, my grandfather took Dad to pick up his grandmother's diamond ring from the family's safety-deposit box. True to his prankster style, my father planned a rather unusual way to propose. He asked my mom to come over and help him fold laundry on—of all nights—New Year's Eve. Begrudgingly, she agreed to come over. With the Dick Clark countdown playing on the TV in the background, my mom picked up a T-shirt to fold. Finding it heavier than it should have been, she turned the shirt around to find in its pocket a tiny box and inside it, a ring.

* * *

At M. D. Anderson in the winter of 1999 to 2000, the doctors who treated my father recommended another aggressive round of chemotherapy. After considering what that would be like for him, my dad reasoned that those treatments would at the very least make him incredibly sick and would certainly give him a poorer quality of life. They also offered no real guarantees of permanently, or even temporarily, getting rid of the cancer. At best, it seemed that these treatment plans might only extend his life for a few extra months. So, instead of following the traditional route that he knew would destroy his quality of life, Dad was very optimistic about trying alternative therapies to boost his immune system and hopefully purge the cancer.

Although our family often all came together at our home in Tucson for school breaks and holidays, after my parents' tour of cancer centers they ultimately decided to spend their time living year-round in our peaceful, isolated house at camp. While I understood their decision, I liked it better when we would meet up in Arizona because it was the only time I could see my high school friends, and there were more options for movies, shopping, and good restaurants—all the things college students want to take advantage of while home on school breaks. Most of my friends had chosen to stay in Tucson to attend the University of Arizona, and I always felt like the odd one out, flying in from so far away. So when we shifted our holidays and visits to be spent at camp, I felt even more detached from the network of support I'd come to rely on.

Still, living at camp during the winter months presented its own unique advantages. I had taken to cross-country skiing like a fish to water and found the times my brothers and I spent together on the trails to be more fun than I'd ever had hanging out at bars with friends in Tucson. Though it was incredibly hard work, skiing came naturally to me, and I loved feeling like I was *good* at something, especially an athletic pursuit since I'd never quite been the world's most graceful athlete. I was a good enough skier to venture off into the woods by myself for the afternoon each day, alone with my thoughts and the sounds of the crunching snow beneath my skis. I'd stop to catch my breath after climbing a hill and kick my skis against the ground to warm my feet, listening for the slap of the wood on the compact snow. Gradually, it felt good to be there—felt right to come home to camp; there were no distractions and nothing to take my attention away from Dad.

Because my father was finding himself less and less able to get outside, the days we spent snowed in, waiting for the county's plows to come down our long driveway, were cozy and welcomed. We had originally planned an adventurous winter break trip to Costa Rica but were forced to cancel at the last minute because of Dad's health, opting for a nice-and-easy Mexican cruise instead. But even this trip had its challenges. Because of his damaged digestive organs and special dietary restrictions, Dad could no longer eat many of the foods he loved. A ravenous meat-eater all his life, he now had trouble digesting even the gentlest vegetarian dishes. The cruise ship's gratuitous displays of buffet tables proved to be a mocking temptation to the culinary luxuries in which Dad could no longer indulge. When we spent the day onshore in Mazatlán, my brothers and I wanted to rent Jet Skis. Dad was always enthusiastic about trying new toys—the bigger, the better—and it surprised me to see him pass up the opportunity to go play out on the water with his kids. Instead, he sat on the beach with my mom and took pictures while my brothers and I made passes back and forth across the bay.

At camp for most of the year now, my parents spent almost all of their time educating themselves on alternative cancer treatments, searching for the best possible roads toward remission. They lived simply, eating only fresh, organic foods and researching constantly. They prayed in the pristine surroundings, and most of all, they hoped.

Chapter 11

ON ROAD TRIPS
AND HEMORRHOIDS

After my first semester at college, my parents agreed that I could take my Jeep Wrangler back to school with me. However, my parents didn't think it was safe for me to do the drive alone, and it was too expensive to ship the vehicle from Tucson, so we planned to fly from camp to Tucson, and from there Dad would make the 2,000-mile road trip with me to Tacoma. I was nervous about him spending so much time in the car while still undergoing chemo, but he was enthusiastic from the start and never backed down when we pressed him to let someone else drive with me.

Initially, we thought the road trip would be fun and would be a good way for the two of us to spend some time together before my next semester began. But as winter break wound down and the time came closer for us to start packing up the car, it was clear that my dad wasn't feeling well at all. His third surgery had fatigued him further, and he suffered excruciating belly pain almost constantly. The nutrient depletion he had from so many rounds of chemo, in addition to the harsh radiation treatments, also gave him unavoidable and uncomfortable hemorrhoids. To add to the hesitation about the trip, Jeeps tend not to be very comfortable vehicles for extended road trips, and riding in one with a bad case of hemorrhoids certainly sounded like a pretty bad idea. So when my dad was feeling sore while just lying in his own bed the day before we were supposed to leave, I started to grow increasingly uneasy about making the trip with him. I didn't want to be responsible for causing my dad any more pain than he already felt. Even though I had been looking forward to the trip, I no longer wanted to go now that I could see how hard it would be on him.

Later that day, my mom sat me down on the couch to talk about the trip.

"If Dad starts getting sick, you need to tell me so we can buy plane tickets," she said.

"Plane tickets for who—what would we do with the car?"

"Well, I've been thinking about this. He'll never tell you if he starts to feel worse. He's too stubborn, and he really wants to go. So I think you'll just have to watch him, make sure he eats, and call me if anything changes. We can fly you both the rest of the way to school and have the car shipped." She held my hands and pulled her face closer to mine. "You're going to have to be responsible. I'm trusting you to watch him, Tan."

I burst into tears as we sat there, feeling the weight of such a responsibility pushing me down; I didn't think that I was capable of monitoring my father that way. Mom and I looked at the AAA maps and decided that Phoenix, San Francisco, and Portland would become our checkpoints—cities we could easily fly from if the need arose.

The following day, we packed up my little piece of tin to the brim and were on our way. With no air-conditioning, no heat, no cruise control, no CD player, and a very short suspension, the ride was at best uncomfortable, and for my dad it was almost unbearable. He found that it felt better for him to have his arms up and away from his abdomen, so he did most of the driving, his arms straight on each side of the steering wheel. It seemed to be such a stiff position to maintain for hours on end, and I worried that he would exhaust himself before the trip was over. I was happy he was with me but felt suffocated by my own concerns for his health. In the Jeep's cramped quarters, I didn't know where I could tuck away such heavy worries.

Heading out of Arizona, we listened to the entire *Godfather* trilogy on tape, a theatrical reading of *Midnight in the Garden of Good and Evil*, and a biography of Franklin and Eleanor Roosevelt. For music, we alternated between selections from my collection and some from his. In that car, we were friends swapping college stories, colleagues discussing contemporary standards in the camping industry, students jointly discovering the grandiose commentaries of Francis Ford Coppola's epic saga.

We only drove about five hours each day before stopping for the night to keep Dad well rested, drawing out the trip to last an entire week. When we passed through Los Angeles my dad made me drive in the rush-hour traffic, thinking it would help me build some strong character and toughness. He wouldn't let me pull over to the side of the highway even after I started crying, begging him to take over.

"You're okay," he said calmly. "You can do this. Just stay inside your lane and don't let the semis or faster cars intimidate you." He knew I could do it, and indeed I did make it . . . for about 10 minutes before I ignored his encouraging sentiments and pulled off at the nearest and friendliest-looking exit. When the Jeep finally stopped and I turned off the engine, I looked over at Dad, arms folded high across his chest, a Cheshire cat grin slapped widely on his face. He was clearly reveling in every second of my torment behind the wheel.

Later, heading through the northernmost-tip of California, I drove up an ominously steep, snowy mountain ascent. Initially, the L.A. traffic had significantly boosted my driving confidence, and I sat with my back relaxed into the seat as we ascended the winding mountain road. But as the shoulder narrowed and then disappeared into a three-foot space between my top-heavy little car and the plunge to imminent death, I grew far less sure of myself. I could contain my unease if I just looked straight ahead, using the hood latches of the Jeep to guide my gaze like blinders on a horse. Finally my father noticed how I had gradually stiffened upright. The more the road bent and wound, the further forward I'd move until my chest was nearly flush with the steering wheel. My fingers were wrapped tightly around the leather so that when I changed positions, my skin stuck for a second or two. Again I pulled over at the first opportunity and pleaded with my dad to switch. This time, he started hysterically laughing at me.

"Wha-at?" I whined. He didn't answer but instead put a hand on my shoulder until I relaxed and then started laughing with him. I was too old to be whining about my fears of driving. I was too old for it, and I knew it. Dad clearly wasn't going to let up on me if I didn't at least try to conquer *some* fears on this trip. We were road comrades, glassy-eyed worshippers inhaling the clean, cold air that rested on top of the strange, early-winter California snow.

Watching the mountains split the road and rise alongside it, scenes passing through my windshield's small rectangle, I played the image against the landscapes of my childhood. This was neither the snow-heavy flatness of Wisconsin nor the wild, monsoon-drunk washes in the foothills of Tucson near my home. Neither the humid summer days at camp—all the mosquitoes, ticks, and sweat—nor the cotton-mouth heat of Arizona that I never grew to love. And soon I'd be back in my new home, my own landscape—the wettest season of all.

I forced in thoughts of returning to school with a car and renting a house with friends next year in order to make myself excited about school again, trying not to feel wistful or nervous about being on my own.

"Hey Dad," I said, "remember our botched ATV trip?"

"Oh God, that was so embarrassing." I turned to look at him, surprised to hear that he'd ever felt embarrassed around me. Didn't he know how untouchable I thought he was?

"Oh man, I was so excited that you even let me start the three-wheelers to load them onto the trailer with you. I was scared as hell that I'd drop them right off the side and break everything."

Dad's smile stretched tightly across his whole face now, his mind scanning the memories of our happy times in Tucson. Dad adjusted the pillows around and beneath him, and reached over to turn the music down.

Firm in his belief that it's important for kids to understand how to drive a vehicle with a clutch, Dad had brought out our old ATV one day in Tucson a few years earlier to teach me the nuances of driving a manual engine.

"I thought that thing was so hardcore when you first got it. I thought I was gonna be a badass extreme-sports junkie like the boys." I laughed at the thought now, knowing I'd never be any such thing. "That ATV seems pretty tame now though, doesn't it?"

"Aw honey, it always was." Dad laughed a little at this but caught himself by just slightly bracing his arms against his sides, absorbing the painful movements of the Jeep over the rough mountain road.

My dad's 1977 CJ-5 Jeep, so much different than the newer model we drove now, had taken us into the mountains that day in Tucson. Our three-wheelers secured on the trailer behind us, the thick desert that surrounds Mount Lemon stretched out around us like a desiccated moat around a castle. The desert air was starting to cool by the time we arrived at the trails, and I was anxious to get my nervous little fingers on those handlebars. We parked the Jeep and my dad climbed up onto the trailer to start unlocking all the chains and bungee cords. I explored the trailhead and looked at the map for a few minutes, and when I looked up at my dad his forehead was all wrinkled, eyes squinting at the still-burning evening sun. He first rummaged through his pockets and then the Jeep. We quickly realized that my dad had certainly remembered the keys to start the ATVs but had forgotten the keys to unlock the chains keeping them safely on the trailer.

"It was classic," I said now, laughing at the memory of his face as he realized his blunder, standing confused on the trailer.

"I felt like such an idiot," Dad said. "I'd prepared this extensive lesson that would teach you not to be fearful of high-powered vehicles and have a well-studied grasp of the concept of the automotive clutch system—"

"And then you forgot the key! Amazing."

"One of my most bozo moments. I admit it."

We'd laughed at ourselves for a few minutes that evening before climbing back into the Jeep and heading home, just as we laughed now remembering it. I didn't care about the ATVs and neither did he. It wasn't the destination—on either that trip or the current one—that mattered to me most.

With each passing road sign and mile marker, I felt myself shifting back and forth between child and adult. While the weather and terrain changed as we moved further north on interstate 5, I tried to see myself through my father's eyes. I felt myself sprouting outward but did he still see me as a little girl, *his* little girl? Would he appreciate my thoughts on the world if I were to share them? Was he taking me seriously when I talked with him about my views and opinions? What kind of adult did he expect me to grow up to be?

Somewhere in Oregon, Dad turned to me and said, "Let's treat ourselves to some really good Chinese food tonight."

"I don't know, Dad." I tried not to look worried but shifted my eyes downward a moment. "Mom would freak out if she knew you strayed off your nutrition plan, and it seems like it'll probably make you pretty sick."

"Well, we don't have to tell Mom. And . . . I just need to eat something tasty. I won't go overboard. I just need something other than rice and oatmeal." His face grew hard, and he pressed his lips tightly together. "I'm so damn sick of eating for the cancer. Tonight I want to eat for myself and enjoy a meal with my very grown-up daughter."

I smiled back at him, excited to see his feistiness still intact. Besides, there was no talking him out of it, and so we searched for the most authentic-looking Chinese spot in Roseburg, Oregon.

A charm hung over us the whole week; somehow my father's delicate health held, and we realized that we wouldn't have a problem making it all the way to our final destination.

When we arrived in Tacoma a week after we'd set out, I was thrilled to be back at school and also relieved that we'd made it and that I hadn't needed to go over my father's head by calling Mom to request two plane tickets home. Having a full week in which to soak up Dad's stories and strange jokes had been, I realized later, such good medicine for us both.

I wanted to soothe his pain, wanted to find words that would make his worries fade, but those words never came to me during that road trip. Instead, it was all I could do just to keep myself strong enough to get through the week without crying, hoping he wouldn't notice the extreme effort it took.

Chapter 12

MARINATING

The winter passed with a lot of trips back and forth between school, Tucson, and camp, and soon again it was time to prepare for another summer season. Dad's spirits were high and he had regained some energy. He looked like his old self again and being able to fully engage in his role at camp seemed to fill him with vigor and resilience. Every summer, staff members would start arriving at camp as early as the middle of May to help prepare the property and buildings for the upcoming season. Before the official staff-training week even started, about a dozen counselors, trip leaders, and specialty staff had already arrived to help with everything from roof maintenance to buying new ski boats. My dad was a firm believer in positive reinforcement, and he often took the pre-camp work crew out for dinner and ice cream to show his appreciation for their hard work. One such busy summer evening, my parents took the staff out to Dairy Queen.

There were about ten of us in our group and it took a few minutes to order our ice cream. There was another family in line behind us, waiting patiently to place their order. Once he finished paying for our treats, my father added a $20 bill to the total amount to pay for the family behind us. Just because.

The father of this family didn't know what to do; he had obviously not been the recipient of random acts of kindness very often. At first, he looked at my dad as if he was a total lunatic, and then he insisted on paying for the ice cream himself. For a brief moment, the Dairy Queen parking lot in Gordon, Wisconsin, became thick with tension.

Throughout my life, I often felt embarrassed by my father's boldness; as a kid I'd cringe when my father hugged instead of shook hands with my teachers at the parent/teacher conferences. I'd see the surprised look on my teacher's face and then watch as it slowly melted the instant he or she felt my father's open-hearted, impossible-to-ignore intentions. In high school, I used to pull into the driveway to find my friends' cars already parked in my spot and walk in the house to find at least one or two of them crying on my dad's shoulder over some crisis or another. He'd help us all gather a pile of snacks and then listen while we poured the emotional contents of our day out onto the kitchen table, taking in our trivial bits of gossip as if it were the highlight of his day. Whenever Dad made friends with strangers in line at the grocery store or dog park, which was often, he'd find a way to effortlessly put his hand on their shoulder or at the very least come in for a high-five. This was his way: He felt that in disarming people's rigid personal space issues, he could make a lasting connection with that person, even if they never met again.

With this philosophy in mind, my dad walked up to the man at Dairy Queen, a total stranger, and shook his hand while casually placing his other hand on the man's shoulder. I saw him squeeze the bewildered stranger's shoulder with almost parental warmth, while shaking his hand vigorously and firmly. At once the situation was calm again, and we walked to our van. Pulling away from the Dairy Queen, I saw the man's face one last time as he waved goodbye: It held a gigantic, silly grin, splashed across his face before he bit into a Dilly Bar, paid for by a new friend.

* * *

In the fall of 2000, Dylan and his best friend, Andrew, moved to Seattle after working at camp over the summer. They had only been in the city for a few weeks, looking for houses to rent while staying with friends. I was down in Tacoma, renting a big house close to campus with three good friends, but Dylan and Andrew stopped by a few times a week for dinner. One night, my roommates and I came home from a movie to find Dylan's blue truck parked in front of the house. Having Dylan and Andrew over was normal, so I walked inside and said hello, then headed straight to the refrigerator to start making dinner. As I held the chilled silver bowl of marinating veggies I'd set in the fridge earlier against my hip, I looked up at Dylan's face as he followed me into the kitchen and knew immediately that something was wrong. I set the bowl down and started stirring, knowing that Dylan wouldn't tell me whatever it was with our friends in the room; As long as I didn't let him take me out of the kitchen, I wouldn't have to hear whatever this bit of bad news was.

"Why don't you leave that for a second, Tan."

He was trying to control his voice, but his face was flat and hard. Dylan and I moved quickly upstairs to my room, walking past Andrew in the doorway. Andrew squeezed my arm and gave me a downward half-smile, warming me for a moment with this rare break from his usual shyness.

Our grandfather had been ill in recent months, and my mind turned immediately to him. "It's Papa Sammy, isn't it?" I asked, looking straight into Dylan's nervous face once he'd closed my bedroom door behind him. "Is he back in the hospital?"

"No, no. Um, Papa's fine. He's still at home. He's fine."

"What's going on then?" My heartbeats began to crescendo in my ears.

"Mom and Dad want to talk to you so I'm going to call them, okay?"

My heart sank into my gut, ripping and burning as it went. I sat on the edge of my bed while Dylan stood, then paced in circles after handing me the phone. "Hi, sweetie." Mom's voice was heavily accented with our Midwestern dipthong, a sure sign that she'd been crying.

"Okay, just tell me already. What's going on, Mom?"

"While we're down here in Milwaukee, honey, Dad had a CT scan of his liver and colon." Dylan folded his arms and lifted his left hand to his lips to chew on a fingernail.

"So what did they find?" The words came out of my mouth in sharp staccatos. My heart matched the beat, rushing and pumping hard in my chest.

"They found four new tumors in his liver." I swallowed hard, my nose and eyes tingling with the promise of tears. "So . . . we're just going to talk to some new doctors now and think about the plan . . ." The rest of her response was muffled as I dropped my shoulders and slumped over my knees, body folded in half, resting the phone on the floor and burying my shaking shoulders against my legs.

Chapter 13

THE MARKS OF A GOOD MAN

My father was devastated.

All year he had been visualizing the cancer slowly shrinking away, eventually disappearing, while in reality the tumors had been growing and spreading. I had my own feelings about the recurrence of his tumors, but what worried me more was the likelihood that my father's hopes had died when he learned that the cancer had not, in fact, slipped quietly into the darkness, had not gone into remission, had not left our lives. Like a bubbling pot of clarified butter, my stock of worry had cleared over the years: The confusion, anger, and self-pity had boiled away, and what remained was just the pure concern for my father. How *he* must have felt given the news, not how I felt.

I'm still here; I can work through my worry, angst, fear, or pain as time passes. When I am sad now, so many years after his death, what I am sad about is how scared he must have been that day he learned the cancer was still inside him, how shocked and unsure he must have felt. The surgeon who operated on my father twice before told us there was nothing further he could do. We'd reached the point where my father had run out of options.

While my dad was at a new intersection in his illness, my Papa Sammy was nearing the final turn of his own road. My mom shuttled back and forth between camp and Milwaukee, between caring for her sick husband and watching over her dying father. That fall, I began dropping classes to accommodate a more flexible travel schedule. I wanted to be able to visit my parents as often as possible and frequently flew back and forth between Milwaukee, Minong, Tacoma, and Tucson, where we still had a house and where I'd retreat to when visiting my high school friends. Throughout college, my wardrobe was split between the four cities, and I racked up enough frequent flyer miles to support an entire traveling basketball team.

For a short while, as my grandfather's condition rapidly deteriorated, my family made plans to consult surgeons who would operate on my father's liver. They would remove, freeze, or heat up the tumors in hopes of stalling their growth, depending on how many were found once they opened him up. My parents visited one surgeon in Milwaukee and another in Madison, but both would only perform the operation if they could place a permanent pump in the liver through which a constant infusion of chemo would flow, indefinitely. Essentially, they each were certain that the tumors would persist in returning, making the installation of the continual-release chemotherapy device necessary to combat their regrowth.

Dad thought a long time about this and in the end decided that surgery was too risky. In fact, the doctors were unsure of what they'd find once they cut him open. There was a strong possibility that they would discover too many tumors or tumors that had grown too large to be removed safely. It was also possible that the liver would fail to stop bleeding, causing my father to bleed out and die right there on the operating table. Considering his medical history, Dad also worried about recovering successfully from another surgery and dealing with the possibility of bowel obstructions again. Ultimately, he didn't want to live the rest of his life with poison continuously running through his body. And I had to agree with him—who would?

As my parents weighed all their options and tried to decide which next step to take, Papa Sammy passed away. Although my grandfather was a strong, stubborn man—and often made it difficult to get close to him—he and my father had developed a meaningful relationship throughout the thirty years of my parents' marriage. The loss affected Dad almost as much as it did my mother.

In his final years, my Papa Sammy had worked hard on his relationships, finally opening up to give and receive love without his trademark grumpiness and resistance. I'd always seen past the coldness of my grandfather's demeanor and had especially treasured the way he maintained a solid, constant presence in our lives; for Sammy, simply "showing up" was one of the definitive marks of a good man.

Papa Sammy had been especially eager to help as we made the transition to camp life in those early years. Back when we used to drive back and forth to Minong and couldn't afford two sets of computers, fax machines, and monstrously heavy Gestetner printing presses for our monthly newsletters in the days before email, we had to tow these items in a trailer behind our van twice each summer. We'd leave our house locked up and in the care of family and neighbors before driving the 343 miles up to Minong. My brothers and I looked forward to leaving for a few months, in part because of the way our departure always turned into an exciting event.

Our relatives and family friends would arrive at our house to help my parents strategically pack and secure the car and trailer full of camp necessities and to see us off for the summer. Among them, Papa Sammy would stand at the head of the driveway and shout instructions to everyone, while we kids ran around the yard getting in the way and delaying progress.

"Richard, don't put that damn keyboard there, it'll be toast if it rains. It always rains in Eau Claire," Papa Sammy would bark at my dad. "And Barbie" (my mom's father was the only person who ever called her by that nickname), "don't forget to tie the tarp down in the corners so it won't flap in the wind."

My grandfather never actually lifted or carried so much as a toothpick to help, but he sure enjoyed standing in front of everyone with a cup of coffee, making a big show of grumbling and scowling as if he weren't having the time of his life telling the grown-ups what to do and watching his grandchildren run laps around the house. Later, when my family moved to Tucson, we simply adjusted this routine to include air travel. The only thing missing in those days was my grandfather.

And now he was gone and would be missing from all that was to come. He wouldn't see me, his youngest grandchild, graduate college or marry or grow up to make him proud. Papa Sammy's funeral was the first I'd ever attended, and I was comforted to see the room fill up with people eager to pay him due respect. I remember one of my cousins watching as my family cried in a group huddle, the five of us, having by then learned how to lean on each other for support. She later told me that she had looked on in awe and respect that day, jealous of our closeness. But I never heard her say anything about being jealous of the means by which we came to be so close. No one could be envious of that journey.

My mom managed to maintain the level of strength she had achieved throughout my father's illness and applied it to the loss of her own father. Knowing she still had miles to go with my father before she could rest, she somehow absorbed all the pain of watching my grandfather die and simply carried on. Losing her father while trying to save her husband changed her in ways that I will probably never understand.

* * *

A few months after Papa Sammy passed away, Dad went to see a man named Dr. Gregory, a medical intuitive who restored my father's foundation of hope through their work together. Dr. Gregory uses his intuitive abilities to diagnose and recommend treatment for physical ailments. My dad was skeptical; he'd spent his thirty years of marriage making fun of my mom for believing in holistic healing, but his options were limited at this point. Chemo and surgery were off the table, and Dad was learning to consider every alternative, no matter how bizarre or taxing they seemed.

But at their appointment, Dr. Gregory eclipsed all of my father's doubts with the precision of his diagnosis. From that point forward, Dad enjoyed his meetings with Dr. Gregory and respected his remarkable abilities as a healer. They worked together throughout the winter months using herbs, oils, and teas that were specially created for my dad's body, trying to boost his immune system in order to fight off the invading cancer cells. Regardless of what those unconventional treatments did to the cancer, they did make Dad feel a little better. No one bothered to question how or why. By phone, Dad also began working more frequently with his therapist from the Simonton Cancer Center for support.

All this searching and studying led my parents to consider an alternative cancer treatment center in Baja, Mexico, called Sanoviv. They were impressed with the innovative therapies offered there, including a heat treatment called hyperthermia; knowing that tumor growth requires specific environmental conditions, Dad believed that this process had a good chance of prolonging his life.

In March of 2000, my parents temporarily moved to the Sanoviv Medical Institute, where my father underwent various methods of both traditional and alternative healing, including the hyperthermic therapy. He would lie in a long white tube, while a nurse closed the rounded lid over him. With just his head poking out from the top, Dad would lie still for as long as he could stand it, as the machine clicked and hummed, gradually raising his body's core temperature to over 104 degrees. When he had reached his limit, he'd emerge from the iron-lung-like chamber barely able to walk. He also underwent a complete detoxification through raw foods, hoping to cleanse his body of food-borne toxins. He had intravenous infusions of vitamins and immune boosters. Chelation treatments. Vigorous exercise. Vega machines. Bioenergetic treatments. Homeopathic energy treatments. His veins collapsed and rolled. Hundreds of CT, MRI, and PET scans; gallons of barium prep liquid for dozens of colonoscopies. His blood was removed from his body. His blood was treated. His blood was put back in. Needles, blood. Needles, blood.

Dad always felt some kind of pain, discomfort, or fatigue throughout his entire illness. Either he was weak and sore from the surgeries, had stomachaches from his shortened colon, suffered nausea from the chemo, felt pain from the radiation, or became sore from going to the bathroom so frequently. Once his gall bladder was removed, he was unable to eat many of his favorite foods and had a lot of indigestion and gurgling in his stomach.

Day after day he watched himself shrink in the mirror, losing a great deal of weight that he would never regain.

While still at Sanoviv, the doctors performed a CT scan to re-evaluate my father's cancer. Despite all the hard work and the many excruciating treatments, the tumors were still growing. His condition had not changed at all.

* * *

The truth is we will never know if those treatments gave him a longer life and let him live through another summer; if they hurt him; or if they did nothing at all. When my parents returned to Wisconsin after their stay at Sanoviv, my dad's oncologist urged him to consider chemo one more time, hoping to extend his life, but Dad didn't want to compromise the quality of his life again just to gain another month or so of life. Every time I came home for a visit, I'd find dozens of small glass bottles, filled with prescriptions from Sanoviv or Dr. Gregory, housed in the crevices between salad dressings and condiments in the refrigerator door, as well as tubs and jars lining the counters like a multicolor backsplash of holistic remedies. Dad was also now receiving injections of mistletoe extract, a controversial alternative cancer treatment used throughout Europe. These vials were kept chilled in the freezer, and Mom administered the shots for Dad. I watched her practice on oranges first, her fingers pushing down on the rind, feeling for rough spots. She'd rock the syringe back and forth a few times, trying to find the right amount of force before jabbing the tip of the needle into his skin. Dad never complained about the pain of the needle snapping down into his already tender body, nor the stinging of the plant extract as it coursed through his muscle tissue. Eventually this process fell smoothly into the rest of their daily anti-cancer routines—routines that were becoming a full-time job for them both.

Dad had been through so much pain already, had endured the physical torture of so many barbaric treatments—both traditional and alternative—as well as the emotional suffering that came from desperately trying to heal. But he'd only grown sicker each year.

He also had a consistent pain on his left side, sensitive to even the lightest touch. My dad often spoke of his pre- and post-cancer pain thresholds—how "cancer pain" seemed to exist on a whole other scale far beyond anything else he could imagine someone experiencing. We waited for him to scream or cry, to demand that he be given no more. We waited for him to complain, waited for him to bow beneath the ceaselessness of his physical discomfort. But, instead, there were only two nights when he simply rolled over and whispered to my mom a modest "I don't feel good." This was the apex of his complaints.

I can still picture him with those NG tubes down his nose, throat, and stomach, in so much pain when his insides were in spasm, so sore from the radiation. Still, he never complained. His strength and resilience were a testament to how much he loved his family and how much he loved life—he just kept on going without drawing attention to his discomfort because he wanted to be here with us so badly and wanted to make the most of our time together to the very extent of his diminishing ability.

When we were all home together, we'd spend our days doing things that accommodated my father's needs. Dad spent a lot of time mentoring Gabe, preparing him to eventually take over at camp. Though he had very little energy, Dad also wanted to be outdoors when he could, if even only for five minutes at a time, taking slow, deliberate walks around camp with Gabe, Dylan, and me by his side.

Mostly, though, we watched movies or read inside, the wood stoves at the north and south ends constantly whispering a steady susurrus into the house. All around us, the expanse of autumn and isolation stretched on, a great presence of silence that almost nothing could pierce. Of course our friends and family knew that Dad was getting worse, and the phone calls came without interruption. But Dad didn't have the energy to talk so much, and we simply took messages and passed them along, keeping the house cloaked in a hush. The only person Dad did want to talk to was his best friend, Alan.

Chapter 14

DOWN THIS ROAD

In early July of 2001, I was talking on the phone with my mom's friend, Cheryl, when she said to me, "Oh honey, isn't it so sad about Alan?"

"What's so sad about Alan?" I asked her. "What happened?"

"Oh . . . hmmm . . . oh dear, you should call your mom, honey. She'll tell you."

* * *

Alan: a tall drink of blond Norwegian heritage. My father: a short, bald, stocky Jewish guy.

Alan loved to eat Lox with capers and cream cheese, and my dad savored *lutifisk* with fresh *lefse*. Together they made an odd, but perfect, pair.

My parents met Alan and Susan Huse when their son, Mark, and my brother, Gabe, entered preschool together. The Huses had another son named Mike, close to Dylan's age. Years later, they and my parents were still good friends, and on the day my parents came home from the hospital after I was born, Susan called to say she was pregnant with Stephen. With kids so close in age and several favorite activities in common, it was easy for my Dad to become best friends with Alan.

The boys all went to camp together in the summers, with Gabe and Mark in a cabin together for several years. Dylan and Mark were a year apart but convinced their camp director to let them stay in a cabin together. Dylan and Mark reigned over the camp with constant pranks and mischief, including their famous impromptu trek into town on "borrowed" camp bicycles.

When I was about eleven years old, I decided to take a few weeks away from camp to spend some time with my friends in Milwaukee. I stayed with school friends for a week, and then spent a few days with Stephen at Alan and Susan's house. My dad's birthday was approaching in a few days, and Alan decided to drive me back up to camp earlier than planned so he could surprise my dad on the big day. I was excited to go back up to camp even though I had some anxiety about a whole day spent in the car with Alan. He was my dad's buddy, after all, and seemed too old to be good company for someone like me.

Alan stood at about six feet four inches tall and drove a tiny, red Miata convertible. When it was time to pack the car and start our trip from Milwaukee to Minong, Alan didn't think my duffel bag would fit in the small car. In the busy parking lot of his company, Milwaukee Millwork, Alan unzipped my bag and started rearranging its contents for all to see. As a prepubescent, eleven-year-old girl, the last thing in the world I wanted was for my dad's friend to manhandle my underwear and dirty socks in front of a crowd. Alan never had a daughter and clearly didn't know any better, so I let it slide as we finally fit the bag in the trunk and made for the open road.

In the car, Alan made it easy for me to open up and before I knew it, I was talking to him like I would any friend my own age. By the time we reached Madison, I started to understand why Dad would want to hang out with this guy. We passed the hours by sharing the things we loved about camp life, and we talked some about my favorite subjects in school, before moving on to discuss Frank Herbert's *Dune Chronicles* and the possibility of intelligent extraterrestrial life.

I knew that Alan was a regular churchgoer and even taught Sunday school, so his open-mindedness and candor caught me off-guard; I had no idea he was so tapped in to my generation's zeitgeist, or at least my version of it. The drive took us a few extra hours due to a lengthy summer downpour, but even cramped and crowded as we were inside the little convertible, time flew by. Being quite the chatterbox, I loved that Alan let me talk as much as I wanted. Usually my brothers, teachers, and friends would grow tired of my endless chattering, but it seemed to amuse Alan. He said it seemed like we were making good time even though we weren't, and I was elated. By the time we pulled into camp almost seven hours after setting out, Alan was no longer just another adult; he was now my friend and confidante.

Our families had fun taking ski vacations together and over the years, the ten of us sampled the slopes of Snowbird, Arapahoe Basin, Keystone, Whistler, Blackcomb, and the upper peninsula of Michigan. Alan was particularly easy to spot on the mountain, not only for his light blond hair and towering height, but also for the neon-pink windbreaker he always wore while skiing. He found the jacket on clearance at a local Milwaukee sporting store and couldn't resist buying it because it was so cheap, never mind that it was actually a ladies' jacket.

Like a lot of kids, I learned how to downhill ski without poles so that I could master the fundamentals of the sport before attempting the more nuanced elements. I loved following my brothers and Alan's boys as they attacked the ski runs. Whether or not they meant for me to trail behind them, I'd ski wherever they skied: over jumps, into the backcountry paths, and down the Black Diamond runs that were much too technical and difficult for my small, uncoordinated body.

Dad always told us when we took a tumble in the snow that if we didn't fall at least once, it meant we weren't trying hard enough. With this in mind, I took to the mountains hoping to get down with as much speed as possible. Dressed in a cumbersome snowsuit and hand-me-down goggles that never stayed in place, I bombed down the slopes, my arms pushed back behind me with the force of the wind, now zipping noisily in my ears. Though I knew it was dangerous, sometimes I even closed my eyes and let my skis point straight down to the bottom of the run. I was small enough to have passed between people's legs and made this my default plan should I run into skiers blocking my path.

My daredevil style seemed to amuse the older boys, and it positively delighted my father. More than anything, I think he loved being able to share one of his most beloved activities with his most beloved people—especially when my brothers and I had taken to the sport just as naturally and enthusiastically as he had. But when I really picked up more speed than the slope called for, Dad would race to catch up to me, yelling down the hill, "Turn, Tanya . . . you have to make turns!" Whenever I clumsily landed a jump or slowed to a stop at the bottom of a run all wind-bitten and red-nosed, my dad would lift me up by the back of my snowsuit for a quick kiss or a high-high-five, my feet dangling in the air, before we'd turn and head toward the chair lift to do it all again.

At lunchtime during these trips, we'd enter a lodge on the ski slopes, only to stare wistfully at the kids eating gooey, grilled cheese sandwiches, slices of pizza, and sourdough bread bowls filled with chili. Instead of sampling such tasty-looking mountain fare, Dad would pack peanut butter and jelly sandwiches on wheat bread with a few Fig Newtons—the whole lunch by midday having amalgamated into a soggy, pasty mess because my Dad never wore a proper backpack to carry such items. He'd either wear a fanny pack, which of course was far too embarrassing for us to tolerate, or he'd stick the lunches in the front pocket of his ski jacket where they'd mush together and disintegrate.

Alan, however, wouldn't even go this far. He'd simply peruse the aisle with silverware, napkins, and straws and begin collecting the complimentary jam, crackers, and condiments. These he would line up in rows according to flavor. Next he used a plastic knife to make little sandwiches out of the assortment. He'd bring back several of these morsels to our table, lay each one out in front of him like a delicacy, and eat like a king.

* * *

Alan was one of the most physically fit men I'd ever met. His family's medical history was littered by cases of heart disease; many of his relatives, including his father, died at a young age from heart-related problems. To combat this likely end, Alan often ran long distances and even biked a nearly-fifteen-mile round-trip commute to and from work when the weather permitted. Riding his bike with a friend around the Fourth of July in 2001, Alan took a nasty fall. By the time he got home and his wife came to see him, she knew something was off. His face was bright red and covered in sweat, but more importantly, Susan could tell that he wasn't acting like himself. Thinking perhaps he had a touch of heat stroke, Alan drank lots of water and rested a few days.

Alan always walked too quickly for Susan; she struggled to keep up with his pace throughout their thirty-three-year marriage. A few days after the bicycle fall, Alan and Susan took a walk through the Whitefish Bay neighborhood of Milwaukee. Susan was, for the first time, leading the way and was glad to finally show Alan how it felt to be left behind on the sidewalk. Still, she noticed that it seemed as if he couldn't walk quickly. Throughout that week, Alan's behavior continued to deviate from the norm; he backed into a neighbor's car, stumbled and lost his balance several times, and drove too far to the left in his lane on the freeway, nearly driving into oncoming traffic. Finally wondering if perhaps Alan had suffered a small stroke, Susan convinced him to see their doctor. Just three days later, Alan was diagnosed with melanoma, which had spread to and metastasized in his brain.

"You have a number of small tumors. There's nothing we can do," the doctor had said to Alan. That number was eventually clarified as twenty-three small tumors positioned throughout his brain. His oncologist told Susan that Alan would most likely live as little as three to five more months.

The news of Alan's cancer set my dad back a great distance. He had always planned for Alan to take care of us after he died, and now Alan would likely be gone by the time Dad also passed away. Such a bizarre twist of their two fates surprised us all—my dad never expected their friendship to end in this way—but each tried to comfort the other as death drew nearer for both. Because it was detected so late and the cancer was so aggressive, Alan's illness worsened very quickly. Although Alan did undergo some radiation treatments, surgery was risky and there wasn't much else to try. Alan lost his balance and fell frequently, which sent him to the hospital or an ambulance to the house several times. Still, Alan insisted on going into work every day, though Susan now had to drive him to and from the office. She understood his need to go, understood the pitiful resignation in simply waiting at home. However, she was jealous of my mom—jealous that even though my dad also did some work each day, they were together for all that would be left of his last days.

Chapter 15

GOING HOME

That summer of 2001, my father's liver started to fail. His liver enzymes increased and then steadily began to poison him, turning him the sickly yellow shade of jaundice. I was away in Tacoma most of the summer and didn't really know how badly Dad's health had turned. Gabe called in early July to tell me that our parents had been sugarcoating things on the phone when I spoke to them and that he was beginning to worry about Dad's health and stamina. Gabe told me that our father's skin was turning yellow and that he had been forced to exclusively wear pants, long-sleeved shirts, and sunglasses to hide his jaundiced condition from the campers and staff.

The discoloration started in his eyes, turning the corners a highlighter shade of yellow, and then traveled to his skin, which slowly paled before matching his eyes in a sickly hue. Gabe said that some days the color wasn't as bad as others but that it seemed to be getting steadily worse. I was furious with my parents for allowing me to go on for so long thinking everything was all right, though I knew a break from all the stress I'd been under was all they had wanted for me. Nevertheless, I wished that they had given me more time to get ready, wished they would have let me watch the inevitable approach from the distance like the darkening sky of an afternoon thunderstorm.

"I'll come home for the fall semester, at the very least," I told Gabe.

"Yeah," Gabe said, quiet for a minute as we both thought it through. "You probably should."

"I guess I can just take the semester off. Right?"

"Or you could think about going to UMD with Dylan. He can probably even register for you." After our call, it was clear that it was time for things to change, whether we wanted them to or not.

A few weeks later, the monthly liver function and liver enzyme tests that my dad took at his oncologist's office in Duluth came back with the worst news yet. During an earlier test, my dad's blood came through the syringe thicker than usual and looking very dark— almost black. Mom and Dad knew then that he was not doing well but remained hopeful and chose not to worry my brothers or me by telling us about the experience or what it could potentially mean.

In a healthy adult, the average number of liver enzymes can range anywhere from 25 to 125. During the period of two years before his death, when my mom documented his monthly tests, my dad's enzyme count jumped around from 72 to the 490s. By August, the nurse who took Dad's blood sample thought she'd made a mistake while performing the exam, not believing that his liver enzymes could even reach such high numbers, somewhere around 1,000. She carried out the test one more time, only to obtain the same shocking, ominous result. In the space of just three or four weeks, his condition had severely deteriorated, faster than even his oncologist could have predicted. By the middle of August, Dad's numbers were somewhere in the 3,000s. My father was heartbroken to learn that most of his insides were now completely overtaken, poisoned with the cancer. He would no longer be able to donate any of his organs, an act of human kindness he strongly advocated.

Arriving back at camp after hearing the devastating prognosis, my parents shut the door to their bedroom and lay down on the bed together. They would need to tell the three of us that Dad was dying, and they had no idea how to do it. The two of them grasped hands, each feeling the stresses, joys, ups, and downs of the past three decades fade away; all that mattered in that moment was the realization that they only had a small amount of time left together.

* * *

I was at work, adjusting a set of Thomas the Tank Engine tracks for the three-year-old boy I took care of, when his father yelled that I had a telephone call. I looked at Henry and tilted my head quizzically before scooping him up in my arms and heading upstairs to answer the phone. As I bounded up each step, Henry resting on my hip and curling his arm around my neck, I knew that something was wrong, or at least wrong enough for someone to call me at work. On the phone, my parents calmly and plainly told me that some of Dad's routine test results had them worried and that they wanted me to come home immediately.

"Barney's been on the phone all day," Mom said in a hush. I could hear the click as Dad hung up, letting Mom finish issuing my instructions. "He's got you on a flight tomorrow morning at seven." That was as much as she would tell me until I made it back to my house and had packed. She said we would talk about the rest as soon as I was home. But they didn't need to give me any details—I knew from the tenuously steadied timbre of their voices that whatever they were going to tell me later, it would be bad news.

I was shaking as I hung up the phone, not sure what to do or say first. I apologized several times to Henry's father while running out the front door, leaving my boss without a nanny for the rest of the day and most likely for the rest of the summer.

The father of my sweet little charges seemed an odd man to me—I felt that he sometimes acted aloof and emotionally distant, insensitive even at times. He and I could never quite find a way to comfortably understand or relate to one another, but I loved watching his children, he appreciated how much I cared for his family, and this was enough for us both. We were far from close, but as I stumbled out his front door, just barely keeping the tears in, he stopped me. He wrapped me in a startlingly tight hug, as if he'd needed it too, and told me that he was proud of me for going to my father's side. In a rare moment of candor, he explained how he had been too late in acknowledging his own mother's cancer before she died and always regretted not being there with her when she needed him most. That exchange of stories and embrace was the first time death would connect me with a person to whom I would have otherwise always felt distant. It would prove to be the first of many such connections to be made down the road.

* * *

With the phone call from my parents came a paralyzing disillusion: Hope and strong will alone could not save my father.

I flung my Jeep's small red door wide open on its hinge and grasped the steering wheel to lift the weight of my body up into the car. My arms hung heavy against the pressure of my fingers around the weathered texture of the wheel, elbows resting on my thighs. I drove this way for a few blocks, eyes blinking in a rapid, broken rhythm. Stopping at a red light, I let my head rest on the wheel. As my forehead touched the cool leather, the tears began. The epiphany had struck—it was as if I was finally allowing myself to keep my eyes open long enough to focus my gaze. And what I let myself see in that focused gaze was that life was going to happen as it happens, no matter how much I wanted it to choose a different path. I could only shake and heave great gulps of air, making my chest rise and fall so deeply that my muscles tightened and would be sore for days. After a minute or so, the honking horns made me blink away a wave of tears and push the clutch down, put my hand on the gear shift, and drive on autopilot, until finally I had managed to bring myself into the driveway of my house.

I walked up the stairs to the front door, leaning heavily on the rough wooden railing, stepped through the door, climbed the beige-carpet stairs, and advanced straight into my room. I didn't want to tell my roommates what was happening yet; I just wanted to get my things packed and set them by the door before explaining anything. I quickly stuffed a duffel bag to the brim, not knowing how long I was packing for or if I would even be coming back.

I threw clothes into the green canvas bag willy-nilly, not bothering to neatly board-fold anything the way I always do. I was consumed with worry that Dad was going to die that night, before I could get to him. I tortured myself with guilt over not having been home the whole summer, ashamed for having gone to school 2,000 miles away from him when he had been so sick. I allowed myself no pardon for taking such a long time to grow up.

I didn't say goodbye to anyone other than my roommates and left earlier than necessary the next morning, anxious to get the journey over with. As the wheels of the airplane lifted from the tarmac, I thought about my life at school: my friends, my writing, and my studies. I imagined the mess of them all sticking to the black lines of runway beneath the belly of the plane, staying behind while I lifted up into the air.

When I finally walked into the house hours later and saw my dad, he opened his arms and squeezed me tightly, welcoming me home. Held close to him, I felt for the first time how skinny he now was. The way his skin stretched and reached to cover his collarbone shocked me, as if I could literally see the places where the cancer was feeding off him. Everyone in the room smiled but no one said a word. There was only the heavy, damp heat in the room, the click of the ceiling fan above us, and the nervous smiles on our faces, holding our fears in like corks. I had just seen him while visiting camp three weeks before and already he looked so much worse, seemed so much closer to death.

My parents waited until I settled down on the living room couch to unload the full story on me. Back at St. Luke's hospital in Duluth, Dad's oncologist said that his liver would probably fail completely within a few weeks, and once the decline set in, Dad would become mentally confused as his physical condition worsened. And then shortly thereafter, he would die. At the most, he had three weeks left to live. And at the least—just a few days.

My stomach rolled in and over itself as Mom spoke. I felt deceived, horrified that everyone else had had more time to let this development sink in. But I also knew that had she told me the details over the phone, I might not have made it through that stoplight back in Tacoma.

Because I'd arrived at camp from so far away and without any warning, we spent much of that night figuring out how we were going to make it through the last two weeks of the postseason, and what story we would tell the staff members who remained at camp to cover up the ominous nature of what was really going on.

After we made a plan for the remaining days of the season, I sat with my dad on the couch. As if it were any other night, we watched TV and caught up on what I'd learned in my summer classes. Dad rattled off one joke after another about my obnoxious roommate who slept with the TV on full-blast, making me perk up and laugh for the first time since I arrived home. As I rocked back in fits of giggles, I patted him on the chest. He winced and pulled away from me, his whole body shrinking in one swift movement. No one told me the tumors were now so obtrusive that it hurt him to be touched anywhere on his chest or abdomen. He breathed deeply to regain his repose and said to me, "Tanya, you can't do that." Then he lifted his shirt and showed me the tumors, which were visibly poking out from the skin over his belly.

Chapter 16

A SUMMER DAY ON LAKE POKEGAMA

We've seen it all go and we'll watch it go again. The great thing is to last and get your work done and see and hear and learn and understand . . . but still there were a few things to be said. There were a few practical things to be said.

—*Ernest Hemingway,* Death in the Afternoon

The second session of camp had just ended, and many of our counselors and trip leaders, or "trippers" as we call them, were busy enjoying the various end-of-season activities. This gave us precious bits of stolen private time to figure out what the hell we were going to do. We needed to be prepared in case the doctors had been generous in their final diagnoses. And though he literally could have died at any moment, Dad kept thinking positively.

"My life since the embolism—" he said, "—I have been asking God to give me another summer so I can do this wonderful, wonderful work. And if it's God's choice that I die, I'm grateful that it'll be when camp is over so that whatever grieving the kids have to do, they can do with parents."

But for me, I just wanted them all gone. It disgusted me to have to plan these things out surrounded by so many people. Though I shared my father's concerns for the camp community, I wanted them all to leave—thought at the time that they *should* leave. I'd shared my father my whole life and now, at least in death, I wanted him to myself.

While everyone was milling about, carrying the boats into storage and taking all the hand- and footholds off the climbing wall, my family took a boat out into the middle of our lake—the only place we could be certain of some much-needed privacy. We walked the short distance from our house to the waterfront, took to the dock waving and laughing. In the lake some younger counselors were swimming and rolling round and round—under then over the water on an old lumberjack's log. We hopped into the boat as if middle-of-the-day boat tours were a long-held family tradition.

Smile and say, "Good job—nice one" to that tripper catching a bass on the other dock. Nod to the people standing thigh-deep in the water, taking down the mainsails of the sail boats. *It's fine.* Look around with your best-rehearsed camp-director face, look like it's the best day ever.

We fixed our faces in mock pleasure and cruised on at moderate speeds. My dad drove the boat, even though I saw him arch sideways holding his belly as if with each wave his liver failed him more. He led us to a spot where we could float in view of a bald eagle's nest at the edge of our property. When he killed the engine, we sat facing each other on the boat's vinyl cushions for a few minutes. The gentle, late-summer breeze rocked us side to side, only the water-borne echoes of people yelling and whistles blowing from the shore for noise.

I'm not usually afraid to be the first one to speak and break a silence, but I had nothing to say then. Dad, however, knew that there was much to be said.

"I want time without distractions now to sit with each of you and just talk. Each time I talk to you I feel more pride, and that pride goes such a long way in numbing the pain," he said. He looked up at the sky, squinting at its brightness, and continued: "So we should talk about pain and what's going to happen."

The sounds coming from around the lake dulled, the wind died, and all around our boat the world seemed muted.

"I hope it will be easier for you kids to deal with death if you know how I feel." I stopped my gaze on a bug crawling over the boat's rough carpeting and held it there.

"There are different ways to acknowledge the end of a life," he said, "because as people we are all different. What's important to me are the people who have touched my life and taught me valuable lessons. I hope that I might have had the privilege of doing the same." I heard what he was saying, but I wanted him to stop talking, wanted it all to go away.

"I'd like it if people could share some of those moments or impressions at my memorial, both the good things I may have done and things that reflect my absolutely stupid sense of humor." Now I was listening. Now I was beginning to understand that if we didn't pay attention, we'd risk failing to honor his last wishes, his final words, and it didn't matter even a little bit whether or not I was ready. Here they were. This was our chance.

I tilted my chin up into the sun so I could look at him while he talked. Gabe took notes in a small notebook he always carried with him—an idea he got from Alan. Dylan and I joked that Mom should take back-up notes because Gabe's handwriting was so atrocious that we were worried we'd never be able to read these important details later.

Dad continued on as if he had planned the whole speech, as if it were just another rehearsal of what he had said to us in his head many times. "That's all right if people want to be a part of the group but keep their thoughts to themselves, and I hope that some people will be comfortable enough to share some stories."

This he said while looking at me: "For me, living with the Sword of Damocles over one shoulder was all but erased by the love and kindness of all the wonderful people who made my life so magnificent, so satisfying, and so full. I want people to leave with smiles on their faces." Then we decided on some songs he liked for the service and the people he thought would likely wish to speak.

Next, the more practical matters: There would be no needles in the next few weeks, no hospital beds. "I wanted quality of life," he said with resoluteness in his voice. "The liver will be overcome with tumor growth—making me feverish, itchy, confused." He was calm again now, looking out across the lake to our water-skiing dock where trippers were climbing in and out of the water.

"At that point, hospice should intervene and make me comfortable, let death go as a natural process. Let the body shut down naturally and allow the soul to move." My mom and brothers were crying with their heads down, Gabe frantically writing as Dad spoke.

"That might be hard for you guys, so if that time comes, I hope you'll take comfort in knowing that it's exactly what I want."

He told us to have his body cremated and to wait two or three weeks before holding a memorial service so that the four of us would have enough time to mourn together before opening up our grief to friends and family. While we discussed what would happen over the next few days, it occurred to me that *this* could be the last day that our family would have together—the last time there would be five of us.

My father had known his share of friends and family who lost loved ones, and he was saddened by how little support they were given after suffering such a traumatic turn in their lives. He wanted something different for us; he wanted us to go through the experience of his death with awareness and an appreciation for its beauty. Dad wanted us to lean heavily on the love and support of our closest friends and allow the bond within our immediate circle to carry us through the darkest grieving. It seemed unnatural and terrifying to be discussing these things while he was still here, but I trusted my father and listened as intently as I could manage. He knew what I didn't yet understand: that these events, though difficult to stomach, were better appreciated with an open line of communication. If we were to go through this impending devastation, he wanted us to go through it with our eyes open. There would be no glossing over the importance of what was happening to us; we would not pretend that everything would be fine while brushing it all under the table. Not with him.

I looked at my dad through a marathon of tears running from my eyes with the speed of having someplace better to be. I wanted him to stop talking, wanted him to tell me it had all been a mistake and he would be fine—all of this nonsense could wait for another twenty or forty years. Even then, in my desperation for it to be otherwise I could see that he was sicker and thinner than I had ever seen him. His face had turned gray and muted of its usual vibrancy, his eyes now yellow like a late-October moon.

He began telling my brothers and me what he wanted for the three of us—to move forward in our education and then decide if camp was the life we wanted for ourselves or if another calling held our interests. But as he said this, I couldn't think about whether I'd grow up to pursue writing or working or even camp—all I wanted was to be just like him, in whatever capacity such a thing could be attained.

"How will I know what to do without you here?" I asked between sobs, breaking into his monologue. He looked down at me, then bent down to scoop me up in his arms. Finding some vestige of stored-up strength, he held me next to him while I cried and let the thought of him not doing this again for the rest of my life blow through me. He put his hand on my head and hugged me tightly against his warm, yellow skin.

"You know, I loved waking up with you kids when you were little—the diapers, feeding you, having my coffee, and talking to you. It was my time. The best time." He kept his arm around me and squeezed the top of my arm while saying, "Being a parent is like being in a perpetual state of bliss, interrupted by a few poopy diapers and the only change is what's in the diapers! The hardest thing about parenting is stepping back and allowing you to learn life's lessons, and not protect you too much."

I wanted him to protect me too much, wanted him to forever tell me what to do so I wouldn't need to decide for myself. In light of his failing health, I wanted him to be as overbearing as possible, but he knew better. He told me not to worry about being him or being me. That if I learned how to begin everything I do or say with love, to fill my heart with it, everything would look different. That in the end, being right isn't what matters.

I had so many questions I wanted to ask, uncertainties about what death would look like and how I would know if it was coming. What if it happened in the middle of the night—would I be there? As everyone else talked about the logistics of making sure camp would be taken care of, I looked back on the previous three years of my father's illness, hating myself for being so stupid. Had I really thought everything would be fine? How could I have been so dumb as to go on planning my future, taking classes, and partying with friends while all along my father was slowly dying? I hated my decisions to attend college far from home, to work somewhere other than camp during that summer, to separate myself from my parents when I could have been with my father all that time.

For several months already, my dad had lived with the decision to stop trying for a cure. The only alternative was to attempt treatments only slightly less deadly than what was killing him in the first place. Each doctor presented other options but none were pain-free or even seemed worth trying. Instead, he was clear on his decision to stop and just let go. Logically, I understood the argument but until August came, and with it the realization that he truly was dying, I couldn't digest the outcome of such a decision. Openly discussing the details of his death was subsequently more than I could bear.

As we faced the lakefront and scanned the shore for our cabins, I could see that Dad still felt pretty damn lucky. Watching death crawl nearer, he continued to appreciate how fun and full our lives were. "I have had a lifetime of dreams conceived and exceeded— how can I not be grateful for that?"

* * *

Being as open as we were about all of this was difficult for me. To me, it seemed like all we could, and would, do was just sit around and wait for him to die, and I couldn't accept that. My dad wanted his last few weeks to be spent together doing the things we enjoyed doing as a family. But I hated thinking about what we would do while he was dying, or even how much time we'd have. Talking about it only made me feel worse, at first. But my dad made me see that I couldn't be afraid of those dark questions, those scary emotions, because they were there to help me work through the fear and come out strong, and clear, on the other side.

Of course, I didn't have very far to look in order to find a good role model for pushing past the pain and finding beauty. My dad found the strength and composure to send the rest of the camp crew off in his usual style and waved kisses to them as they drove up the long hill out of camp. And after most of the counselors, trippers, and kitchen staff went home for the season, my father allowed a few key people into our home before they left—those who had worked with us for many years and in doing so had become like a part of our family. There, he told them the truth and allowed them to say goodbye. It couldn't have been easy to face each one of his closest friends, colleagues, and surrogate children to tell them he was dying, but he knew it was the right thing to do. He was able to give his beloved employees the opportunity to tell him how much they loved him, how much he had influenced them. The secret of his cancer was finally out in the open, and it was a great relief to us all to let our emotions show in public after so many years of carefully maintained poise.

As the last car turned the corner out of camp, Dad was already crafting the letter he would send home to the campers' families, informing them of his illness and gently preparing them for what we knew was coming, what they would be guessing even as they read his words of assurance. After the campers had been home long enough to settle back into their usual routines, Dad sent that letter out to all our camp contacts, finally informing the community at large of his illness. From that day forward, our mailbox flooded with letters of encouragement, support, love, adoration, and gratitude for all the lives my father had touched.

Letting the whole world in on what we had been going through so privately felt strange and violating in the beginning, but soon all the phone calls, letters, and emails began to lift my father up a little. I could physically see the effect love was having on him and hoped it could still cure him even at this desperate eleventh hour.

Chapter 17

A FINAL LOAD OF
REMNANT MILLWORK

Alan, too, had always possessed a special love for camp. He'd pack a single change of clothes and a toothbrush and head up north a few times each summer to relax and see my dad. Even though our camp house had two bathrooms with perfectly working showers, Alan would always choose to bathe in his swim trunks down at the waterfront's beach shower, which did not have a water heater. The very act of toughing out a cold shower seemed to satisfy Alan's need for a real outdoor experience, and he'd always walk back up to the house with a big grin on his face afterward. One year during Alan's visit, my dad was in the middle of building a multi-room addition to our house, and when Alan arrived, the roof hadn't yet been finished and only the initial layers of the room's frame had been constructed. As a joke, my dad moved a perfectly made bed into the bare room and set a small nightstand with an alarm clock beside it. When Alan arrived, Dad showed him to the new "guestroom" and laughed at his little joke. Only that night, Alan chose to actually sleep in the unfinished room with the cold night sky above him.

* * *

In early August of that year, Alan and Susan made one final trip to visit Dad at the camp, but the weather was so hot and muggy that the two ailing men could only comfortably spend time together staying inside my parents' air-conditioned bedroom, which was the only air-conditioned room at camp. With both of their health deteriorating quickly, we worried that the late-summer visit would be the last time the two men would see each other. So our two families rushed to make a plan for them to see each other once more that fall.

My family drove down to Milwaukee in late September to make that last visit with Alan. By the time we reached Milwaukee, the health of the two best friends had deteriorated with frightening speed, and they were visibly shocked at the sight of one another.

Dad and Alan had always enjoyed crafting their skills in the "fine art of being cheap." Every dual-family dinner on the town we'd ever shared turned into a competition between the two men to see who could pick the least expensive, tastiest, most authentic, and often greasiest restaurant. Not wanting this time to be any different, Dad and Alan decided to have dinner at a Mexican restaurant called Conjitos down in the Third Ward District. It was one of our regular spots, where we had enjoyed years of eating our meals on cheap paper plates and sharing one root beer between the five of us. No refills, of course, this time around either, in keeping with the spirit of those comically money-thrifty days.

Alan's millwork business had often supplied Dad's camp projects with remnants from old construction accounts, and because the doors and windows of a new building are often the most expensive materials, Alan always saved pieces from his large inventory that had been discarded and sold them to my dad for next to nothing. Over the years they enjoyed collaborating on new and interesting designs for as little money as possible—their signature style.

On the final day of our visit with Alan, we drove Dylan's big pickup truck to Milwaukee Millwork for one last load of remnant pieces. Dad and Alan were too weak to help load the windows and doors, so they stood back and watched while Dylan, Gabe, and a few of Alan's employees lifted everything into the truck bed and strapped it down securely.

"Well, that's it. That's everything," Alan said to my dad. They walked toward each other and hugged while the rest of us looked on in silence.

* * *

The five-and-a-half-hour drive home from Milwaukee to Minong ended up taking us two days because of Dad's unstable health and diminishing energy. We spent the night in Tomah—the halfway point between the two cities—in a motel called the Cranberry Country Lodge. Dad, Gabe, and Dylan walked across the highway to the only other hotel at the Tomah exit in order to sneak in and enjoy that hotel's hot tub. After only a few minutes in the water, though, Dad said he was getting overheated and wanted to go lie down. Walking back across the empty highway with towels around their waists, my brothers noticed Dad looking flushed and unsteady.

Later, while my brothers and I watched TV in our room, my dad started feeling dizzy and complaining of pressure building in his lungs. Mom called us into their room and right away my eyes fixed on the large beads of sweat dripping from Dad's face, his shock-widened eyes, the tinge of blue in his lips. His hands were pressed on his chest, rising and falling so quickly it didn't seem like he could get any oxygen with each breath, one after another empty and terrifying. We gathered around the bed, and Dad started to cry. He told us he thought this might be *it*, that it was happening right then. The rest of us started crying too, hugging him, and praying aloud that he wouldn't die—not like this, not at the Cranberry Country Lodge.

After a few minutes, though, Dad was able to breathe a little easier and the pain he'd felt in his chest slowly dissipated. Perhaps he'd had a small heart attack, or even a panic attack, but for the moment he seemed stable enough to keep traveling, so the next day we got back in the car and drove home at a desperate pace.

Back at camp, my dad didn't have the strength, energy, or time to talk with anyone over the phone, though both the house and camp lines rang nearly constantly most days. Often we'd simply relay well-wishes or let the machines load up with messages. However, there was one call my dad made each night, and that was to Alan. Dad would slowly and deliberately walk to his bedroom, close the door, and lie on his bed with the old black office phone tucked into the curve between his shoulder and neck. Then the two of them worked out theories on what dying was going to feel like, how close it seemed, and who would go first. With Alan, my father could finally be as candid as he wished about the insecurities and fear he felt, knowing that he might simply fall asleep and not wake up again. Dad had been on this road alone for such a long time, and while he was heartbroken about Alan's illness, he felt somewhat soothed knowing his friend could definitively understand his fears and trepidation. For Alan, too, having a guide to help him navigate the pain and uncertainty was also comforting.

In preparation for what was to come, they promised to each write a eulogy for the other, to be read by family members should they die at the same time. What a strange source of comfort and also uncertainty—to know that you would not be dying alone, that you'd have your best friend waiting to join you for the journey, and knowing that both of your families would be left behind without you.

Chapter 18

THE CHURCH OF THE FOAMING BRUSH

In early September 2001, when the air was becoming sharp and the leaves were turning, my dad was turning too. His physical abilities were steadily declining, making such basic tasks as getting dressed and walking to the office more difficult and time-consuming than he was at first willing to admit. The autumnal crisp had only just arrived in the evening winds, and the long days were still sunny and warm, at least by Wisconsin standards. My father wanted to go on performing his daily routine as long as possible; it seemed wasteful to simply sit around the house and wait to die. True to form, he held on fiercely to his activities and independence.

He'd often walk the hundred feet or so between the office and house a few times a day, accomplishing small bits of work even though it wasn't necessary; Gabe, Michelle, and my mom had all the camp work sufficiently covered. But I could tell that Dad felt anxious about the abrupt end to his work, especially since he'd spent his entire life working in some capacity and toward some goal. Whether it was being an inspirational teacher, an accomplished lawyer, or a well-loved camp director, his work ethic was undeniable and not easily shaken loose. I think that in his mind, the day he stopped being himself would be the day he died, but he never allowed that to happen—he was too busy squeezing the last drops of normalcy and pleasure into his cup.

Car care had always been tantamount to religion in our family; although we attended synagogue growing up, and my brothers and I were properly bar mitzvahed with all the appropriate fanfare, we were never a seriously devout family. On the occasions we did go to Temple for the High Holidays, we'd often take turns goofing around in the hallways behind the building's grandiose synagogue. When I was in seventh grade, I sat at the end of our balcony pew on Rosh Hashanah. As the cantor took the stage to lead the congregation in song, I looked over at my family to find that everyone except my disapproving mom was asleep, though even she looked back at me with sleep-heavy eyes.

Instead of using our Jewish faith to bring us closer, we'd regularly gather together at early morning on the lawn or driveway, dressed in shorts and flip-flops, to attend my father's Church of the Foaming Brush. Although we never owned expensive, luxury vehicles, my father loved to be on the road and got very excited about cars that handled well and were fun to drive. He drove a motorcycle for many years and, when we were younger, took us on short trips with Alan and his sons. We even had a sidecar that could fit two of us if one of my brothers held me in his lap. Getting picked up from school on the back of my dad's motorcycle made me a much cooler kid than I would otherwise have been in the fifth grade. Eventually, the three of us grew older and wanted motorcycles of our own, at which point—terrified of that prospect—my father promptly sold his Honda Nighthawk and transferred his passion to sports cars.

The last car my dad would ever buy was likely his favorite—a 2001 Subaru Impreza 2.5 RS rally car. The purchase was a bit out of character for him because once he'd received his cancer diagnosis, he didn't want to spend any money on himself or on anything for his unknown future. He didn't even want to spend money to go to the dentist if he was only going to die a short time down the road.

But at one point after yet another of his many procedures and after a hopeful prognosis, he felt like he could actually buy something for himself, as he believed he might still have a long future. One day, while visiting me at school, my parents and I decided to test-drive Subaru's new rally car—just for kicks. Finding this sort of thing to be an incredible amount of fun, my dad drove the car up over curbs, did doughnuts in a dirt parking lot, and revved the engine until the tachometer floated back and forth uneasily in the red zone. I sat in the backseat with the Subaru salesman, who looked like he was going to nervously smile his way through cardiac arrest. A few months later, despite not needing a new car in the least, my dad bought the 2001 Subaru Impreza 2.5 RS he had driven in Tacoma. He told me that it felt like the most irresponsible thing he had ever done, and he loved it. We all loved that he felt hopeful enough to actually buy something fun for himself, and we encouraged his near-giddy worship of the little speedster.

We also never were a very materialistic family, and so keeping our cars well-maintained had less to do with keeping up appearances or worshipping store-bought things than with being responsible for our property.

The anxiety my dad felt waiting for death to take him each night made it impossible for him to fall asleep, so he began relying on sleeping medication to help him rest. Soon, he and my mom started doling out half a dose here, a whole dose there, to each of us when we found it increasingly hard to get to sleep as well, which was most of the time. We'd take turns helping Dad to get into bed at night, resting his arm around our shoulders. Often, he'd already have taken his nightly sleeping pill and would be seconds from sleep as we walked him through the hallway, the TV still flickering its shadows on the walls behind us. The sleeping pills made him a little silly, and as I eased him down to the bed one night, lifting the blankets over his legs, he looked up at me almost giddy with love—the way I must have looked when he tucked me in as a little girl. He wasn't childlike, though; he was simply filled with gratitude for having lived to see another beautiful autumn day with his wife and children.

We all figured that in those final months of his life, Dad would stop trying to exert the energy necessary for washing his car, especially when simply getting up from the couch and walking the twenty feet to his bed had become a regular challenge. Though he allowed us to help him into bed each night, Dad remained adamant about washing his car all by himself. Because he was so weak, though, he was forced to do the washing in stages. First he pulled the car as close to the house as possible. There, he would pre-rinse the car before taking a seat on a nearby bench to rest. Next, he'd scrub the car and wheels before having a drink of water and another rest on the bench. He then rinsed the suds away and quickly dried it with a chamois. After a long nap, he'd return to the car to clean the interior and squeegee the windows. He did accept help on occasion but only for the company, and even then he would frequently offer suggestions and criticism on my brothers' and my detailing skills. I didn't mind the critique, though, because as he and I would work on the hood, Dad would teach me about the different parts of the engine and how they worked together. Or he would tell me about when he first learned to drive and how he even snuck his father's car in the middle of the night without permission. I kept these bits of knowledge and stories tucked away, knowing I would soon be left to pass them on.

When we were finished and the car was clean, I'd help Dad lay his tired body on the couch and talk with him until he fell asleep. Watching him lie there exhausted but pleased, I felt that I could almost see his face advance in age with each passing hour. He was becoming an old man right in front of my eyes, with unnatural speed.

Chapter 19

THE LAST CRUMB

By the end of September 2001, it was just our family at camp—everyone had gone home for the winter. I loved the privacy, the seclusion, the time alone with my family that I'd always craved. I took a walk one afternoon just as the aspen leaves were starting to turn and could so clearly remember my first impressions of camp. I looked around at all our land and thought about what camp looked like when my parents first bought the property so many years ago.

During one of Dad's first visits as a potential buyer, he called home to fill us in on what camp was like. Being so young, I was still mastering the skills of holding and speaking into a telephone. But I remember this conversation vividly.

"I miss you so much, Won-Ton. So much!" he said first. "I can't wait for you to come up here next time."

"I miss you too, Daddy. When are you coming home?" I cooed, as if his answer would be a turning point in the plot of one of our bedtime stories.

"Oh, soon, soon. You're really going to love it here. There's a big hill with grass all around and only one little piece of sidewalk in the whole place."

As he said this, my three-year-old mind began painting the scene: a cartoonishly steep hill covered entirely in grass, with a continuous section of sidewalk cantilevered around the hill like the rings of Saturn. So when I arrived at camp for the first time, I was disappointed to find that it didn't look like the image I'd pictured at all.

"You have an imagination just like mine, honey!" Dad said with excitement before taking my small hand in his and walking me around all the buildings. As we strolled, he told me about one morning before school when he was nine years old. He and his mother, my Nana Mimi, were playing a quick game of cowboys and Indians before he began his walk to school. As part of the game, my dad tied his mother up to a chair and ran circles around her for a few minutes. When she told him it was time to get his backpack ready and leave for school, he was still in character. So he pulled her—still tied to the chair—backward into a nearby closet and closed the door. He then promptly picked up his backpack, walked down the stairs, and out the front door. She stayed tied to the chair and locked in the closet until my Papa Ben got home later that afternoon. I comforted myself by remembering and retelling those stories I loved so much— stories of my dad as a child, as a young man, a newly married twenty- something, a law student, a brand-new father—because in those stories and memories he was healthy and strong. Though I'd been cold when I set out that afternoon, I was warm now and unzipped my jacket halfway to let in some of the fall air to cool my neck and chest. The path I walked was flanked on one side by stands of wheat and thistle, and on the other by the innocuous, meandering bend of the lake that hugged the north end of camp. The road was soggy and un-manicured, but bare enough of branches to accommodate me. Walking our land and seeing how much it had changed over the years made me think back to the early days and try to imagine how scared my parents must have felt signing up for all this.

Arriving at camp our first summer, my parents must have looked around at the unmowed grass and weeds stretching out for 400 acres, the disheveled buildings, and the winter-bruised trees in abject dread. My mom first cleaned and organized the house we inherited from the previous owner—the house where we would spend half our lives— making sure that at the very least we had someplace welcoming to sleep at the end of each exhausting day. Next, my parents tackled what lay outside our cozy little cabin walls.

The property presented a maintenance nightmare with the majority of the buildings needing to be restored, or in some cases entirely rebuilt. Many cabins were turn-of-the-century structures from the time the camp was called "Sunset Cove Resort." Though these buildings still housed valuable and curious antiques such as water pumps and wood-burning stoves, they no longer met the standards of safety and cleanliness required by the American Camp Association. Dad immediately started diving into lumber costs, local construction companies, and lakefront property restoration laws, only then understanding what a huge commitment he'd made by accepting the business, the land, and this lifestyle. He stayed up late each night, hunched over his desk with only the light of a green-shaded banker's lamp he'd taken from his office at the law firm. He'd pore over blueprints and invoices, address books and camper lists. I loved sitting at his desk and looking at the neatly stacked piles of papers and pens lined up according to height. He was always so organized, even when he'd taken on more tasks than he could handle.

* * *

But as September wore on into October, Dad's liver quickly stopped filtering the toxins which flowed through it, and those toxins began traveling up to his brain. This not only caused him to blurt out random and disjointed statements, but it also made him sleep most of the day. We soon realized that we would need the assistance of hospice workers to make sure Dad was getting the best possible care during this time.

One afternoon my mom sent me to town to run some errands. By then she had stopped leaving my dad's side for even a few hours, and

I still liked getting out of the house even if it was just to drive into town and get the mail. Camp gets an eerie, empty sort of quietness without all the kids to fill it, and at times it made me uneasy to be there for so many uninterrupted days.

Driving around Minong, I did the grocery shopping, refilled my father's prescriptions, and dropped into Walker's hardware store. Next on my list was to stop by the town clinic to pick something up. Mom hadn't written any other notes for this task so I assumed I was to get a new medication or perhaps some paperwork for her to sign. I had no reason to suspect otherwise until I told the desk nurse my name. The look in her eyes as she consulted her chart made me stand a little straighter.

I understood the reason for her expression when she handed me a small, unsealed envelope. I spread the sides apart and looked inside to see my father's name printed on a "Do Not Resuscitate" bracelet. It was printed in small hospital lettering inside the unadorned envelope.

It occurred to me, as I held the paper in my fingers, that it had been someone's mundane task to look up the correct spelling of "Richard Bruce Chernov" and print it on a blank medical bracelet before casually dropping it into an envelope. What kind of job title did he have, and what else did he do all day? Did he know that this patient's daughter would have to pick it up and hold it in her hands, face her father's death so plainly?

I'd been given nothing in life to prepare me for dealing with something that upsetting. Of course, my mother never dreamed they would leave the bracelet in an unsealed envelope for me to see; she simply thought I would pick up a little package and be spared any unnecessary heartache. The nurse held up a clipboard for me and rested it on the speckled beige counter between us. I had to hold my right hand with my left so that I could sign for the DNR. As if I had just learned to write, the letters of my own name were oversize and sloppy. I walked out of the tiny Northwoods Clinic stunned, mouth hanging open, eyes squinting at the autumn sky, footsteps irresolute and timid. The sun was too bright and the manicured grass seemed all wrong. I clutched the white envelope in my hand, afraid to look at it again. Such a small piece of paper and plastic had in an instant stripped me of any remaining innocence I spent my teenage years denying. There had still been some naïveté inside me when I left the house that afternoon, just a little crumb of childhood, and by the time I stepped foot out of the clinic it was gone.

As I walked toward the car, I fixated on the thought that Dad was the one father I would ever have in this life, and I felt like I held the key to his death in my hands. Any remaining doubts of what the immediate future would hold for my family and me were unceremoniously expunged with the existence of that tiny piece of plastic. I had spent the previous weeks hoping, perhaps believing, something could still cure him, could bring him back to us so that we could move on with things the way we'd always imagined. But with this simple errand and this plain, machine-printed bracelet, I was forced to acknowledge the tangible confirmation of what I didn't think I could face: that I was going to watch my father die. I held proof now that it *would* take place—and that it would be against the law for anyone to try to save him. Standing at the door to my car, unable to will myself to enter and go home, I was no longer a child—I was tarnished with the burden of adulthood.

Watching someone you love die changes all the rules you thought the universe followed, or at least that you thought would not apply to you for one reason or another. To this day, I don't blame my mom for unknowingly sending me to run such an errand, my father for wanting the DNR order, or the nurse for handing it over to me. A member of my immediate family was required to walk through those doors and sign that piece of paper. I happened to be going into town that day, so I ended up being the one to do it, and so, somewhere on the highway between the clinic and our driveway, I willed myself to buck up. Life was getting tougher by the minute, and I couldn't keep up; it was throwing monumental hardships my way, and I knew I'd need some Herculean courage to stay in the ring. Picking up Dad's DNR made me see that sometimes you just have to bite your lip and do whatever needs to be done, no matter how badly every inch of you wants *not* to do it.

Driving home I felt like nothing could ever faze me again after what I had just been through. Of course I was wrong, but at the time it was the hardest task I'd ever had to carry out. On the short drive home, I rested the envelope on the seat next to me and kept glancing over at it as if it were my passenger. I didn't go so far as to brace it with my arm when I stepped on the brakes, but I did feel a need to protect it until it arrived safely at home. Though I didn't want it, and knew I had just experienced something no child should have to go through, I sensed that there was a purpose to what I was doing. It was Dad's wish to have an uneventful death at home, and I had tangible proof of it now. Though I fantasized about chucking it out the car window—so that I could call an ambulance if Dad started to die—I knew it was not for me to deny my father a death on his terms.

Chapter 20

MAKING IT DOWN THE HILL

When Dad was moving closer to death during the fall of 2001, his was not the only change taking place. My brothers and I were struggling in our relationships with each other, trying to sort out all that was happening to our family. Growing up together, we went through the necessary ups and downs as kids, tormented each other with various forms of verbal and physical fighting as all siblings do. Though we had grown up feeling close to one another despite these common sibling rivalries, my brothers and I were fast becoming three very different people. As we were thrown back together under one roof to watch our father die, we gradually resumed the dynamic we'd had as children. This quickly proved to be an ineffective way to carry out our relationship, especially considering the difficult circumstances.

When we first came back together in August, the three of us clung to each other, to help us deal with the possibility that Dad would die within the month. But as the weeks passed and Dad continued to fight, the uncertainty of our time with him and the sheer isolation of living at camp understandably made us irritable. Because there were no alternatives, my brothers were the best targets for all my frustrations, and they acted similarly toward me. Not only were we living together again under the rules of our parents after having experienced life on our own at college but we were doing this in—of all places—Minong, Wisconsin. The quasi-literal middle of nowhere. Our house felt confining even with 400 acres of open land surrounding it, and somehow grew to feel smaller with each passing day. The isolation was by far the most tormenting element in an already exhausting situation. Perhaps if we'd had friends nearby or some other outlet for our mess of complex emotions, we wouldn't have turned on each other the way we did.

As the weeks progressed into October, Gabe and I challenged each other constantly, arguing over the most trivial problems. Our childlike regression saw no bounds but instead ran rampant as our fears and exhaustion increased, intensifying with each passing hour. One moment we were best friends, sharing a laugh over some esoteric joke; the next moment we'd be volleying insults like long-standing enemies begrudging each other the arbitrary grievances of youth. Because we are alike in so many ways and have always had a natural connection, Gabe and I just couldn't resist pushing each other's buttons—even into adulthood, even while Dad was dying. Our antics did not go unnoticed by my father, who voiced his disappointment in our behavior.

"We don't have time for this," he'd say. "There's just no more time. You kids have to figure out how to get along, and you've got to do it now."

Dad was concerned for us but also fascinated to see how we went about working through these issues. We had each grown into our adult selves; to come back together under one roof presented a myriad of challenges. Though none of us had endured such tragedy before, I felt as if my brothers—especially Dylan, being the oldest—thought they knew more than I did about what we were all going through. My brothers frequently spoke to me as if I were still a child, and this absolutely infuriated me. Being stubbornly independent by nature, I did not easily tolerate this treatment. As far as I was concerned, we were all in the same position: We were scared, impatient, bored, nervous, and exhausted. I didn't think it was their place to tell me how to act or how to feel. I know now that all they wanted was to protect their little sister—to insulate me from and prepare me for what was to come. And even at the time, I thought I understood their desire to watch out for me, but I couldn't help feeling belittled by their condescension.

At the very least, though, what the three of us had in common was our commitment to our family. Even when we poked fun at each other or picked fights, there was always an undertone of love, trust, and fellowship; no amount of petty bickering could ever undo the knots that bound us together, and we knew it. Sacrificing our personal lives for what could have been an indefinite amount of time, we each came home because we knew it was the right thing to do—to be together as a family. Though we often fought, we could at least agree on the fact that none of us hesitated to be by Dad's side. We had only each other to rely on, only each other to love.

* * *

Because of our seven-year age gap, Dylan had always been old enough to seem out of reach as a peer. Though we played well together when we were young, and Dylan always treated me with a protective, sort of amused demeanor, as adults we found that family vacations and school holidays seemed to be the only occasions during which we spent large blocks of time together. Once I was old enough to have anything interesting to say about the world, Dylan had already moved out and gone to college. Coming together to take care of Dad was the first time we tried to actually get to know each other, not simply as siblings but as individuals.

That fall I took an official leave of absence from my studies at UPS in Tacoma. Dylan was trying to finish his master's degree in musicology, so we both decided to enroll in a few classes at the University of Minnesota at Duluth so we wouldn't fall too far behind. Twice a week we would make the hour-long drive together and leave camp behind. Those biweekly trips to Duluth became the arena in which we learned how to be grown-up siblings together—to become friends. We found that we shared a certain camaraderie as fellow students, and the conversations we had in his truck between Minong and the Minnesota border set a foundation for the two of us to develop a relationship unique from the rest of the family.

UMD was a different kind of school environment than UPS and much larger. I didn't take time to explore or become familiar with the campus except for the routes I used in order to get to my classes. I didn't officially transfer to UMD and wasn't planning on staying there any longer than was necessary—I always planned on returning to my life at UPS no matter the circumstances or how long it took. It felt strange to take classes in Duluth and to consciously try *not* to make friends so I wouldn't feel tied down there.

Most of my classes never reached the academic standard to which I had become accustomed at UPS, and I had no problem doing the bare minimum work in order to receive good grades. Students at UMD were loud and boisterous during class, interrupting the professors and having open conversations or talking on their cell phones mid-lecture. I found this behavior appalling and felt an even stronger urge to get back to Tacoma. The male students in Duluth didn't interest me at all, and the girls all blended together into one blonde, pale, Fargo-accented creature. Dylan and I took to referring to this particular type of girl as the "Midwestern Goddess." And since we both tried to squeeze a nearly full load of credits into two days of the week, each class day was long, and when Dylan and I met up on campus and walked to the truck it had already been dark outside for several hours. We'd grab a pizza to bring home with us and head back to camp, the hour-long drive allowing us plenty of time to unload the stresses of our day.

Meanwhile, Gabe and I also tried to find ways to spend time together away from camp. We'd usually go see a movie about a half-hour away in Hayward every few weeks. Mindless blockbusters worked best to serve our purpose, and during the ride to the theater and while watching the movie, we always had a good time. But somehow by the time we drove back to camp, each of us attentively scanning the highway's shoulders for the reflective eyes of deer, we'd resort to fighting once again. It didn't seem to matter what we were discussing; somehow we'd end up bickering so fiercely that as soon as we pulled into the long driveway, I'd make Gabe stop and let me out. I'd slam the car door and walk the rest of the way down the big, dark hill. But then the next week a new movie would be playing, and Gabe and I were friends again. Eventually, by the middle of October, this childish routine grew wearisome, and I stopped picking fights with him. We agreed to work hard at mending our relationship and after a few weeks of effort, of being kind to one another, we found that we could once again make it all the way down to our house without any hostility or bickering.

As difficult as it was to re-adjust our sibling roles, the three of us knew it was important. We assumed that Dad didn't want his final days filled with our petty bickering at the dinner table, and I was embarrassed at having participated in such behavior in the past. It only took a few weeks of seeing the disappointed look on Dad's already exhausted face to make me more civil toward my brothers.

"This is the time for the three of you to reintroduce yourselves to each other. You are the only ones who will ever know what this feels like. You'll want to respect that," Dad said to us one evening.

Dad always had a way of snapping us back to reality and making us forget what we had been arguing about. As our father grew sicker, and spent less and less time awake, my brothers and I stopped fighting altogether. The toll of watching him die took up all the space inside us—there was no room left for petty squabbles over who left the TV on, about the correct definition of "osmosis," or whose turn it was to wash the dishes.

Though it only helped to ease some of the fears I had about Dad's impending death, the closeness I began to feel with my brothers made me stronger. Because of their support, I felt I was able to take the best care of our father that I could. When we'd waited with him, so anxious and terrified that with each passing moment we had less and less of ourselves to give, I'd just look at my brothers as they read in the corner of Dad's room and would find a little more energy to keep going, simply because we were in this together.

*   *   *

When Dylan and I weren't traveling to Duluth, we filled our time building new mountain-bike trails at the southeastern end of the camp property. It was ideal work for autumn; by now the aspens performed for us, spinning their quivering green leaves into gold, into shavings of sunset that exhibited the season's memorial to all that had come before. Most of the time, Dylan would drop me off and head to another section of the trail, leaving me to work alone for a few hours. I'd leaf-blow a narrow path as I moved along, shuffling through the decadent, detritus-filled road. I watched in ear-plugged semi-silence as the dirt revealed itself, clean and solid, untouched by rain or wind under a blanket of waving yellow leaves.

In an instant I felt like Moses: the leaf-blower my wand of faith, the glowing dead leaves my Red Sea. Ghostly pale aspens and soft-peeling birches leaned against the wind in gradations of white. Before me the lake was the kind of azure only fall can offer, a blue so jewel-like that you know it will end in a brilliant flash of color before turning pale and frigid.

Our lake was only a mile or so long, and even less by width. It dried by the year, overwhelmed with weeds and muck. I thought of it as a shrinking reminder of the glacial march that pushed down on these lands. Still, I always felt it big as night behind me.

Leaf-blowing, cutting brush away, or maybe raking, I'd walk the crest of a small hill and clear a balance-beam-narrow ridge. I loved to navigate the brown among the yellow, the white against the blue.

Chapter 21

TO HURRY UP AND DIE

Each day we were told could be Dad's last, according to his doctors, but every morning he kept waking up, paler and thinner than the day before. It may seem cruel to phrase it in these terms, but we had nothing to do but wait. Wait for him to die.

Sometimes Dad seemed almost like himself, watching football or taking a nap with a book. Other days he was someone else entirely—sleeping most of the day and absently shuffling around the house while he was awake. I knew he wouldn't make it much longer and a significant part of me just wanted it all to end—for his sake as much as for my own.

Dad was rapidly becoming a fragile old man at the age of fifty-six, and each morning I could see how he had changed overnight, how much further he'd drifted.

"I feel like I am gradually separating from my body—feels like I'm on a different plane," he said to me once after a long nap.

"What do you mean by that, Dad?"

"My body is declining. So it's freaky to look in the mirror, but it's okay—I have help when I need it, and that's the love—there's love here," he said, pointing at his chest and then waving his arms above him. "I'm talking about love."

I tried to absorb what he was saying, what it must have been like to watch his body fail him while his mind was becoming spiritually stronger than it had ever been. He said sometimes it felt like he was just beginning to figure things out and then the floor began to crumble beneath him.

There was also the isolation of being at camp, which seemed to make things seem even more intense. Trapped inside the little house, trapped in the gut of a hard Wisconsin winter, I felt monstrously claustrophobic as the days passed in seclusion. I know now that for my parents, this secluded setting was comforting and private in a way that was perfect for what was to come.

While Dylan and I were off at school or working on the trails, Gabe was busy keeping camp afloat after having recently decided he would take camp onto his own shoulders. Our mom devoted every minute of her day to maintaining Dad's comfort, seeing that his every need was met. The four of us were like soldiers keeping watch, guarding against the knock of Death at our front door. At night we would pick at plates of thrown-together meals, watch TV, sit and talk, or rest in silence. Time became a series of waiting for the next thing to happen, for something to change and snap us out of the haze we'd been functioning in for months.

In this isolation, we clung to each other for comfort while simultaneously and frequently pissing each other off. We challenged each other over things both large and small, each one disapproving of the others' methods of coping. But in Minong there was nowhere to escape to, no group of friends to hear my complaints, and certainly nothing within myself solid enough onto which I could hold for serenity.

On the days when my father was lucid and upbeat, we all let ourselves linger in the far-off hope that this was some kind of prophetic worsening right before things would miraculously get better. Only things didn't get better. Soon my dad was no longer able to do any camp work and instead spent most of his time resting, listening to his favorite worn-out Harry Chapin and Randy Newman CDs, and watching the Green Bay Packers play a respectable season.

I, however, was becoming increasingly restless in Minong and decided that I wanted to go back to Washington to visit my friends for a weekend. As I discussed the idea with my parents, they told me they felt torn—although we were exhausted and a break seemed like a reasonable request, there was always the possibility that something terrible would happen while I was away.

"It could be so good for me to see my friends," I said casually. "It'll just be for a weekend."

However, my family couldn't understand why I'd be willing to take the risk of leaving for a weekend. Gabe had taken short trips away from the home, visiting the homes of current and prospective camp families, but he hadn't taken any trips farther than half a day's drive from the house. Dylan didn't want any of us to leave, for any reason.

Knowing in my gut that it wasn't a good idea, I convinced myself that I needed to seek the support of my friends, that it was necessary for me to leave in order to take care of myself and stay levelheaded. I knew it was possible that Dad would get worse or even die while I was away, but I didn't want to give in to that thought. I convinced myself that since Dad had made it so far past the doctors' prognoses that he'd certainly keep going or even get better. And while my family told me, again and again, that the decisions I was making would turn out to be the unalterable things that would haunt me forever, I didn't care to listen. Throughout his illness, I set myself up for one after another bad decision, each time sensing more clearly the pressure of how little time we had left as a complete family unit. I earnestly, desperately wanted to grow up in time for my father to see it happen but couldn't sort out how to do that without panicking and choosing to do the wrong thing at every turn.

The night before I was scheduled to leave for Washington, my dad sat down next to me to talk about my decision. He told me he didn't want me to go, but he also didn't want to see me upset. He could see my anxiety mounting and loved me too much to ask me to stay. We sat together not saying anything for a while until I finally became frustrated.

"I just think I should go," I said plainly, "because it's been really hard to just wait like this." I wanted to tell him that I was exhausted, that I was scared, that I couldn't imagine him not being there when I woke up in the morning. But none of those things came out of my mouth. I simply left the room and went outside. When I came back to the house, my mom was waiting for me outside the door.

"Do you have any idea what your father is thinking about right now, Tanya?" she asked.

"No, I guess I don't. Why?"

She kept her voice low and calm so my father and brothers wouldn't hear what she was about to say.

"After you left, he walked into the kitchen and said, 'Well, I guess I better hurry up and die then.'" She took a deep breath and steadied herself. "You need to figure this out and fix it, Tanya. You need to apologize to him. But I wouldn't do it just now. Go wait in the office."

I realized that without meaning to, I had made my dad feel guilty for still being alive. I turned on my heels and as soon as Mom was back inside, I ran the rest of the distance to the office, sobbing and shaking as I made my way up the stairs and through the green-trimmed glass door. I relived the scene between me and my father, feeling no sympathy for myself, and after an hour of sniveling I walked back home. I wasn't upset because I had been yelled at but because I knew that I would never be able to take back those hurtful words I'd said, never swallow them back down forever. To this day, the memory of what I put my dad through by saying that I was tired of waiting for him to die will never go away, will never be undone or forgotten.

I avoided my dad when I got back into the house. I was painfully ashamed for being so insensitive. After an hour of pretending nothing was wrong, I allowed him to sit down next to me at the edge of my bed.

"Honey, you're going to become an intelligent, strong woman," he said. "I think you just need to take some time to reflect on how to get to that place."

"I didn't mean that before—I didn't mean it the way I said it, the way it came out. I didn't want you to—"

"It's okay, Won-ton," he said, bringing the pre-emptive tear-tingling into my nose. "I know you didn't."

* * *

I ended up going to visit my friends back in Washington anyway, and fortunately nothing devastating happened while I was away. As badly as I wanted to go at the time, I don't even remember the trip now; it did me none of the good it was meant to.

When I returned home, there were even more hospice workers and doctors coming and going from our house. They seemed so sure of themselves while administering a new medication or asking questions about Dad's comfort. But when I pulled one of them aside to ask what I could expect when the moment came, she had no answers for me. I so badly wanted to know what was normal in a case like this—when he would go and what it would look like.

"What should I do?" I'd ask each worker.

"It's different for everyone. I really can't say," they replied every time.

Searching through the pamphlets and books our hospice nurse brought me, I still didn't find the kind of information I was so hungry for. There was a lot of advice, a lot of neutrally written sentiments meant to comfort, but they did nothing to quell all the uncertainties I felt. For answering these questions I would be on my own—a conclusion that surprisingly soothed me. After that, the waiting became something different, something more settled. I still felt torn between wanting my dad to stay with us and knowing that as soon as he died he would be at peace. I wanted things to move on to the next step not because I wanted my dad to die, but because I just wanted to feel a different kind of pain—I knew that whatever happened next, there was going to be more hurting, but at least it would be of a different sort.

I simply felt sorry for myself. No one could tell me how to handle what was happening to me, how to protect my mom, how to help my dad die. No one seemed to know anything and that wasn't good enough for me. With so precious little time left to strengthen my relationship with my dad, I instead squandered most of my days shopping online and watching movies in bed. Mom thought it might help for me to talk with her brother Michael—my beloved Uncle Wooby.

He wasted no time with small talk once I got on the phone. "Tell me, sweetheart, just how long do you think you have to straighten things out with your father?" he asked me. I didn't have anything to say back.

"Well, listen—I don't know either, but it's not going to be a very long time. And there's nothing you can do about that. I understand you wish you could, but you can't."

"Yeah, I obviously know that, but—"

"See, I don't think you do get it, Tanya. There's nothing your dad can do about it, nothing I can do, nothing you can do. It's *happening*. So what are you going to do with the rest of your time together?" His words struck me down and I was speechless. The softly written platitudes in the hospice literature had said nothing like this.

After a long silence, he said, "Your dad is going to die. Very soon. So just . . . be . . . loving." As we hung up the phone, I heard Uncle Wooby start to cry. I realized that he was losing my father, too—was losing a brother and friend—but I was lucky enough to actually have the opportunity to take care of him if only for just a little longer.

There was nothing I could do to stop my dad from dying. The feelings and situations that were causing me this pain would only get worse. Even though I had no say in the final outcome, I did have the ability to control how I behaved in light of it. As badly as my dad wanted to continue helping kids at camp, to continue loving my mom, to continue raising my brothers and me, none of it had any effect on the destined outcome. All he could do was be as brave and as purposeful in the few days he had left to live. In turn, all that I could do was be as supportive and loving as possible while I still had him with me.

So I worked hard from that point on to just love him as much as I could, and doing so made room for a flood of energy to come bursting out of me and straight to my father. The second I walked through my fears of his death, uninhibited love poured outward and helped me be the person I wanted my dad to see before he died. As soon as I released the need to control what was happening to my family, I felt incredible relief from the previously unceasing anger and bitterness. If my dad could face death with courage and acceptance, then I would have to do my best to support him and follow suit.

* * *

One afternoon a few days later, I took a nap on the bed next to my dad in the muted, early-winter sunlight. Beneath the pillow we shared, I could feel the tiny vibrations of the BBC news report pumping through the small, disc-shaped pillow-speaker my dad always slept with. His mind was so active—always running—so he used this tiny amplifier, tuned to NPR, to keep his mind occupied enough to fall asleep. I reached under the pillow and held the speaker in my palm. I imagined it as a sand dollar made of plastic, with holes meant to spread the sound in place of the ocean creature's bilateral symmetry. I pushed the volume dial to the left, its ridges under my fingertip like a dime, then put my hand in Dad's. I waited for him to squeeze back or open his eyes and smile at me, or breathe differently . . . to notice me, notice me next to him.

Nothing happened. The speaker remained, a dried-up, make-believe sea animal. Dad didn't move and he didn't wake up. But he knew I was there. I curled his fingers around mine and felt that his hand, like the rest of his body, was swollen and warm to the touch. I put my other hand on top of his and waited with him. Though his chest was lifting and falling with the regular movements of sleep—just the steady, slow breath of a man taking a nap—for a moment it felt like he was already gone. I caught myself starting to grieve for him even though he was still alive, still breathing, still sleeping right next to me, though for how much longer I didn't know. That afternoon, none of the unkind things I had said to him over the years mattered anymore. It was just him, slowly drifting away from me and continuing further, bit by bit, on his path toward death, while we napped in the late-afternoon sun. But at that moment, all had been forgiven.

Chapter 22

THE CRUELEST PREVIEW

Alan went to work one more time on a Sunday in October, and by the following Friday had retreated quietly into a coma. He died as the sun rose the following morning, Saturday, October 20, 2001. Susan was with him when the moment came, and his death was peaceful, quiet. Instantly, the world became to us a little emptier and a little colder in the wake of his absence. With Alan's death, the road before my father curved and fell.

* * *

When Alan passed away, Dad was already too sick to drive down to Milwaukee for the funeral, so Dylan, Gabe, and I made the trip in his place. We planned to stay less than twenty-four hours before heading back to camp, worrying that Dad wouldn't hang on much longer now that Alan was gone.

Attending Alan's funeral was a bizarre experience; watching Mark, Mike, and Stephen go through what I knew my brothers and I would very soon be going through ourselves was a cruel preview. I looked on as Susan and the boys forced smiles and gave handshakes in the receiving line before the service started. I thought about how tired they must have been standing up there for so long, how tired I felt just watching them.

The service began and Dylan read the eulogy my father wrote for Alan. I watched from my seat as his hands rattled the pages in front of him. I found Susan at the reception and hugged her for my mom, visualizing some kind of osmotic transfer of the love and positive energy my mom had given me when we left for Milwaukee. We held each other for a long while, Susan and I. When I started to pull away from our embrace, she lovingly looked into my eyes and whispered to me, "When Alan was dying, taking his last breaths, I told him it was okay to go. I told him that Richard would be right behind him."

"I'm glad he knew Dad would be with him," I mumbled, shocked and sad. Even though I was truly relieved that Alan had the comforting thought of my father following right behind, I still wasn't ready to let go of my dad. I didn't want him to follow right behind Alan. I wanted him to stay with me.

Early the next morning, my brothers and I rode north through the state in silence. The drive between Milwaukee and camp was a well-practiced routine for us, having made the trip about a dozen times each year for most of our lives. Over the years, we learned to fill the five or six hours with car games, music battles, and lots of junk food. But on this particular day, the drive was nothing to pass through quickly. The three of us had now seen with our very own eyes what we were driving home to.

That night in bed, I lay awake until it was nearly morning, trying to quiet my brain for even just a few hours of respite. But I couldn't seem to shut off my worries or push away the memories of all that I'd been through in the last twenty-four hours long enough to let myself drift into welcome, silent unconsciousness. Insomnia had been steadily making a nest in my psyche and was at its worst now that Alan was gone. How could Dad not follow quickly behind?

Ruminating over the things I wanted to change but couldn't, I tried all the tricks I knew to fall sleep with no success. Reading was no good anymore—I'd lose track of the words as they mixed with my constant, anxious inner monologue, and end up rereading the same paragraphs again and again. Eventually giving up, I sat and looked out the window, missing the simple, pampered bedtime routines I always enjoyed as a child.

As the baby of the family, and growing up in a uniquely creative and compassionate household, my usual nighttime ritual was ridiculously self-indulgent. Each parent and sibling would make his or her way to my bedroom to help tuck me into my canopy bed, which was decadently awash in pink lace and peach frills. The dark wood floors in the den outside my bedroom would have been perfect for tap-dancing; there, I could tell by the sound of approaching footsteps which family member was coming toward my room.

First, my mom would sit next to me on the bed and sing her repertoire of good-night songs while smoothing out my hair on the pillow. Relaxed and close to sleep as my mom left the room, Gabe would come in and get me all riled up again with his traditional "Tushie Dance." Switching on a glass, swan-topped music box on my dresser, Gabe would dance around in circles, shaking his butt around in time with the music. Next, Dylan would bring his guitar and play a song from his series of self-composed lullabies to calm me down again.

Finally, I would hear my father's heavy footsounds growing louder as he approached the door. He'd sit down at the edge of my bed and start spinning together a story that was somehow always equal parts comedy, adventure, and made-up foolery. Together we created imaginary worlds from which we'd draw tales with ever-increasing silliness. Our favorite stories came from the life of "Blubber-Butt," an obese, washed-up warrior whose rear end was so huge, it flapped against the ground as he walked. To illustrate this, Dad would make slobbery *thppppt plbbtt* noises with his tongue between his lips every time Blubber-Butt went for a walk. Blubber-Butt existed in a spoof universe based on *Star Wars*, one of our very favorite sci-fi sagas. Instead of Princess Leia, we had Princess Summer-Fall-Winter-Spring-Cookie-Tushie. Our Luke Skywalker was named

Duke Moonrunner. And in place of Han Solo, we had Flan Tandem. Dad spun out epic, intricately woven ballads that told the adventures our characters had, and as I got older I helped him create each night's episode in the saga. As a Darth Vader/Jabba-the-Hut hybrid, Blubber-Butt lashed out when intruders broke into his palace, and ran *thppppt-plbbt-pppthbtting* through the hall. Eventually, he would corner his enemies and sit on them with his gigantic butt, squashing them as flat as pancakes before sticking them up on his wall with chewing gum.

And when we finally did put Blubber-Butt and his elaborate misadventures to rest almost twelve years after Dad told the first story, we created an ending that saw our strange hero returning home to the wife and family he'd had in his life before turning to the dark side. As we closed the series and set its characters to rest forever, we imagined Blubber-Butt walking through the grass to the front door of his house in the suburbs, ringing the bell, and embracing his teary-eyed wife.

*   *   *

I must have settled back into bed and fallen asleep eventually, because when I opened my eyes again it was bright early morning and my mom was just walking into my room, picking up my discarded funeral clothes from the day before. She smiled a tired, pleading smile and folded my clothes into a neat pile on top of the window seat. Her gaze lost in the scene, she looked outside, assessing the snow and finding—for a moment—a bit of solace in its newness, its fresh and clean state of being. I sat up bleary-eyed and smiled the same smile back, then threw the covers off my legs, standing up to meet another day.

Dad and me, Milwaukee 1981

Dancing cheek-to-cheek, Milwaukee 1982

Gabe, Dylan, and me,
Milwaukee 1982

The five of us, with Annie, at camp, 1986

Little girl at the big camp, 1987

Riding the chairlift with Dad in Whistler, B.C., 1995

Dad and Alan: two best friends, Utah, 1996

Dad and me
visiting Dylan in
Fairbanks, Alaska,
1998

Heading out along the Southeast coast of Alaska with NOLS,
Petersburg, 1999

Never was there a father who loved his daughter more than Dad
loved me, Tucson, 1999

Dad and me setting out to drive from Tucson to Tacoma, January 2000

Dad paddling his favorite solo canoe, Camp, July 2000

Dad and Jimmy at the north end of camp, Winter 2000

Mom lighting the candles on my twenty-first birthday cake, my first birthday without Dad, Camp, August 2002

Mom and me at my graduation from the University of Puget Sound, Tacoma, May 2003

Gabe and Dylan packing my bags before traveling to Europe, September 2003

Chapter 23

LIVING IN THE DIM

The deepest thing we share
And do not talk about
But have to have, was there,
And by that light found out.
— MAY SARTON

After arriving back at camp, we all felt Alan's presence in the house and it wasn't long before my dad started saying Alan's name in his sleep.

All through the end of October, Dad sat limply on his favorite leather chair in the back corner of the combination dining room/solarium. With the light pouring in from the windows and skylights, that room made Dad happier than sitting on the big couches in front of the TV or lying in bed. While Dylan and I sat around the table doing homework, Dylan with a guitar in his lap as he scribbled notes and key signatures on his sheet music, Dad dozed in the corner or looked outside at the leaves falling around the house. Though it had been weeks since he was last outside, Dad was still fully dressed with his shoes on while he took in the sights from the inside.

Observing how his shoulders failed to fill out his shirt, how his thin wrists and knees showed through his clothing, I suddenly felt an odd affinity for all the special ways both my parents tried to fulfill their roles as camp directors, including their proclivity for wearing outrageous outfits to amuse the campers. My mom had an enormous collection of silly earrings and would choose a different pair to wear each day. She became so well-known for her wacky earrings that camp families began sending her crazy earrings as gifts. She had rubber mouse earrings, credit card earrings, globe earrings, and even a pair of miniature tennis shoes. After a few years, her collection grew so large that she began storing it in a large tackle box; the many compartments meant to hold fishing lures were the perfect system for keeping all her earrings organized.

Dad started playing with his wardrobe, too, by donning obnoxious Hawaiian shirts, colored sunglasses, and—best of all—the ugliest shoes he could find. In the mid-'90s, Dad struck up a deal with a few outdoor gear companies who allowed him to test products still being prepared for the market. A pair of shoes, sunglasses, or watch would come in the mail, and Dad fulfilled his end of the deal by wearing the product for a few months, keeping documentation of performance, design, and comfort. Then he'd send the item back and in exchange received a big discount on a portion of that company's catalog. Throughout the years, he arranged these "pro-deals" with brands such as the North Face, Chaco, Snow Creek, and Nike All Conditions Gear. Every time he opened a package from the Nike ACG manufacturing center, something horrid would peer back at us from inside. But for some reason Dad thought these items were cool. The uglier the shoe, the more he wanted to wear it. And soon, this gave him an idea. Whenever we passed a Nike outlet store, our family would go inside for just one purpose: to compete in an Ugly Shoe-off. We each had five minutes to find not only the ugliest but also the cheapest shoes we could find. When the allotted time was up, we would meet up near the cash registers and compare our hideous treasures. Shopping this way was almost better than looking for things I would actually wear.

The only bad part about winning these contests was that whoever picked out the worst-looking and lowest-priced pair of shoes was then required to actually wear them in public. As a teenager, I backed out a few times when the rest of the family thought I should wear my game-winning shoes, but Dad was the opposite: He was thrilled every time he could wear his ugly shoes out of the house. It was when he had to dress nicely, or at least more traditionally, that he moaned and groaned.

Now Dad only had his crazy attire to wear inside the house— there were no campers to amuse with his loud clothing or wacky shoes. No audience but his own children. And though he had slept away most of that late-fall afternoon, the neon-green Nike half-sandal, half-shoe monstrosity he loved so much still covered his wool-socked feet. He wore a matching green Nike pullover that came up around his neck.

He opened his eyes after his nap, turned to me, and said, "Tanya, since you're so good at sewing, do you think you can make me a new zipper? One that's less pointy?"

"Sure, Dad," I said, as I watched him grab at the place where a zipper would have been on his shirt if it needed one. The toxins flowing freely through his body were now reaching his brain, forcing seemingly random statements to leave his mouth unchecked with increasing regularity. He made comments about people who weren't in the room with us and asked questions about trips we'd never taken. Seeing him this way was such a stark contrast to the sharpness of wit and intellect I'd only ever seen from my father; the only small solace I could take was in knowing that when he did slip out of lucidity, he never seemed to notice that anything was off.

Among those traveling thoughts, though, were moments of brief lucidity: recommendations for an oil change in this or that camp vehicle, reminders to renew the *Consumer Reports* subscription, and other such everyday tasks. But other times he knew exactly the right moment to call my attention to something important. One day while I rubbed his wool-socked feet in front of a football game, he said to me, apropos of nothing we'd been talking about, "Have lots of dogs in your life, Won-ton." I looked up at him with raised eyebrows, only half paying attention to what he was saying. "They're so good, aren't they?" I followed his gaze to our dogs, Jimmy and Sophie, sharing the dog bed in the corner of the living room. The smile, the shine in his eyes, told me all I needed to know about the love he felt for them, the gratitude for all the nights and afternoons those dogs had spent guarding his bedside, protecting him.

Only a few weeks after Alan's funeral, Dad stopped eating and drinking on his own. He slept all but a few hours each day, and when he did wake it was into a drowsy kind of semi-twilight.

By the middle of November, Dad had started bouncing between being lucid and not, being with us and someplace else. One cold, early-winter day while I sat on the couch in the living room with the TV on, I watched him move into the kitchen. Dad shuffled atop the multi-green pattern of the vinyl flooring, taking short, measured steps. He seemed so small now, had grown so skinny that I was afraid to touch his skin. His neck and chest shriveled down until I could see perfectly the concave scoops around his collarbone, even through his clothing. He wore a green fleece pullover shirt and pajama pants.

Dad had never worn pajamas before—he always slept in undies to keep from getting too warm. That is, until he got cancer. Immediately after his diagnosis, people began giving him pajama sets all the time, as if pajamas were the ubiquitous, official uniform of cancer patients around the globe.

I looked through the doorway at his face while he fussed with the twist-tie around a loaf of bread. His cheeks were gray and flat, making them look even more pulled, even more thinned. His socked feet made quick *shushing* sounds as he moved around the corner toward the toaster. While my eyes were still fixed on him, he lost his balance for a moment and started falling.

When his left arm fell back against the wall to brace his body as it dropped downward, I jumped from the couch and rushed toward him. Before I could get to the kitchen, his left arm folded in against the pressure, and gravity took him the rest of the way down. As I moved forward, I knew I wouldn't get to him in time, knew I should have gotten my lazy ass up to help him in the first place. The weight of his frail body pulled him back and then down on top of a small, wooden baker's rack. And all the while, our eyes were locked together in a direct line as he shrunk into a fleece bundle against the wall, onions and sweet potatoes all around him on the kitchen floor. He looked up at me, simultaneously confused, amused, and embarrassed. I helped him up off the floor, his hands wrapped around my elbow. Neither of us said anything as I steadied him back on his feet.

While Dad slept more and more, the quality of his waking moments diminished. The four of us took turns sitting with him in my parents' bedroom, reading or lying next to him. Every few hours we'd take a break and space out in front of the TV for a while, letting the flickering images of the rest of the world numb us enough to head back into Dad's room. In there together, we'd read and re-read the same lines over and over in our books, brains recognizing the words but focusing instead on the gaps of time between Dad's breaths. I'd count to forty sometimes, and then lock eyes with Gabe. We would lean forward, heads tilted inward for better hearing, hold our books in our laps, and keep each other's stare until Dad rattled out a long, gasping breath. Each hour the last hour, each breath the last breath. Then we'd go back to the line we'd been skimming all day. Wait to start the deathwatch count again.

My dad didn't need any lights on in his room for his own sake. For months already, his eyes had been hypersensitive from the jaundice, making the harshness of house lights extremely painful. So instead, my mom used candles to light the room, casting a dream-like tint over the whole space; as winter blustered at the windows and the pipes threatened to freeze underneath us, the room inside always looked warm and soft. Observing this scene at times made it easier for me to understand my father's decision to die at home; the image of a well-lit hospital room now seemed unbearable and unnatural.

While I waited to feed Dad a Popsicle, place a pain pill on his tongue, or do whatever else I could to keep him clean and comfortable, I'd play with the candles at his bedside. I would dip my fingers into the little puddles of melted wax surrounding the wick, test how long I could keep my fingertip in the hot, liquefied mess before pulling it out. I'd let it dry and dip again into the soupy well before peeling away the curved wax with my fingerprint embedded on the inside. I'd turn the candle upside down and make a cradle of my hand, letting the wax drip into my waiting palm. If I made a particularly well-crafted finger mold, I'd line it up on the shelf behind me in a display of perfumed, miniature statues.

One night we accidentally left a candle burning, and it dripped down the bedside in streaks, creating bumpy stalactites that splattered their offspring onto the carpet. For the next two days, I entertained myself by picking the tiny wax dots from the green carpeting and piling them together on a plate. Though I knew I was only busying myself with these inane tasks to keep my fear at bay, they were often the only things keeping me from completely crumbling under the prolonged intensity of our situation.

* * *

Each night my mom would join my dad in bed, and Gabe would go off to his own cabin about a hundred yards down the road, having moved down there when space in our small house became too cramped for comfort. Dylan and I remained in the living room, splitting one of Dad's little white sleeping pills, and watching TV until we got sleepy enough to stumble off to bed. Without the Ambien, we'd stay up watching TV all night long, unable to shut our minds off, or lie in bed waiting anxiously for Mom to come into our rooms and tell us, "It's time." Even though we were supposed to take the pills in bed and wait the few minutes to fall asleep while safely horizontal, those few minutes before the medication took us under were spent torturing ourselves about not being alert enough to focus if the time really did come. So every night as Dylan walked through his doorway and I walked through mine, we'd say to each other, "Good night. I love you. Wake me up." *Wake me up if he starts to die.*

* * *

One night in late November, mom woke me and helped me out of bed at 3:30 in the morning. I thought to myself, *Okay, this must be it.* But instead she said that Dad had been asking for me all night. As I walked into the room, I could see the one light above my parents' bed switched on and Dad below it, his eyes closed. He kept saying over and over, "Please bring me my daughter, my sweet beautiful baby daughter." I bent down to him and grabbed his hands. "Where is my daughter? Bring me my gorgeous daughter," he kept saying.

"I'm here," I said. "I'm right next to you, Daddy." His eyes never opened but I felt him squeeze my hand. He turned his chin a little and though the corners of his mouth were smiling, he puckered his lips to kiss me.

* * *

From the hospice literature, I gathered that most people will pass away a few days after they stop taking food or water. Ever the individual, my dad lived for eighteen days after he stopped eating, drinking, blinking his eyes, or waking. During the time we spent with him during those final days, he mumbled a lot of things we didn't understand. We wrote many of his ramblings on the legal pad my mom had used throughout the ordeal, thinking that maybe we'd be able to make sense of what he was saying later on when we weren't so tired.

"Alan is coming in to get me," he'd say with his eyes still closed. "I am hanging with Professor Dixon. I'm all packed with my favorite backpack."

"Who's Professor Dixon?" Gabe asked.

"I think it was one of his law professors. I'm not sure," my mom answered. Dad kept on talking, more clearly now than he had in days.

"Alan and Dr. Dixon are waiting for me. Alan and I will continue the plan. Stop and have a drink. It's still a good thing."

A few minutes passed with each of us bewildered. Dad continued, "Hey there, Gabey-boy. Alan and Dr. Dixon are talking to me. Alan will make it easy for me. Sounds like love. A miraculous thing is going on."

Through tears we'd answer him back, "It's okay to go, Dad. You can let go now."

We reminded him over and over that we loved him enough to let him go, even though it was the one thing in the world we didn't want. As much as the words hurt me each time they left my lips, I wanted him to know that it *was* all right to leave us if it meant he wouldn't be in any more pain. Though we never discussed it then, my mother and brothers thought similarly during that time; none of us could bear to watch him wither any further.

Sometimes he'd say shockingly poignant things, like, "Too short a ride—I want to stay and do it all over again. I don't want to leave you. I love you," and "I don't understand. It's not fair. I'm going on my one-way trip." Even though his mind was already someplace else, the things he said were often astute observations on what the four of us were going through.

On our last day of classes in Duluth, when Dylan and I made that long and lonely drive one more time, we hit a deer, striking the large buck while coming into a curve; there was no way to see him standing there until it was too late to swerve out of the way. I lost my wits and let out a shrill, girly scream just as the deer made impact,

Dylan gripping the wheel as straight as he could hold it. The deer flew up and over the car, and we screeched to a dusty, smoky stop on the highway's shoulder. It was clear that the van was totaled, or nearly so, and the struck deer was nowhere to be found. While we waited for Gabe to come pick us up, we searched through the winter-dry grasses and snow for the buck, finding only a little blood on the gravel.

"It must've run off, right?" I said, kicking the ground to warm my legs inside my jeans, which were stiff from the frigid nighttime temperatures and felt sharp against my skin.

"Or something," Dylan said, heading back to the car with his hands in his pockets, nose and cheeks pink from the cold.

Once we were in Gabe's car, the three of us decided that we would deal with the insurance company in the morning. We obviously weren't going to say anything to Dad; we were certain that he probably didn't even know we had left the house. My mom had told Gabe it was completely unnecessary to give Dad such trivial news about the accident, considering his condition. But when we got home that night and went in to say hello, my dad seemed to know a lot more than we gave him credit for.

"Did you go back to see if it was okay?"

"If what was okay?" Dylan asked.

"The deer—did you check to see if it was hurt?"

* * *

We had no idea how long he would keep going. Our hospice nurse had nothing to offer; she had never seen anyone hold on this long in all her years of helping families care for a dying loved one.

"His resilience is truly rare," she said to me, her eyes quickly brimming with tears as she tried to speak without cracking her voice. "This has never been an easy job for me, Tanya. But knowing your father has affected me more than I was prepared for." She was quiet for a moment, and I felt unprepared for this rare personal moment, unsure of whether or not I was supposed to comfort her or wait for her to do so for me. "I wish I could tell you more than what I know." It seemed like she wanted to keep talking, but she quickly turned away and busied herself checking my father's medications on the bedside table.

At times it felt like Dad would hang on this way forever by the sheer force of not wanting to leave us. My mom even said that she thought maybe this was him slowly working his way back to us—that he would wake up one day and start to feel better. I almost believed her, wanted so badly to believe her.

All we wanted for my dad was a quick and easy death, but that wasn't what happened. He seemed to be in a lot of pain despite the morphine we gave him through patches stuck all over his body. In turn, the four of us lived in the dim—in a pseudo-twilight of exhaustion and resignation. Not talking unless there was something important to be said, not thinking unless it was absolutely necessary.

Chanukah came early that year and though none of us were in the mood to celebrate, my dad had planned for the holiday far in advance. Knowing he most likely wouldn't make it as far as December, he spent some of his last remaining lucid days buying Chanukah presents for the rest of us. By the middle of December, he was now permanently bedridden and unresponsive. He didn't mumble anything or open his eyes even when we gathered together next to him to open up these final presents.

I carefully pulled apart Dad's shabbily executed gift-wrapping, bright blue electrical tape holding together two large sheets of newspaper. Inside, I found that Dad had bought me a turtleneck shirt made from neon-green, outlet-priced polypropylene. Next, I unwrapped a set of collapsible camping chopsticks and a portable, pocket-size roll of toilet paper. Someone who didn't know him might question the lucidity with which my father shopped for these items, but I knew better. He thought these kinds of gifts were hilarious. I could imagine his high-pitched laugh while watching us unravel each silly present, could picture his rough hands clapping as we cocked our heads in confusion. But he didn't do any of those things this time. Would never do them again. He remained asleep or unconscious, in or out of this world, with us and trapped inside his body, or drifting freely in another plane.

He bought similar things for my brothers, and we thanked him with kisses while he lay motionless on the bed. I tried out my new fold-up chopsticks and looked at the clock. It was midnight. It had been seventeen days since he'd opened his eyes.

Chapter 24

THE NOTABLE ABSENCE OF AMBER

To prepare for winter, Dylan and I spent an entire day pulling plastic over each window, trimming it down, taping it to the window frame, and then using a hairdryer to shrink it to size. For supplemental heat, we used two wood-burning stoves placed at opposite ends of the house. At night, we'd take turns getting up to put another log on the fire if the cold woke us. As I lay awake with the winter chill pressed against the windows behind me, the soft, orange glow of the wood-burning stove filtered into my room. It was the one thing that could reliably slow my thoughts enough to allow me to close my eyes and sleep.

On Saturday, December 15, at around 11:00 PM, my mom came into my room and gently woke me up. She didn't say, *It's time.* She didn't have to say anything; I felt it. She led me to the doorway and coming out of the Ambien haze in which I had just been immersed, I noticed how dark it was in my room. In our exhaustion we'd let the fire burn out, and the warm amber light of the fire's reflection on my walls was now gone, replaced by the moon's weak reflection through my plastic-covered windows. The walls and carpet were tinged blue from the brightness of the snow, which must have just started blowing as I fell asleep. As I came out of my room, Dylan was walking out of his. Gabe was on his way up from his house—Mom had already called him.

We crawled back to Dad's bed and leaned over him, each taking a hand or an arm.

"I think his breathing is changing a little. I wasn't sure," Mom whispered. "I thought you should stay in here just in case." The room hushed and still. "It's different in here."

It was back. I felt it. Death—that heavy-breathing creature—was once again devouring the space in our room. My clothes felt heavier against my skin, the candlelight seemed muted as if sheets had been thrown over each of the glass hurricanes that housed them. We stayed like that on the bed for a while, but nothing happened. Dad's breathing came out rattled and sporadic, but it had been that way for almost a week already. It seemed like we waited there for an entire year, waiting in drawn-out, breathless worry for some confirmation of whether or not this would be the moment we'd feared for so long.

I still had no idea what kinds of signs I was looking for, what signal would usher him away, or how I would know one if I saw it. We waited for death, and death would not come. After a few minutes we all began to relax, settling into corners once again to watch and wait. I crawled into a sleeping bag on the floor and thought about going back to sleep. The sleeping pill's venom still ran through my body, making everything seem warm and soft as if I were sun-drunk, lying on sand and grass on a sunny summer day. Dylan and Gabe each took chairs and my mom stayed exactly where she had been the whole four years: attached to my dad's side, whispering how much she loved him over and over again. She told him once more that it was okay to go.

* * *

After an hour of resting uneasily, something did start to change. Mom called us back to the bed to look at Dad. The four of us strangely started breathing at the same pace—my inhales matching theirs and our eyes moving quickly from each other, down to Dad, and back up. Suddenly, as if someone had shouted his name, my dad opened his eyes wide and clear and moved them side to side, as if searching for one of us. We moved closer to him to try to catch his gaze until we were holding his hands tightly in our own, our legs folded up next to his, my mom kissing his head.

Lying in bed all those weeks, he didn't seem like my dad anymore—he didn't speak or laugh, didn't hug me or tell me how much he loved me. He'd stopped telling jokes, stopped asking to hold our hands. But when he opened his eyes and looked at me right then in those last moments before death, he was my dad again. His breaths became quick and tight, and I could see so clearly that it really was him again, fighting so hard, fighting to stay with us. Watching his chest lift and sink so deeply, I understood why he had hung on for those eighteen days—he just wasn't ready to leave.

Then he stopped breathing. I panicked, my face feeling hot and my forehead tingling. No one else breathed, none of us made a sound. It was silent in the room and weighted down with a powerful stillness, as if winter had swept in and frozen us all where we sat. After a minute, the candles started flickering under the wind of our sobs.

And suddenly my dad's chest heaved upward one last time and tried to move death out of the way. Dad gasped a huge breath inward and with all the last bits of energy he roared a great, loud roar. And then he was gone.

* * *

It seemed as if I had waited for this for so long and now that it was here, it felt so rushed, so unexpected. Though I wanted more than anything for him to just not have cancer anymore, the moment he was gone, I wanted desperately to have him back in any way I could. The pain of him being gone, only minutes fresh, was already oppressive. It was suffocating me.

The hours that followed passed in a heart-wrecked blur. Around four o'clock in the morning, I went back to my room and slept for an hour or two. When I woke up, more snow had fallen around us and the whole house seemed awash with its light. I didn't want to go back into my parents' bedroom again now that it was morning. I didn't want to see him lying there, dressed in the daylight that streamed through my parents' windows on mornings like that. My mom told me she'd just called the hospice worker to come and get him—we couldn't put it off much longer.

Passing through the front hall to get dressed in my room, I saw that the lights had been switched on in my parents' room for the first time in weeks. I didn't want to, but I looked in. Our dog, Jimmy, still wouldn't move from the side of the bed and Mom was standing over him, snapping her fingers and telling him to go. He just rested his head down between his two front paws, nose half-hidden under the bedskirt, and stayed where he was. Mom let her arm fall to her side and sat on the bed; her movement didn't change my dad's position. I stood there, watching, waiting for him to roll over and wrap his hands around her waist, or to sit up to kiss her and then wave to me. His eyes were closed, and he looked so small on the bed. My mom had turned on the lights for the first time in weeks so she could dress him in his favorite shirt and cozy socks for the journey, for the cold outside.

"Someone will come to plow the road, but they won't be able to get the stretcher up to the house," she said, seeing me standing paralyzed in the hallway. "Can you shovel a pathway for them to get through?"

Chapter 25

BOROMIR ON THE SCREEN

By ten o'clock on Sunday morning, the four of us had already gathered together at the dining room table to compose a letter to the campers and their families—to tell them, in our own words, that Dad was gone. Since only a few immediate family members knew what had happened that morning, we figured we had until about noon that day before word of my father's death would spread. Hoping to pre-empt any rumors or misinformation, we tried, collectively, to put into words what we had just experienced, what was still so jagged in our hearts.

I was shock-exhausted, numb and cold to my core. Sitting in the snow- and winter-sun-lit dining room, I had trouble staying awake at the table. Though usually copywriting came easily to me, I had nothing to offer that day. I almost never keep my mouth shut, but I didn't want to contribute to this letter. Applying the camp-friendly rhetoric to the news of Dad's death felt grotesque; for me, the obligation to write that letter so soon cheapened the loss, however much I understood the need to write it. I knew that thinking of the campers and their families as well as our own relatives and friends was the right thing to do—they had lost him too, after all. And because I knew that I would soon be sharing laments over his passing with hundreds of people, I just wanted him for the four of us a little longer. Even though it was nice to have some fresh company, the sudden piercing of our long-held seclusion felt like an intrusion—a violation, even. We were the only ones with him when he died; it had been private. It was ours. And now it was gone.

Everyone struggled to agree on the nuances of how the letter should be composed, more out of exhaustion than actual disagreement. We labored over the details, threw heartsick demands back and forth across the table. I sat quietly and let everyone else work out the problems, and by noon the letter had been sent out via mass email. It was a strange feeling, knowing that in a matter of seconds, the overwhelming pull of this massive community sharing in my grief would set in.

That afternoon, I went into my room and closed the door behind me. I kept an old, curly-corded phone on the nightstand next to my bed for late-night phone calls to friends. I'd turned the ringer off months before and, as I went to the bed to make my own phone calls, I turned the ringer back on. There was no need to keep the house so quiet anymore. I called my best friend, my most recent ex-boyfriend, and a few others who deserved to hear my voice as they heard the news of my father's death. Though I know those calls took place, I have no recollection whatsoever of what I said or what was said back to me.

*   *   *

The next day, my mom's good friend, Cheryl, and my Uncle Wooby arrived to be at our sides, and they quickly took to busying themselves cooking and cleaning, organizing the kitchen cabinets, and sorting the laundry that messily covered the couches. They moved as a team from room to room, throwing away the junk they thought we didn't need. They alphabetized, they organized, they scrubbed, and they tried to fatten us up. As if the brush of broom and wipe of cleaning cloth could erase the imprint of loss at our house. And if the house itself were tainted now, what had I become?

I imagined every crumb of dirt or grain of sand that had made its way from the beach into our house as a piece of the person I had been just days earlier, now dropped from dustpan into trash bag, thrown in the dumpster out back.

* * *

That week we worked on locating a meeting hall that could fit all the people planning to attend Dad's service. It was close to the holiday season by then and making arrangements from out of town was especially challenging. As we made phone call after phone call, trying to get the service organized, mail started piling up on our table. Each day that passed, Michelle, our assistant director, would bring us more and more bags of mail from the post office in town. Emails poured into our inboxes and overflowed the camp website. At every meal, we'd gather in the kitchen and hold a stack of cards and printed-out emails in our laps, reading for hours with the one empty chair beside us. We traded back and forth the good ones, cried as we read them over one another's shoulder.

In an explosion of camp connections and the unyielding web of Jewish geography, people all over the world let us know that we were on their minds. Having a new pile of letters at each meal gave me something to do with my time, gave me the feeling that what had happened to me was important. Soon, we learned that camp families were holding their own memorial services in Houston, Nashville, and Chicago for my father.

Gabe took a list of Dad's friends—his lawyer buddies, teaching colleagues, and fellow camp directors—making sure to give each one a personal phone call to tell them about Dad's death. Gabe would take the list and cordless phone in his hands, close his door, and finish calls one after another. He emerged from his room hours later looking exhausted and weak. I finally offered to take a few names off the list for him, and started by calling Tom Haebig, Dad's best friend from his teaching and political activist days in the '60s. Holding the phone in my hand, I knew that this task shouldn't fall on Gabe's shoulders alone—it was my duty too. Still, I sat down for a few minutes with the phone in one hand and the piece of paper with Tom's number in the other, steeling myself for the pain of saying the words aloud. Finally I dialed the number, waited a few seconds, and pressed "Send."

"Hi," I croaked nervously. "Tom? This is Tanya Chernov."

"Oh, hi Tanya," he said pleasantly. "How are you, sweetheart?"

"Tom," I lifted the phone away from my face for a moment, breathed in, and continued, "I wanted to call and tell you that my dad passed away on Sunday. We just . . . wanted you to hear it from us."

* * *

My mom made sure each of us read every new letter as it came in. She had piles on her dresser, on top of her nightstand, and on the kitchen table separated into categories. For a few days, she kept her favorite one on top of all the rest, written by a camper's mother who was also a family friend: *Just got the news. Dammit, dammit and dammit! We're thinking about you all. Emily fell asleep with a picture of Richard next to her.*

Still, some families weren't as thoughtful. One family wrote saying that they wouldn't be able to attend the service because they would be on vacation in Hawaii. They just wanted to let us know what a shame it was that we were making their girls miss the service. One camper ended her email telling us to "have a great winter break."

Another camp mom spoke to Michelle on the phone just two days after my dad died. "It's just that nothing like this has ever happened in our family," she said in her thick, slow Southern drawl, "and I don't know what to say to her in this kind of situation. It's been very hard on us." Michelle could hear the woman putting away dishes and closing a dishwasher door in the background.

"I know," Michelle reassured her. "None of us know what to say right now."

"Well, the thing is, I'd really appreciate it if Barbara could give me a call sometime today and talk to my daughter about Richard's passing."

"I know this is hard for everyone," Michelle said calmly, trying to contain her repulsion at the woman's selfishness. "But Barbara just lost her husband. She's a little busy to be calling camp families herself right now. I'll let her know you send your best, and good luck talking to your daughter."

* * *

A week passed and it was time to make our way down to Milwaukee. Mom and Uncle Wooby drove in one car while Dylan followed behind in his truck. A severe winter storm blew in as they left camp, and Dylan prepared himself for the long drive down at cautiously slow speeds. As they merged onto the highway, Uncle Wooby pulled his car in front. Dylan had expected to take the lead, being the expert winter driver he had become after living in Alaska for several years, and was worried that Uncle Wooby had forgotten how to drive on icy roads after living in New York City for a few years. In his emotionally drained state, Dylan was furious with Uncle Wooby for proceeding down the highway like everything was fine—he had just lost one parent and was convinced that he was about to lose another.

Before leaving camp, Dylan had placed pictures of Alan and Dad on the dashboard in front of him. Glancing down at those pictures now, the icy road stretched out before him with his last remaining parent in perceived peril, Dylan anxiously tried to pull in front and act as the pace car for their caravan. When they finally pulled over for gas, Dylan scolded Uncle Wooby for driving in a way that he thought was careless, and ordered him to slow down. Already we felt the intense, panicked fear of losing another family member. Not just for Dylan but for each of us, this would become almost as crushing as the loss itself—the anticipation of more loss.

I drove down to Milwaukee with Cheryl a few days ahead of everyone else, anxious to get out of Minong and away from the house. It rained the entire drive down the state, and I was happy to flee the scene of our loss, still so unbearably fresh. I would stay at Cheryl's house until the rest of my family came down a few days later. Cheryl's husband, Howard, and their two children, Adam and Rachel, had been a surrogate family to me in recent years, and I thought that staying with them would do me good. Remembering it now, I know it was the unimaginable reality of being in our camp house that drove me out so quickly. I'd reached my limit and could take no more of my new reality.

But when we pulled into the driveway, my surrogate family members were slow to approach the car. Everyone hugged me and told me they loved me, but I could tell they were afraid of me, as if my nearness to death were contagious. I settled in as best as I could, ate dinner with everyone else, and struggled to just keep myself upright.

The first *Lord of the Rings* movie had just opened and everyone wanted to see it, thinking it would be a great distraction for us all. The first two hours were indeed a great distraction; it refreshed me to be out in public again, to appreciate the conveniences of city life for a change. The isolation I had endured all those months at camp seemed overwhelming, and I pushed away thoughts of ever going back there again, focusing on the movie as best as I could.

One-hundred-and-eighty-seven minutes and fifty-one seconds into the film, one of the story's central characters, Boromir of Gondor, dies on his back in the woods. The experience of having seen someone die in real life only days before turned the scene on the screen in front of me into an insult, a direct violation on my delicate state of self-control.

Crying heavily now, watching a dramatized death scene play out in front of me, the scenery cast aglow with the grotesquely perfect finishing touches of movie magic, I looked in disgust at the people sitting all around me in the theater. Why was no one screaming, or crying, or demanding that the film be shut off? How could everyone be *okay* with this? Couldn't they all see how much this was hurting me—couldn't they tell by the tortured look on my face that I just lost my father, that I watched him die right in front of me? What sacrilege, what mockery this was. For us there had been no makeup, no costumes, no script telling us what to say. There had only been the raw reality of my father being taken away.

* * *

On the drive home, I stayed quiet, pressed against the cold leather of the car's backseat. I listened to everyone talk about how great the movie was, how close or how removed it was from Tolkien's original vision. I said nothing, though I'd read the series with vigor as a child. Even in the company of people who had known me since the day I was born, had always loved me as if I were one of their own, I felt like an alien. Like everything was changing.

Away from camp that night, I felt that I wasn't allowed to have the luxury of sleeping pills anymore and was so exhausted that I figured I probably wouldn't even need them. It was my first night without the Ambien and though I was afraid of lying awake all night with my thoughts, I wanted to go straight to bed and get away from the rest of the family.

I went up to Rachel's room where we shared a bed, sleeping like the false sisters we always wanted to be. As a teenager, she'd almost killed me one time, passing a car on Milwaukee's busy Lake Drive one afternoon in her smudge-marked, white Celica convertible. She was sixteen; I must have been eleven. I didn't grab the seat or flinch.

I imagined her as a rebel goddess in her belly-baring shirts, $100 clog shoes. I stole a bouclé sweater from her in high school, tried to scrunch my hair by the heater to copy her curls. Make-believe sisters, wannabe family, we compared bodies and popped pimples in her bathroom mirror for years. But that Friday, my sixth night as a fatherless child, it was clear that we were not family after all: My father was dead; hers was still alive.

When she asked me if I was all right while crawling into bed next to me, I didn't answer. When she told me to say something, I stayed silent. After a while, she pressed her hand flat against my back and kept it there, the warmth of her palm searing into my back, pushing through my chest, and coming out my mouth in wet, syrupy sobs. Then my face stretched tight, held tense in mid-sob with the pressure of a tornado trapped and struggling inside a glass of water. My body was paralyzed by the wails now sticking in my throat, mouth open its widest and eyes clenched tightly together. I pushed my head down into the pillow and wrapped the ends over my ears. Squeezed my ankles together, small frame curled like a snail. Maybe she wondered why I didn't make any noise.

Chapter 26

3:43 PM

By December 26, my best friends from Tucson had flown in to Milwaukee to be with me. Christmas had been largely uneventful, except for the logistical difficulties we encountered trying to make arrangements for Dad's service during the holiday season. My friends and family reserved a wing in the Wisconsin Residence Inn in Fox Point (just outside of Milwaukee) where we could orchestrate the funeral preparations. It was nice having so many people around to help me accomplish the pre-funeral tasks I'd been assigned.

After spending so much concentrated time with just my family, it felt good to be separated from them. It was difficult to look into their faces—to see reflections of my father in their expressions and features—and until the service actually arrived, I didn't want to think about how that would affect my future relationships with them. Would I ever be able to be with my family and not be overwhelmed by the feeling of his presence all around us, with constant reminders everywhere? I couldn't imagine ever not feeling the pain I felt at that moment, in the very darkest well of grief and terror.

The days passed in a blur of exhaustion, to-do lists, and airport runs back and forth across the city. Without fanfare, the morning of the service arrived. Around five o'clock in the morning on Saturday, December 29, I woke before the alarm clock to paint my nails. I turned on the vanity light near the bathroom, hoping the harsh light would not wake up my friends, Emily and Stephanie. My funeral clothes were laid out on the bed—tights folded next to shoes and shirt tucked inside sweater. I pulled out a bottle of maroon nail polish and started painting; the familiar stroke of brush against fingernail soothed me, kept my mind occupied just enough so I wasn't thinking about the events to follow. Drowsily hypnotized by the quiet darkness in the room, I let my thoughts about the day move to the back of my mind, but when I got to my right thumb I stopped, remembering that evening back in October when I had been chopping wood with Dylan by the side of our house. We loaded large stumps into the truck and drove them closer to the house, making it easier to chop them into fireplace-size pieces. We rolled the thick logs down the truck bed and off the tailgate onto the ground, but as I looked down to move my feet out of their path a log rushed forward, pinching my thumb against the side of the truck. I pulled it back, tucked my hand into my belly, and turned around so Dylan couldn't see me cringe. I walked straight into the laundry room where I could be alone and cried while looking at the purple-black stain under my thumbnail.

Now, on the morning of my father's memorial service, the bruise had nearly grown out. I felt a sense of dread that it would soon be gone—this mark that had originated while my father was still alive—and I didn't want this physical reminder of my father's presence to be gone so quickly, as if it were one last lingering connection to him that was slipping away before my eyes.

As I put on my makeup, hoping I'd look at least somewhat presentable, my friends joined me in front of the mirror and talked me through the morning. They helped me sweep my hair up and away from my face, letting the grief that was already settling in to show plainly, unhidden, on my expression.

When my family and I arrived at the location for the service—at a historic and architecturally treasured venue on the east side of Milwaukee—it was still dark outside with the eerie calm of an overcast winter day. The lights of the hall were turned on with an electric click, and the heat began pumping into the giant space as the sun rose through the windows under the massive, sloped ceiling. As people began coming through the front doors, the four of us stood in a line at the base of the stage. The crowd swarmed toward us, separating and squeezing us together at the same time. With each handshake and encouraging sentiment, I felt appreciation for their well wishes but also a sense of isolation—so many of their faces were vaguely or completely unfamiliar to me.

In honor of my father's habit of setting unusual times for events at camp, the service started exactly at 3:43 PM. Uncle Wooby took to the podium and cleared his throat to signal that the service was starting. I swam back through the thick crowd of people taking their seats and sat down in the front row next to my mom and brothers.

As I slouched down into the chair, the weight of standing instantly subsided and I started to cry—as if some internal trigger had been switched by the shift of weight. The surge of grief I felt that moment was almost deafening and I worried that I was having a panic attack; at once my heart started beating like a hummingbird. As I reached under my chair for a box of tissues, I closed my eyes and silently thanked my dad for instructing us to take the time we needed after he died, to make sure we were strong enough by the time the service came. I thought back to what he told us when we sat on the boat together in August: *It's scary with our culture on death. Funerals give space for loss and grieving, and so little for celebrating life. I want you to have time for both.*

Throughout the service, a number of people shared their stories about my father, and we told some of ours. Gabe steadily, stoically, read what he'd written for our father, maintaining noble composure the whole way through. I was glad he took the stage before I did, so that I could steel myself and follow his lead. Now, as I look back, I know what I said as my short eulogy but I don't remember having gotten up and said it. I don't remember looking out at the crowd, making eye contact with recognizable faces, don't remember if I used the paper in my hands or recited the words from memory. I shared my father's favorite poem, "A Creed," by Edwin Markham, line by line, with the personal changes my dad had revised into the short piece to better serve his purpose:

> There is a destiny that makes us brothers:
> None goes his way alone:
> All that we send into the lives of others
> Comes back into our own.

> I care not what his temples or his creed,
> One thing holds firm and fast—
> That into his fateful heap of days and deeds
> The soul of a man is cast.[2]

I sat back down, blinking at the bright lights above me, the winter sun pushing through the windows. Again, I've seen this replayed on the video we recorded at the service, but I have no memory of actually going through these motions. Bits of the day have been blanked out entirely in my memory—empty white space in my mind—while still other moments stand out like hot metal in a roaring fire, red and throbbing.

Dad's three favorite songs piped through the PA system during the service, and as I listened to their melodies, I knew in that moment that these songs would always promise to transport me back to that day. We passed a microphone around the room so that people who felt compelled to voice their remembrances of my father had an opportunity to contribute to the memorial service. Many of Dad's lifelong friends and colleagues spoke, along with several of the people to whom my father had been like a surrogate brother,

---

[2]Marham, Edwin. "A Creed." *Lincoln & Other Poems*. New York: Doubleday, 1913.

friend, or father. A former longtime staff member from camp, Seamus Ford, picked up the microphone from the back of the room. We didn't expect him to be at the service as we'd been unable to contact him after Dad's death. Hearing his voice and seeing his friendly face made me feel a sense of complete warmth and delight.

Seamus had been particularly close with my father during a time when he was quite distant from his own family. "I met Richard at a very important time in my life," he said, pacing at the bottom of the stage. "I was a year out of college . . . and drifting. I was asking the kinds of questions that so many people do at that age. The primary ones for me were, 'What is important? What do I want to do with my life?' Richard recognized that and gave me a chance to discover the answers to those questions for myself."

I looked over at my mom, her gaze fixed devotedly to Seamus, with a tissue pressed up to her nose.

"He listened to me and related to me as a person who was bigger than I knew I could be at that time," Seamus continued. "Being able to spend those years with the Chernov family has contributed enormously to my life, in ways that I express every day. While time and distance have separated us, I have never forgotten you. The Chernovs are my family."

Then Seamus set the microphone down on the carpeted stage and walked toward my mom, who by now was crossing the front of the room toward him with her arms outstretched. He swooped her up in a big bear hug and spun her around a time or two before setting her back down. He then turned to the crowd, motioning for everyone to stand up and join him in starting the silly song he'd introduced to camp years before, called "Father Abraham." Soon the entire room was standing, following the wacky dance and simple lyrics, which was something of a wonderfully bizarre sight to see with everyone dressed in their somber funeral attire.

My mother was laughing with wads of crumpled tissues in her hands, and our elderly relatives, babies, children, Nana Mimi in her wheelchair—even the reception hall's hospitality director—everyone was on their feet, waving their arms in the air and sticking their tongues out while singing as Seamus led the group. Dancing on one foot with my arms raised and wiggling, I thought Dad would have eaten it up with a spoon.

After the song and dance, the service continued with a palpable energy flowing throughout the whole room; everyone seemed to be tuned into the same emotional wavelength. This is the part of the service that I distinctly remember: I turned around in my chair for a moment while Alan's brother, Jack, read the eulogy Alan wrote before his death, and I noticed that the room was completely full, with several rows of people forced to stand at the back and out the main doors. The building could seat 300 people, and I guessed that there must have been at least another hundred overflowing into the hallways. I felt Dad's spirit filling the room with warmth as people shuffled out of the hall with somber, yet genuine, grins on their faces. His hope of putting smiles on the faces of his loved ones one final time had worked—he got what he wanted, and each one of us would be forever changed by the experience.

While I picked at a plate of food that my friend, David, had gently placed in front of me, I talked with one of Dad's lawyer friends during the meal following the service. She told me a story of how Dad accidentally answered an after-hours phone call that was being transferred to her desk. He remained on the line just long enough to hear her husband call her "Sweetikens." Of course, Dad never let her live it down and even once blared the embarrassing moniker over the office intercom for the whole floor to hear.

She spoke also of when she adopted her two infant sons and brought the babies into the office to show them off. She described the two boys in disparate ways: one was jolly and easy-going while the other was reserved and shy.

"Anyway, I took them to the office to be passed around," she said, "as one does with all new babies, and jolly Stuart promptly fell asleep and was no fun at all. Then, as I was talking to various people about my experiences as a new mom, I heard baby noises behind me. I turned around and watched as your father held Harry over his head, and my solemn baby was dissolved in a giggle fit."

"Yes, that sure does sound like Dad," I said.

"He had taken that sad, cautious baby, won him over instantly, and delighted him to pieces. Me too. If anyone else has a more wonderful gift, I don't know who it is. As far as I'm concerned, that is your father's greatness."

As I talked to more people, I got the impression that most were not at the service simply to pay their respects, but instead to mourn the loss of their collective second father, as a community—a special society of people who'd been lucky enough to know him.

Camp's longtime waterfront director, Caleb Knight, had been working with my family since our very first summer and managed to return each year despite familial and professional obligations. Sometimes a rigid, good-natured curmudgeon, Caleb always warmed up in my father's presence. Though he was living in Hong Kong with his family, Caleb moved mountains in order to be at the memorial service, and when he approached me to give his condolences, I thanked him for coming such a long way. He shrugged his shoulders and said, "Your dad was my dad."

Though I've known Caleb since I was three years old and grew up watching his relationship with my dad grow, it had never occurred to me until then how different life without my father would be for him now as well. He squeezed me in a long embrace, as if he needed reassurance of his status as a member of our extended family. I felt the pull of it just as I'd feared, but rather than stealing anything away from me and my grief, the realization of just how important my father had been to all these people filled me up, gave back to me in a way that I could never have anticipated. I'd expected this to be the worst day of my life. Instead, it was the day I felt the safest I'd ever felt— and even better, I felt important.

I started to think that perhaps because my dad was so special to all these people that I must also mean something to them, just by virtue of being his daughter. With so many mourners claiming ownership to my father, it helped to know that I had been a part of their loving him; and in doing so, I had a place in the world—an important one. There was a sense of security that day, knowing that no one expected me to be "normal" yet, because for me there would be no normal again, no getting back to my "old" self. That girl was gone. Someone new was now living in her place.

Chapter 27

NIGHT SKIING

For the listener, who listens in the snow,
And, nothing himself, beholds
Nothing that is not there and the nothing that is.
—WALLACE STEVENS

After Dad's memorial, everyone went back to their own lives, dispersing away from us in a hundred directions. In stark contrast, it felt as if there were no life to go back to for my mom, brothers, and me. Our tattered and shaken little family unit collectively hesitated, wondering how we'd find our way back to life again. Caring for Dad and watching him die had not only depleted every last store of energy and emotion we had, but it had also completely derailed any plans the four of us had for the future.

We stayed in Milwaukee for a week after the service before feeling ready to face our reality head-on. Pulling up to our camp house again was like entering an abandoned country: The buildings looked cold and empty; the weeks of snow had further changed the landscape until it looked foreign, almost alien. The house, the cars parked in the gravel driveway, the lake, the ghostly pale birch trees—it all looked alien to me.

The four of us—just four of us now—lingered in our rooms as if cast off to disappear inside the winter season. The house was clean and quiet and though it no longer retained the immediate feel of it, the imprint of death was still palpable. Trying to fall asleep was even worse than when Dad was alive; now I knew for certain what waking up would bring, and the whole of it seemed endlessly painful, tremendously more than the sum of its parts. I planned then, quaking under the weight of the silence at home, to stay at camp for another month and then head back to school. Though I wanted to be near my mom, I knew that I either had to return to school quickly or likely never go back.

When I finally made the decision to go back to Tacoma, we sold my old Jeep and I inherited Dad's Subaru Impreza, since I was the only one of us in need of a newer and more reliable vehicle (and Dad's treasured Impreza had only been driven a few times). Dylan volunteered to accompany me on the long drive back to Washington. We set a departure date a few weeks out, and with each passing day I eyed the Subaru, imagining that with it I'd be taking a piece of Dad back to Washington with me.

* * *

My family stopped watching TV and movies after Dad died. Pop culture no longer had a necessary or satisfying place in our lives, and I had already learned well my lesson with *The Lord of the Rings*. Ill-prepared for another trigger of that heart-wrenching grief, I preferred to spend my time trying to stay active in both body and mind.

Mom floated in and out of her bedroom all day, and my brothers and I had trouble understanding how she continued to sleep in the bed she had shared with Dad—the bed he died in. At the memorial service, Mom was beautiful, graceful, articulate. She was able to slip back into her "Everyone's Mom" role for the day—to comfort all the people who felt only a fraction of the loss she was enduring. But now back at camp, she hardly said anything at all. Gabe, too, didn't seem to be around much. Having decided to take Dad's place at camp, he dove right into the difficult matter of picking up all the pieces that had scattered when Dad died. I was proud of Gabe for grabbing the reins the way he did, hoping to help keep at least that part of our lives intact. But with Gabe traveling to support our livelihood and Mom descending deeper into her grief, Dylan and I found ourselves alone much of the time.

Before my departure, Dylan and I completed the finishing touches on the house Dad and Gabe had built together at the top of the hill. Dad was always trying to upgrade the staff housing at camp and as his last construction project, he and Gabe co-designed a side-by-side duplex. Every member of our family ended up having a hand in the construction of that building at one stage or another, with my father's trademark, innovative use of space present throughout.

When the house was finally finished, Dylan and I took to the inside. We'd sand and then paint layers of polyurethane on the walls with masks on, going outside in the freezing cold every half-hour to give our brains a break from the chemical smell in the crisp, fresh air.

When we finished our work at the end of each day, we would drive a few miles down the highway to ski on the local trails, dressed in the armor of fleece and grief. With granola bars stuffed into our pockets to keep them from freezing solid, Camelbaks stashed in the backseat of Dad's car, we no longer had anything to wait for but more snow. Most days, the sun was already half-down by the time we reached the trailhead. We stood in the winter-laced twilight and busied ourselves with the business of knocking clots of snow from our boots, stepping into our bindings, and fastening the straps of our gloves and poles. I'd let the air crawl inside me army-style, commandeering my lungs. Stiff, clean, pleasant. We carried out the pre-skiing ritual in the absence of small talk. Strange how in the cold, only the most important things get said.

Dylan started in front as he always did—as effortless in the snow as ever. We both knew I couldn't keep pace but I never stopped trying, and just like every time we took to a trail, he set out and forged the distance between us.

With him disappearing in the far-off curve of the trail, it was just me and the nighttime winter, thighs beginning to itch as blood pumped fast and heavy through my veins while I sewed myself into the right tempo: glide . . . kickglide . . . kickglide . . . kickglide. Dylan waited at the big hills or turns and when we rested, we'd lean on our poles, elbows bent until our gloved hands leveraged our weight against our shoulders. Together, breathing hard, we'd stand there in the evening silence, flexing our feet in our boots. Any words that passed between us were about the weather, the night, or the snow. Nothing more. All else was rendered irrelevant on the trails. Once the cold air chilled our skin enough to get us moving, we'd separate once more on the trail after a minute or two.

I could never see Dylan in the flats; he's a far better skier than I, and he's earned it. As I lost sight of him, I'd watch for the snow to turn its miasmic shades of slate and porcelain as I rushed by. I kept waiting to sense the need to reach up for my headlamp, but never did; the moon grew bold above me, lighting the way so brightly I had trouble judging my speed, but didn't mind the recklessness. At my sides, the snow stayed gray, bouncing the mildest of light all around the winter woods. The branches of the tree above me leaned into one another, entangled in the dim as if holding hands to block out the sun. Nose over toes, I counted each kickglide off in beats of twos.

The last few miles were perfection—slow and sloping. Gravity wrapped me in a windy embrace as I stepped inside the groom-slicked tracks, letting the stiff packing of each ski-shaped indent in the snow carry me sailing me through the forest. The wind shut my eyes for me that night, kissed them closed against the cold rush of it; I could barely see in the dark air with them open anyway. The whistle of my speed grew louder in my ears, louder simply because it was dark. Too quickly the trees opened up and I slowed to a stop, crestfallen, at the end of the trail. I pulled off one glove and turned on my headlamp to find the parking lot, where I'd find Dylan already changed back into his brown and black Sorel boots, the car started and the engine long since warming. Flushed and clammy inside Dad's car, the snow outside looked once again white to me, restored and clean in the headlights.

As the snow melted off our boots and onto the mats, I looked at my brother and asked, "Who will give me away if I get married?"

Neither Dylan nor the winter was able to give me an answer.

Chapter 28

SLIPPING

The way a child knows the world by putting it
part by part into his mouth.
                                    —JACK GILBERT

With our lengthy, mid-winter road trip to Tacoma completed, I dropped Dylan off at a hotel near the airport and hugged him goodbye. As I turned to leave, Dylan slipped a $50 bill into my coat pocket and wouldn't let me give it back. He just shrugged his shoulders and smiled a dull, shy half-smile.

"Keep the car clean," was all he said as he walked away.

A few weeks into the spring semester of my junior year, two months after my father passed away, I went cross-country skiing near Mount Rainier. I traveled alone, enjoying the long and gradual drive up to the mountain. I skied for a few hours, letting my thoughts drift near and then far, like the ocean when she calls back a wave. I let my body take over, let the push and glide of my skis tell me which direction to follow. The last of winter's snow had fallen during the night, and the early-morning sun made a gesture of warming me. Heading back to my car on the last half-mile, I caught an edge in the snow, a rough crust of ice on the grooves of the trail, and started to fall. I slid uncontrollably down a small hill with arms and poles flailing, hitting tree branches as I went, legs attempting to check my awkward balance. Unable to right myself on the gradual slope, I finally landed square on the side of my right thigh. Once I slowed to a flat spot in the snow and brushed the wet slush from my face, I felt just how hard I had fallen. It didn't hurt enough to make me cry, but I thoroughly considered it.

I removed my skis and walked the remaining distance to my car, wiping my wet and cold face with an even wetter and colder sleeve. After I clipped my skis to the rack on top of the Subaru, I pushed the front seat back, stretched out with my feet pressed against the clutch and gas pedal, and pulled my ski pants down on the right side. I prepared myself for what would surely be a bloody welt or bruise the size of a basketball. But there was barely a mark at all. Aside from some redness, probably more from the cold than from the fall, there was nothing to show for my fall, my pain. I was disappointed, then thought this a peculiar reaction; I pulled my seat forward and turned the key in the ignition.

I didn't think much about the fall while driving home, peeling off my sweaty clothes, singing along with the radio, and smoking a cigarette as I re-entered Tacoma's city limits. When I arrived back home, I looked down at my thigh again, a little swollen but otherwise unscathed, and was still disappointed, hoping that at least by now it would have grown into something that might in some way reflect how I felt inside, how devastated and lonely I wanted the world to know I was.

If I in any way premeditated what would happen next, I cannot recall it.

At some point between taking my clothes off and stepping into the shower, I inexplicably decided that since there was no mark on my thigh, it would be a good idea to create one.

I reached into my closet and picked up an orange shelf bracket, a little wooden "L" that was part of an IKEA shelf unit. I turned it over in my hand, gripped the blunt, square end, and jabbed it at the outside of my right thigh, over and over. I looked away and clenched my jaw, pushing it into my skin and then scraping it across. Broken capillaries popped up, polka-dotting my skin every time I pulled the unlikely weapon away. This behavior continued in the shower, me punching a shampoo bottle against my leg until a creeping shadow of blue began to appear beneath the bright pink splotches now littering my thigh.

What I've heard from people who cut or otherwise hurt themselves suggests that they commonly don't feel the physical pain as they cause it. Maybe I wasn't truly committed to the task, or maybe I wasn't doing it right because I felt every grate of the un-sanded wood, every punch from my own fist into the muscle, and it *hurt*. It hurt enough that I had to take little rests and run my leg under the water, wincing as the wound grew dark under the heat. I liked seeing how far I could take the pain, found pleasure in wanting to stop but soldiering on, doling out whatever lashes I thought were owed to me. Now I had something tangible to hold on to—I had something to show for my pain. For the moment, it was delicious.

I got dressed, put on makeup, blow-dried my hair, and moved through my "get pretty" routine as usual. Under my jeans, a contrary desire to show how un-pretty I felt was growing and seeping outward like water through clenched teeth. I went out of the house for a party at a friend's a few minutes away and once I got into my car, I again pulled my pants down a little to see what I had done. Still I did not feel the satisfaction I expected, but not because there was nothing to see on my leg. This time, the wound had appeared in its full form, having had time to grow and ooze. I was shocked at how bloody it was now. It looked new to me, as if I weren't the one who'd just caused it. I stared at its size—the awful grandeur of it—and wondered what kind of monster this made me. How had I really done this to myself? How had I attacked this huge chunk of my own body? In a confused but titillating mess of reactions, I was simultaneously horrified and proud. The welt was fever-hot and tender to my touch, but I couldn't stop poking it as pain shot through my thigh.

On the drive to the party, I created a convincing story, a lie that I would tell again and again that night at the party, and for several months afterward. I couldn't sit right, at the table playing quarters or on the couch taking bong hits, because my leg hurt each time it abraded against my tight jeans. I held the pain secret, treasured it silently as a precious physical sign of the suffering I had felt every day since my Dad died.

I proceeded to get drunk and let the act of self-medication sink its roots deep, seeping into me. Slowly, the pain on my leg dissipated, and I moved on to other, more immediate methods of drawing attention to myself. The alcohol worked its charms all through my 107 pounds until I loosened up enough to start bragging about my injury, claiming the bravado of my adopted persona. Better still, I showed everyone the wound. I pulled at my jeans, showing the right amount of attractive, toned leg in proportion to the ugly, angry section of the welt. By now the blood had started to congeal, making the first weavings of clot and scab. When a friend asked what happened, I told him I fell skiing. It was a little bit true: I had indeed fallen while skiing.

But in this horrifying act, in this egregious fallacy, no one doubted me. No one sensed my lie as I spun it ever more intricately; they'd swallowed it, and I kept shoving spoonfuls into their mouths, desperate for the opportunity to be acknowledged as having *gone through something*.

* * *

I never hurt myself like that again. Ever. I needed to learn that lesson only once. I did a somewhat insane thing, yes. But at the time I had my reasons.

Through the years, I've known cutters—friends and coworkers who obsessively scratched the backs of their hands with Exacto knives and blamed the cat, or who dragged fingernails across their belly so their self-abuse could be easily hidden. As much as I tried to place myself in a different category from them, I had no luck. I always thought that intentionally injuring oneself set a person a breed apart, and so I was astonished at being capable of such an act myself, without much premeditated thought. Misery had found strength inside me, spreading and transforming me in ways unpredictable even to myself.

* * *

I think back to the series of actions that took place that day, remembering the emotions that led me to do the things I did. In a way, I am proud of myself for having endured a pain so raw, so terrible, so all-consuming that it prompted me to grab the closest object and punch myself with it. I endured it, and I learned that the loss I felt was punishment enough; it wasn't necessary to go on adding to that pain.

I don't know all kinds of pain, but I know a few. We all know the desperate crush of a first heartbreak, or of the distinct anguish that belongs to adolescence, the sorrow of loneliness, and at some time in our lives, we will all know the pain of loss.

I've seen it play out both up close and far away: Death strings the experiences of our lives together more powerfully than anything else. The physical scar of that late-winter day lingered for a few years, then eventually faded, but the emotional scar has never paled. The memory I carry reminds me that I have to let go of the damaged girl I see reflected in the mirror some mornings and allow myself to just be, just be, just be, just be.

Chapter 29

A TECHNICAL MOURNER

In May 2002, I spent an afternoon shopping at my favorite craft supply store near campus. I wandered up and down the aisles looking at fancy new wood-burning tools, embroidery kits, paint, and yarn. I needed something to keep me busy while watching TV or relaxing because when my hands were idle, my mind would easily turn to dark thoughts. Looking through the bead section, Jim Croce's song "Time in a Bottle" started playing over the store's PA system. My dad loved Jim Croce, and that iconic song was one of the three we played at his memorial service per his request.

Though I was by now thousands of miles and several months removed from the service, all the feelings I experienced that day came swarming back to me in a flood of paralyzing images. I couldn't keep myself together and, more importantly, I didn't care to. The basket I carried dropped to the floor and with it several packets of bright blue beads from a make-your-own-necklace kit. I knelt down, my fingertips resting on the perforated metal shelving for balance. Without noticing the other people in the store, I let myself give in to tears. I didn't cover my eyes or my mouth and didn't wipe my nose even after it began dripping on the linoleum floor. Other shoppers turned down my aisle and then quickly headed in the opposite direction at the sight of me crouched on the floor. Every bead-seeker walked away as fast as she could without actually running. And no one asked if I was all right.

I was entirely unprepared for a public grieving session and started to suspect that if I didn't release my welled-up sorrow more frequently, it would continue to sneak up on me at similarly inappropriate times.

A few days later while walking from one class to another, I crossed the quad and came to a point where the sidewalk divides in two directions. The path veering to my right led me to my parked car, the other to my next class. As I neared the split, the girl walking in front of me said to her friend, "I hate my dad so much. I wish he would just, like, die." The words struck me, pulled the wind out of my gut. "My God, he's such a pain in the ass," she continued. Hearing her selfishness, her naïveté, and her callous insensitivity, I turned my body around, stepped onto the path heading right, went home, and cried in bed for the rest of the day.

About a month later, I was cleaning out the Subaru when I found an unlabeled cassette tape forgotten in the glove box. I pushed the tape into the cassette player and turned my key in the ignition. At first all I heard was the fuzzy whisper of bad recording quality and then a man's voice speaking very quietly in the background. The man had some kind of Eastern European accent—Russian, maybe. I heard him instruct someone to uncross his legs, noting that it was bad for circulation. Hearing this, I realized that the tape was a recording of one of my father's sessions with Dr. Gregory, the medical intuitive my dad worked with during his illness. I listened with my ear turned quizzically toward the speaker, as Dr. Gregory began expounding on what he saw in terms of spirituality, health, faith, and energy in my father's body.

The tape cracked and buzzed with static, and while Dr. Gregory rambled on in his steady voice, in the background I heard my dad *breathe*. Just an exhalation—not even a full sigh—but I knew it was him; it was a sound that came from him, a sound I would never hear again. I sat in the passenger seat of my car—his car—and cried against the steering wheel, arms held tightly over my head, until my roommate got home and tapped on my car window to see if I was all right. As we walked together up our narrow sidewalk, I felt the undeniable urge to get away from there, get out of the city and into the woods. I went inside and packed a bag, throwing whatever was on my desk into my old skiing backpack.

I took the car on a two-day road trip up the Olympic Peninsula, driving all the way to where the highway ends—spit out onto a windblown beach in La Push, Washington. I got a motel room by myself for the first time, cranked up the heat until it was so hot I had to strip down to a T-shirt and underwear, and ate three dinners sprawled out in front of me on the bed before heading back to school the next day.

I'd had enough of these public outbursts and decided to be a bit more proactive in my grief. I started to sit with an oversize binder my mom sent me, filled with copies of every card, letter, and email we received after Dad died, as well as the obituaries and eulogies written for him. I closed my bedroom door and paged through the letters, waiting to feel the burn in my nose and the ache in my throat before the tears started to flow. But try as I did to illicit the full force of my grief-response, nothing made me cry. Finally I found a card stuck in the back pocket with a note that my mom had attached to it with a piece of tape: *Found this in Dad's desk drawer at camp—he must have forgotten about it.* It was just a silly card my Dad had picked out to send me while I was at school, as had become his habit after his last baby bird left the nest. He had only started writing it before apparently becoming distracted and forgetting it under a pile of papers. In his all-capital-letter handwriting, it read, HEY WON-TON! SO PROUD OF THE—

It wasn't what he had written—I already knew that he was proud of me. It was his *handwriting* that brought the memories back. Finally the release I'd been hoping for bubbled to the surface and flooded over. Sitting on the bed with the binder splayed open on my knees, elbows burying my head as I tucked into myself, I cried for ten straight minutes.

Over the next few days, I felt calmer and steadier. I didn't carry around the same weight in my chest now that I'd unloaded some of my pain out into the world. Though I wondered why no one had suggested that I do so at the outset of my grief journey, it was obvious that I'd need to apply some techniques for managing my grief or risk losing my mind. If I didn't schedule a time each day to reach inside and dig out a memory, to think about Dad and let myself cry as hard as I needed to, my emotions would only accumulate in my gut until they finally blew out of me like a half-quelled Tourette's tic.

As the days and weeks went by, I eventually didn't need to perform this ritual as often, and sometimes I could think or talk about Dad without crying at all. After a few months, looking through pictures or home videos even started making me happy again. I know there will always be triggers, little reminders of my dad that shake me up. For the rest of my life, I will be constantly vulnerable to these sneak attacks, because grief is a ninja. Grief likes to enter the room when all is dark and quiet and unassuming. The grief ninja can take many shapes and forms, can bend and contort to fit into the small crevices of one's psyche. The grief ninja will crouch and hide and wait patiently while sweating in its heavy, black garb until it has the perfect moment to lunge—when all other guards are down.

Sometimes the grief ninja strikes with subtlety and grace, and sometimes it comes for me with hoards of shiny weaponry. It makes no difference. It hurts every time.

I've known this for years, and yet the ninja catches me by surprise with great frequency. Just when I think I am completely consumed by the daily demands of life, or distracted by other emotions, it finds an entry point and squeezes in to crash the party. Some nights as I begin to feel the gentle tugs of sleep, the ninja slips in. Often he comes to me with a single, simple message that floats silently into my mind and becomes my mantra for the duration of my sleepless night: "I miss him."

The time I'd spent living without my dad taught me that I could no longer try to guess how things would be if he were still alive. The person I was when he was alive was unrecognizable to me now; to wonder what I would be like or how life would be if he had survived cancer was a torturous, futile piece of foolishness.

Even so, especially in those early months, if I didn't continue to perform frequent maintenance on my grief in an organized way, I'd never be able to function. So the ninja and I curled ourselves into a corner whenever I felt I was overdue for a good cry, feeling the full heft of my grief. I knew that no matter how things had changed or what my life would look like down the road, I'd have to learn to feel comforted by the thought of my dad, comforted even by the grief itself. If I didn't have him, I could at least have the memory of him, the longing for something so wonderful and so terribly absent. As if the measure of a person could lie in the very size of the void their absence creates, the great magnitude of the gulf left in me became almost a kind of comfort, a reminder of how great he was and how lucky I am to have had him as my dad, to be his only daughter. Life was fleeting and love was fleeting, but grief—grief would stay with me forever.

* * *

Soon I had looked at every old photo of my dad, had read all the letters, watched all the videos, and still needed ways to pre-emptively manage my grief. Throughout his life, my Papa Sammy had regularly performed the ancient Jewish ritual of saying Kaddish for the people he'd lost: his mother, father, sister, and wife. This was one of the most important traditions of Papa Sammy's faith and before he died, he anxiously voiced his fears that none of his children would make the commitment to practice the ritual in his memory.

Showing a remarkable level of psychological astuteness, the ancient Jews believed that death was so sacred, so harrowing an event that mourners would naturally want to isolate themselves from the rest of the world in order to doubt the existence of God, and perhaps even slip closer to death themselves. The Kaddish recitation, in essence, was designed to combat such a lonely and dangerous journey through grief. A mourner, or immediate relative of the deceased (usually male), recites the mourner's Kaddish prayer out loud and in the presence of at least nine other men, who come together to form a minion, or quorum, that serves to bear witness to the grief and to stand beside the griever. In many congregations, volunteers show up every morning at sunrise in an act of community spirit and generosity, just in case there aren't enough mourners to make up the full minion. The prayer must be said at least once every day for eleven months, though some people will carry out the ritual three times a day and up to twelve months after the death of a loved one.

The prayer itself actually makes no mention of death or grief; instead, it exalts God and praises his teachings. At the very time when most grieving people hate God and bring to question the nature of his role in the world, people of Jewish faith simply show up and say the memorized words aloud, believing that the rest will eventually follow. Uncle Wooby recognized the spiritual value of this routine long before his father passed away. He told me that he thought it was remarkable how the ancient Jews knew losing a loved one would be a time in life when we all need other people around us, to keep us buoyed against the pain. So after Papa Sammy died, Uncle Wooby followed through with the incredible commitment and said the mourner's Kaddish for his father for the full eleven months without missing a single morning.

My dad never expressed any interest in having this prayer recited for him; he had fallen out of touch with his faith and long since replaced it with a more secular, spiritual-based path. Still, I liked the idea that at least in this group, at least while saying the words of the prayer, I could still be "in mourning" long after the rest of the world wanted me to be normal again. Although I essentially hadn't been to Temple since my own bat mitzvah eight years before, I decided to check out the only Jewish synagogue in Tacoma; I would try Uncle Wooby's method and see how it worked.

At first, I simply enjoyed having somewhere to go every Friday evening before parties started and friends gathered for whatever college-time debauchery was on the menu. After class and before sundown, I'd dress in my demure temple clothes and lift my own prayer book from my shelf. Arriving at the synagogue, I happily nestled into the familiar sounds and routine of attending a Shabbat service.

I kept going to those Friday-evening services even when I had technically ceased to be a mourner in the eyes of the faith, saying, *Yit'gadal v'yit'kadash sh'mei raba*: May His great Name grow exalted and sanctified. I wasn't in mourning anymore, not by these guidelines anyway. *B'al'ma di v'ra khir'utei*: In the world that He created as He willed. Still, the eyes of the crowd felt good on me. *Ba'agala uviz'man kariv v'im'ru*: Swiftly and soon.

Nobody knew me there; nobody knew what had happened to me or how long it had been since I suffered my terrible loss. In that building, eleven months is what we were allowed. The congregation just saw me, standing among the few, standing because this still hurt, standing because I wanted to be acknowledged for it, to keep death fresh. *V'yit'hadar v'yit'aleh v'yit'halal sh'mei d'kud'sha*: Mighty, upraised, and lauded be the Name of the Holy One. Most of us would at some point let our tears drop down the fronts of our bodies like the fringe of a talis. Sometimes I was the only one to show emotion; other times women I'd never seen before would drape themselves in shawls and wail like animals, the people nearby holding them up by their elbows.

Our stuttering rabbi always made eye contact with me, holding it a few seconds before moving on to the next person. *B'rikh hu*: Blessed is He. *L'eila min kol bir'khata v'shirata*: Beyond any blessing and song. The rabbi would say: *Y'hei sh'lama raba min sh'maya*, slamming into hurdles of words. *V'chayim aleinu v'al kol yis'ra'eil v'im'ru*: And life upon us and upon all Israel. I'd never heard a stutter in two languages, at least never that I understood. And I loved it. I felt somewhat proud to discover that the sounds of stuttering are the same spoken with another alphabet. *Oseh shalom bim'romav hu ya'aseh shalom*: He who makes peace in His heights, may He make peace. I sat down and repeated, *Amein*.

Chapter 30

THE RESIDUAL STAND

The spring semester was nearly finished and as I completed the last of my final exams, I had to make a quick decision about where to spend my summer. I felt that spending the next few months in Tacoma was out of the question—most of my friends had been put off by my depression during the spring semester and had moved on. Within a few months of Dad's death, my circle of friends and even my boyfriend showed their inability to deal with loss and grief— some seemed afraid of me and some never even breathed a word about what had happened in my family—and I quickly found myself almost entirely without a support system at school. But I wasn't sure about returning to camp either.

During that first semester back at college, I found myself becoming more dependent on my best friend, Rachel, who lost her father when she was only nine years old. When we met as freshmen, we had no idea that it would be our fathers who would bring us together as friends. One evening, Rachel and I found ourselves practically alone in the cafeteria. Long after we'd finished eating and pushed aside our trays, we lingered in the dining hall's quiet rotunda, talking about what we'd been through, how we'd changed, and how different we felt from the rest of our friends. Her dad had been sick a long time too, and we spoke a common language that we couldn't share with just anyone else. For the rest of our lives, we knew we'd been bonded together because of it.

Rachel was going home for the summer, and I saw no point in staying at school, so far away from my family. I knew that camp needed what little help I could offer as my father's daughter, if not for any other reason. My family had no idea how the campers and staff would fare without my dad, and we struggled with the decision to open that season. I felt such a sharp sting trying to imagine how camp would look, feel, and sound without Dad's welcoming smile, exuberant laugh, and his low, booming voice filling the lodge at every meal.

I hadn't been back to Wisconsin since that winter and pulling into the camp's bumpy driveway was like throwing an old shirt over my head: soft, weathered, familiar. I told myself not to be nervous walking in the front door of our house; so much was different now, and I didn't know how to feel coming home. I tried to remind myself that Dad wouldn't be there and that I couldn't expect to see him walk around the corner or look up from the kitchen table to greet me. Though I wished for it over everything else in the world, I wouldn't see him walking toward me with a hug, wouldn't hear him call my name.

Exploring the house after dropping my bags, I inspected all the rooms to see how things had changed, or not changed, since I'd been gone, and I found that Dad was still there—in a way. His face smiled at me from the hundreds of family photos crowding the walls, narrating the story of our lives with their sun-dulled images. In my parents' bedroom, his clothes still hung in the closet, his shoes lined up neatly on the floor below exactly where he'd left them. I pulled apart the wooden closet doors and pulled the long, white string to turn the light on, the little silver cone at the end of the string bungeeing up and hitting the naked bulb with a tinny *dink*.

Standing at the base of the closet, I scanned my eyes over the flannels and sweaters, the well-worn leather belts and fleece jackets. In a swift and spontaneous movement, I dove forward, lunging my upper body into the clothes, wrapping my arms wide around the hanging shirts and jackets. My face buried in the fabric, I breathed in, sucked the smell into my body as if it were all the oxygen left in the world. Exhaling, I bunched the hangers more closely together until they felt thick and full, then wiggled further into the mass with my arms outstretched, back arched, face pressed in, searching for his smell in the empty clothes.

* * *

What my family experienced together in December had been so private and so sacred that opening up our house and the land to campers almost felt like a bizarre violation of our personal pain. Certainly by then, the sight of our home filled with hundreds of people overnight was a familiar one, but this—this was something else. I saw my father everywhere: his intellectual prowess in the design of every policy and practice; his resourcefulness in the design of every building; his humor in the silly plaques hanging throughout camp; his tenderness in the photos of friends smiling and hugging each other hanging on every wall of the office. As if grief had given me a pair of tinted goggles to wear, nothing looked the same.

In my father's absence, the landscape of the business had changed as well. Without him to keep everyone focused, happy, and motivated, our team of administrators was forced to find new footing, each person feeling his or her own grief begin to work in new ways. In the camp environment, our collective loss felt even more raw and urgent. Gabe was too young and overwhelmed by the responsibilities suddenly dropped into his hands to take everything on by himself, and my mom was simply exhausted, nervous, and, in so many inconceivable ways, heartbroken. None of us knew exactly how our grief would surface as camp was opened up to the kids; my dad had been the cotter pin keeping us all together. Without him, we were afraid we'd scatter.

Because we had been so nervous throughout that winter about the upcoming season, my brother and family spent months consulting

other camp directors who had been through similar situations—
people who had personal and first-hand expertise on how to handle
such a difficult transition. Though we were personally devastated,
as the season approached we found ourselves comforted by the
knowledge that our years of professional experience would keep us
buoyed and focused. By the time we all gathered together at camp
to prepare for the kids to arrive, we were still shaken by our grief
but at least felt prepared. And in the pre-camp weeks, consisting of
maintenance and staff training—all the busy prep work it takes to
get things ready for the campers—we proceeded to check everything
off our lists. Cabins were cleaned and docks put into the water and
anchored into the sandy muck. Paperwork was filed, tennis nets
hung across the courts, and the lodge swept and dusted. We were
ready, but all the readiness in the world still couldn't lessen our
feeling of loss.

    Bolstered by the strength and love of the administrators we'd
worked with for so many years, we at least knew that it would be a
good summer for the kids no matter how hard it would be for us. The
day before the campers arrived, my family and I took a walk near the
council-fire ring to talk about Dad, check in with each other about
everything that was going to happen—the things we could anticipate,
the things we knew we could not.

    We traced the large slope of grass wrapping around the stone
firepit with our footsteps in silence. That day marked the strange
convergence of the six-month anniversary of Dad's death, the thirty-
third anniversary of my parents' marriage, and also Father's Day—our
first without him. We'd had time to start dealing with our winter lives
without Dad, but *camp* life without him was still uncharted. None of
us knew what to expect from the kids now that their hero was gone.
How would they behave in the absence of his watchful demeanor?
Would they laugh without his silly accents and dorky jokes? Could
we reproduce the joy he emanated with such seeming effortlessness?
As we stood huddled together looking down at the freshly manicured

grass, we prayed for the strength to just get through the next two months without losing our way.

What we discovered the moment the campers arrived was that my father had laid down such a strong set of blueprints for us to follow that all we really needed to do was relax and trust ourselves. We found ways to settle back into our tried-and-true methods, focusing on the campers and giving them the individual attention and acknowledgment they were accustomed to. The rest seemed to just fall into place, and the summer carried on as always. Same beautiful play—new cast of treasured characters.

I, however, was still lost at camp that summer. Though I was determined not to let *anything* be good anymore, my job was especially ill-suited to my skills. Wasting time in the office again, I fielded phone calls from nervous parents and put Band-Aids on scraped knees.

My brothers and I struggled to see eye-to-eye on most things—and we quickly pushed back against the closeness we had achieved while Dad was sick. I'd had nowhere else to go—camp was my only home, but it felt like a prison. Living in our cabin again felt stale and suffocating, like breathing your own air too long under a blanket. My room would never be mine in the same way again, too crowded with memories of the sleepless hours, the nights of self-loathing and dread. As the weeks wore on, the migraines I suffered as a teenager returned, occurring almost daily, despite my having largely outgrown them years before. I'd lie in the back room of the office in the hot and humid summer twilight hours, waiting for my medication to kick in, for the edge of the pain to dull and fade. Stifled by the heat of the afternoon, I couldn't help crying, though I knew the effort and tumult of it worsened the pain. It wasn't long before I started taking Ambien again, perhaps not because I needed it to get to sleep but because I preferred its speed and effect. I was slipping into a new kind of depression, giving myself permission to sink further with every passing day.

As the first session of camp progressed, the community's collective longing for my father was palpable. Since everyone missed my dad so fiercely and so persistently, we thought it might help to hold a special Sunday service in his memory. Though I wasn't eager to eulogize my father for a second time, I could see the need for it. We're not a religious camp in any way, and these services didn't preach any specific dogma or doctrine. Instead we used songs, poems, and stories to discuss themes such as global awareness, friendship, environmental stewardship, and emotional self-discovery. "Sunday Services" were always my mom's department—her office was lined with binders full of poems and proverbs helpful in creating these short, kid-friendly gatherings on the things that make us better human beings. With Dad gone, Mom was now busier than ever, and I knew she could use my help. With nowhere else to filter my pain and the longing I felt to have my father back, I reluctantly accepted the responsibility of leading the special program. But even as the service began to take its shape, I still wasn't sure if I wanted to participate when Sunday came.

I selected a few campers and staff to join me in writing the speeches we would give on Sunday morning. Sitting down with each fellow mourner to compose a well-written eulogy for my dad was a surprisingly cathartic experience. Finally, some of the jealousy and territorialism I had felt since his passing began to ebb away. Hearing how empty these other people felt in response to my father's death made me feel increasingly less lonely. Most importantly, it made me feel lucky. All my life, people told me how much they always wanted to have my father as a parent, not just as a camp-Dad, and how much they envied me their whole lives because of what I had. So many people had wished for him to claim them as his children, but only I had been his *real* daughter. Working on the service ultimately forced that notion to take root: I was the luckiest girl in the world because I got to have him as *my* dad. The realness suddenly shed a spotlight on a pride I'd never acknowledged before. Even though I only had him for twenty years of my life, it was twenty more years than anyone else ever had, and for the first time in years I allowed myself to feel blessed for this gift.

During the service, I stood where my dad had always stood on Sunday mornings: under a large white pine tree in the center of camp. His presence filled me and, looking out over the camp community, I understood why he had always been so tirelessly protective of his flock. I wanted to protect them now too—wanted to love them and keep them warm and safe. I slowly paced from side to side as I spoke, looking up into the shadows of the big white pine above me.

This "Service Tree" is the source of many legends at camp, some of which were very likely true at one time and embellished into the stuff of campfire stories over the years like an epic game of telephone. It stands much taller than the other white pines at camp, and its trunk is at least five feet thick on all sides. One theory for this astoundingly old tree's longevity is that it was left as a "witness tree," part of a residual stand from the Northwoods' logging era. Many logging companies would leave one large tree, or sometimes a small stand of trees, to remain in the middle of an area they had ravaged. All over the state as well as the country, witness trees have served as landmarks and meeting places. Their lonely vigil is impossible to ignore.

Throughout my last years working at camp before I started a career of my own, those Sunday services were by far the best part of my job. I loved to carefully choose a cabin group to lead each service, then sit back and watch them decide on a theme for the week and how best to explore that theme with the rest of the campers. I'd give them each a binder or book, now lining the shelves of my own office, and collect each camper's chosen song or story to be printed in the program. We'd rehearse throughout the week, working on speaking loud enough for the whole camp to hear. It was an opportunity for me to grow closer to campers with whom I may not have otherwise spent much time, and I loved watching the expression on a camper's face as she took her turn reading a poem or quote aloud, finding her voice in front of the crowd.

* * *

I loved to stand with my back against the solidness of the white pine bark, while the kids in front of me sat on benches below the low-hanging boughs of the service tree. Sometimes I walked around the group as I spoke, just as my dad always did. In my brief stewardship of this tradition, I found that leading services and following in my father's footsteps by teaching our girls how to be good friends, respectful global citizens, and conscientious environmentalists made me miss Dad just a little less. When Gabe edited all the video footage from that summer during the post-season weeks, I was anxious to watch the videos of Sunday services. Seeing myself on the screen as I faced the crowd didn't make me particularly sad, but seeing myself in Dad's place at the tree was a different matter. When Gabe fast-forwarded through the frames, I made him stop at the end of each service so I could watch myself walk forward with my hands in my pockets, in the very same stance and stroll as my father had. Instead of his face in that setting, I saw my own, and the finality of his absence sunk in. He was never coming back; I'd never see his face again, would never see him captivate the audience of campers and staff. I would never again have the luxury of being part of his audience.

Chapter 31

THROWING ROCKS

Our first summer without Dad passed by, and as it did, I felt a longing for a traditional cemetery plot and burial for my father. I knew it was his wish to be cremated and for his and Alan's ashes to be spread together whenever the rest of us were ready to let go of those last physical remnants. But even knowing this, I found myself wishing desperately for a place I could go, a place where he was, a place where I could grieve properly for him.

By the middle of August 2002, camp had closed for another season and we had survived, mostly intact. I was eager to head back to Washington and escape some of the festering emotional intensity camp had created for me. But again I felt torn about leaving my mother; the summer had worn her down, and I could tell when we said goodbye that she would worry herself ill about me while I was away, wondering how I was doing when she needed to just rest and take care of herself. I reassured her that I would come home again in a month or so, and tried to wrap my head around the task of returning to school in order to finish out my senior year.

By the time I left to go back to school, we still hadn't spread Dad's ashes because of the lake's late thaw. Our family, as well as Alan's, was still trying to plan a weekend before the lake froze over again to come together and spread the ashes.

The year before, as we were all sitting in the boat on the lake, my father told us exactly where he wanted his ashes spread: "My ashes—at the north of camp, in view of the eagle's nest. My heart is here. I am a local, a Minongian."

"Pick a night with a good sunset and face east because the sun rises in the east and brings new life, represents the seasons," he continued, now pointing over to a small peninsula blocking the view of his favorite spot from the rest of the lake, keeping it private and secluded.

"It's the Native American way of life, it feels clean and healing, a need to embrace the possibility of the closure of life. The eagle is flying over us right now, look—it's a messenger from God, a good omen."

* * *

After Dad's service, I didn't see Alan's family again for almost a year. When we finally did all come together again, it was the middle of October and the leaves up north were just turning their peak colors, twisting glimmers of orange and red in the wind. It felt good to get a little escape from school and to see my family again now that we had all recovered from the camp season. It was nice to see Susan and my mom together; just as Alan and my Dad had walked toward death together, so, too, were their wives now holding hands through widowhood. It seemed as if they were each reaching the various landmarks of grief at the same time, helping each other along.

It was a comedy of errors trying to determine how to get the eight of us out onto the lake, which included going down a narrow passage of water, over a small portage, and back into the water on the other side of the narrow spit of land. We paddled across the lake dressed in fleece and wool tucked inside our best life jackets, imagining Dad and Alan looking down on us and laughing their asses off at the scene we made while clumsily piling into the old aluminum canoes. We managed, with some difficulty, to get each one of us up and over a long-abandoned dam, slipping over water-slimed sticks and layers of packed mud. Once again in the canoes on the other side, we floated silently in the small pond.

Mom and Susan opened the lids from boxes in their laps and pulled out thick plastic bags filled with pale-colored ash. No one spoke as we aligned the two canoes so that we could face each other, dipping gently side to side in the low waves. Once positioned with our two canoes forming parallel lines, Susan and Mom began drizzling the ash onto the surface of the water. I rested my chin on the gunwale and looked over the edge of boat, its cool aluminum chilling my neck. I watched the ashes spiral down into the indigo, mixing with muck, weeds, and the sand beneath. We cried into the pond, our tears chasing the sandy ash. *Don't go, don't go.* My eyes followed the cloudy mixture as it expanded and sank like a plume of smoke, disappearing beneath us.

When there was nothing left to see in the water below our boats, I was glad that my father had chosen this spot. I knew I would enjoy coming there to be near him and felt foolish for having wanted such a traditional farewell. Our smiles returned during the paddle back to the beach, the sun now already dipping behind the pines across the lake. The sky was getting dark by the time the canoes and paddles were back in their rightful places, locked up once more for the season.

Walking back to the house, we passed an old cabin, one of camp's original turn-of-the-century buildings. We hadn't used it for years but kept it for empty duffel-bag storage and the like. It would be torn down soon, stripped away to the studs next spring along with a few other dilapidated buildings to make room for newer structures. Gabe stopped walking and stared at the cabin, into the darkness behind its windows. The rest of the boys and I took notice and slowed our steps, turned our bodies back toward the lake, and watched him. Without speaking, he picked up a rock from the road and turned it over a few times in his hand, then cocked his arm behind him and threw it at the cabin. It hit a peeling section of log-siding with a *thud* and disappeared into the grass. No one spoke or tried to stop him.

He picked up a larger rock and threw again, this time smashing clear through a window. Still, no one said anything. Then Dylan and Mark found rocks at their feet, held them in their hands to feel the weight before chucking them at the cabin almost in unison. Steven and I looked at each other as if for permission and joined our older brothers in a quest to break every window. Each of us took a moment to rub the rocks in our fingers, allowing the significance of what we'd just done to sink in a moment before pulling back to hurl them at the cabin. When one of us hit a particularly good throw, the rest would simply nod in approval. Mom and Susan walked backward the rest of the way to the front door so they could watch us, their hands still clasped around the empty, ash-lined bags.

Chapter 32

I HAVE SEEN NOTHING AND EVERYTHING

As my senior year moved into its winter months, I expected less and less of myself academically. I could think only of my pain, could feel only my loss. What's more, I saw no reason to alter the situation. It felt good being sad all the time, felt right. It felt necessary and safe. Trying to fit in among my peers was impossible in my state of mind, but more importantly, the effort was simply more than I was willing to make.

I stopped setting my alarm for class each morning, thinking that if I woke up in time, I was meant to go to class that day; I'd leave it in fate's capable hands. I'd fantasize about sleeping in—sleeping until it got dark outside again, skipping all classes and calling in sick to work. But then each morning I could sleep no later than six o'clock, sweating beneath too many layers of pajamas and down blankets. In silent protest to the world for carrying on as usual, I did my best to care very little for my appearance and affect, though that kind of apathy didn't come naturally to me at all. I consciously stopped choosing coordinated outfits for class and instead considered it a good day if I dug up the motivation to put on a fresh pair of pajama pants. I took up an obnoxious, defiant bubble-gum-chewing habit even while in class. No one bothered me about any of it. I believe they were scared of me—professors, TAs, students—no one wanted to touch what I had going on, and certainly no one wanted to risk making it worse.

* * *

All the well-wishers at Dad's service told me that I wouldn't always feel so awful—that life would slowly, eventually, get easier. But as time passed, none of it got any easier; it just became more familiar. Time hadn't softened the edge of my grief and in fact as time passed, I only missed Dad more. Perhaps the tone of my pain had changed, yes, but the plain, pure feeling of *just missing him* worsened as milestones and days marched by.

Friends and relatives kept telling me how strong I was, how brave. *You look great, honey. Really good.* As if my clear complexion could right all that had gone wrong. But inside I felt ugly. I felt ruined. I stopped caring about living—stopped putting on my seat belt when I got in the car or looking for traffic as I crossed a busy street. If this was what life was going to be like, then I didn't want to keep living it. This mentality did not seem brave or strong to me—not by any definition—and people's well-intentioned platitudes only served to infuriate me further. It was becoming difficult to build up the energy just to flip the covers over my legs each morning and break the seal of warmth I'd worked on all night. I felt the opposite of everything people kept telling me I was, and it made me question why they continued to offer these tidbits of mock wisdom to my clearly heartbroken face. Did they see something I could not? Did they have some special window to the future that was being denied to me?

In her own search for answers, my mom spent her first year of widowhood devouring books written by other widows. She sent many of them along to me, but I never saw in them what she did. To me, each memoir was just another therapy session, another sentimental series of whining statements about how badly grief hurts, and even though much of it did ring true to what I experienced, I was looking for something more.

I wanted to learn a secret from these books—wanted to discover some hidden benefit of grief. As if there were one book meant just for me out there, I read every bit of nonfiction I could find. The books my mom read and mailed to me always ended with the author still locked inside the darkness—there were no rainbows on the other side of grief, no sparkling pool of glory waiting to congratulate me for the journey. And this wasn't good enough for me; though I didn't want anyone to tell me everything would be fine—because that was most certainly not the truth—I also didn't want to hear that it wouldn't all be all right in the end. I knew now that my pain wouldn't ever really go away, but I suppose what I needed was to know that somehow I'd be okay in the end.

I made a good writing friend through the very small English department at school, and after class one day he handed me Dave Eggers's innovative memoir, *A Heartbreaking Work of Staggering Genius*. I devoured it. I loved the gruesome bits he shared about his parents' deaths and the brave way he admitted his own shameful thoughts or behavior. His blunt candor satisfied all the lingering needs I still had to know what death would always look like, smell like, feel like. About halfway through the book, I felt Eggers's torment and began an imaginary conversation with him:

Please see this! I am the common multiplier for 47 million! I am the perfect amalgam! I was born of both stability and chaos.

No shit? Me too! I had both the stability and the chaos of which you speak. And it has messed me up.

I have seen nothing and everything.

Yes, you are right. I have seen everything now that I have seen death, yet it has humbled me. I am young; I am mortal. I haven't even begun to see what there is to see. I know nothing—possess nothing to show for myself. Dude, I totally get what you're saying.

I am twenty-four but feel ten thousand years old.

I am twenty-one. And I feel like a forty-seven-year-old recovering alcoholic: barely making it through the day while trying to pick up the scattered pieces of my former self. We would make fine friends, Dave. You and I would get along thick as thieves. Hilarity would ensue. No doubt.

I am emboldened by youth, unfettered and hopeful, though inextricably bound to the past and future by my beautiful brother, who is part of both.

Now this is getting bizarre. I, too, feel bound by my brothers. Though I am not raising them, they are a constant reminder of what I have lost, and because of this I am terrified of ever losing them, ever letting them slip through my fingers. I love them and I hate them for looking like our father. I love them and I hate them for having been a part of my past and being part of the future that will not involve an intact family. But hopeful? This, I am not. What do you still hope for, Dave?

All this did not happen to us for naught, I can assure you—there is no logic to that, there is logic only in assuming that we suffered for a reason.

Well, you're right. There must be a reason. There must. I'll die if there isn't.

Just give us our due . . . I am rootless, ripped from all foundations.[3]

Yes, Dave. We are owed. We are due for something magical. We deserve to be repaid. Things have been stolen; things have been replaced without our consent. Life is at once different and never going to change. How must we navigate, Dave? How will we search to find that which was supposed to be delivered?

---

[3]Reprinted with the permission of Simon & Schuster, Inc., from *Heartbreaking Work of Staggering Genius* by Dave Eggers. Copyright © 2000, 2001 by David ("Dave") K. Eggers. All rights reserved.

* * *

It made me feel less selfish knowing that I wasn't the only one looking for some hidden treasure I was sure would be waiting for me soon—some nugget of esoteric wisdom that only mourners have the opportunity to possess. It seemed greedy to expect life to repay me, but I didn't care. I'd spent the years that were supposed to be the "best" of my life shuttling between hospital waiting rooms and cold, barren airports in Washington, Arizona, Minnesota, and Wisconsin. Even when I went to parties, hung out with friends, and exhibited all the signs of having a good time, it was only a pretense. From the moment my dad was diagnosed until several years after he died, my thoughts were with him at all times. Senior prom was filled with an unnatural sorrow. College was stressful, lonely, and alienating. My coming-of-age years were filled with more pain than joy. None of those landmark experiences were for me what they are supposed to be. Everything happy was compromised and weakened into, at best, bittersweet. And the future only held more of the same. Graduation without him. Traveling in Europe with depression as my only companion. My first apartment. My first real job. Falling in love. Having children of my own. All of it a reminder of his absence.

Reading Dave Eggers's book made me realize that things would definitely not get any easier and for this, both he and I deserved to be repaid.

Of course I knew that I'd never get back what I'd lost, no matter how well-adjusted I became in my grief and no matter how much time passed. For my trouble, then, I wanted to be given something in exchange. For the first time since my father's death, I was mad as hell. I wasn't just angry that he had been taken away from me, but also angry that I had not been given something in return. I felt filled with the realization that whatever I thought I was owed, it was late in coming.

Feeling so cheated, I couldn't stop thinking back to the night after Dad's memorial service, lying in bed and feeling certain that I had just survived the worst day of my life, that things would surely be easier from that point forward. In the months that followed, however, I had grown steadily more impatient with myself for getting bothered or upset by the everyday stresses I encountered. I expected some kind of super-resilient shield to suddenly rise up around me, fending off both major and minor distresses with dignity, ease, and grace. Where was the magical veil of emotional badass-ness that was supposed to blanket me from all things painful? Dave Eggers seemed to have found his pot of gold at the end of his grief-rainbow: He had a *Time* magazine's "Best Book of the Year." And he was funnier for what he had been through, obviously smarter and wittier for the path he was forced to walk. I envied him, and I hated him. He was strong, and I was not. I looked up his picture on the Internet, hoping he'd at least be ugly.

* * *

Eventually I gave up looking for my post-grief treasure. Instead I gave myself permission to hate life for as long as I wanted. When I saw drugs or alcohol around me, I used them with intentional abandon. I hadn't been dependent on drugs at any time before in my life, but without my father to help me navigate such temptations, I didn't even try to resist. I made friends with one of the many drug-dealing and -using cliques on campus and spent time with them exploring an incredibly diverse pot playground. As self-professed culinary aficionados, we cooked an ever-changing milieu of pot-laden banana breads, blondies, and scones. In addition, we tried an assortment of gastronomy-free methods for getting high. We used a gas mask pumped full of pot smoke, hookahs, vaporizers, gravity bongs, knife-hits lit by flame torches, and our favorite: the five-foot red, plastic bong named Clifford, the Big Red Bong. I loved smoking from Clifford because I could then brag about being able to literally smoke my height in weed.

After smoking several five-footers and eating a piece of dense ginger-pot bread one afternoon, I lost a few hours to the drug. Somehow I woke up back at my own house, in bed, my car awkwardly parked in the driveway. Though I couldn't remember any of it, I'd spent almost two hours driving the two miles to my house. Lying face down with my arms spread out to each side, I was so high I felt like I was dying. I obsessed over the notion of death coming for me in that moment until it became my reality. For the first time since my father's death, I began to consider my own. There would always be an increased likelihood of my brothers and I having cancer, with such a direct line of it coming at us through our father. I'd already imagined and worried about losing my mother or my brothers, but now, thinking it could happen at any moment, I faced my own death. Would history repeat itself, would death come knocking for me in the very same way? I wondered if I'd die young, younger even than my dad. Would I live long enough to have children of my own, and if I did, would I die at the cusp of their formative years and leave them to the same sad fate I'd endured?

Though I was frightened and absolutely convinced that this was my time, I felt strangely relieved: I could go be with Dad again.

* * *

Twice a week, I took a three-hour alternative processes photography class. Many of these methods of print development incorporated long waits of up to two hours while an image was exposed to UV light or developed in water baths. During the wait, I'd drive to a friend's house nearby to smoke our traditional mid-afternoon gravity-bong hit. We used a modified plastic soda bottle, which was cut in half and fitted for a bowl. Next, we'd fill a sink and put the bottle into the water, light the bowl, and then pull up to create a vacuum. The suction drew air into the container along with the smoke and because of the large two-liter chamber, the smoke inside was much denser than possible in a standard bong. This was McGyver-smoking at its finest.

The darkroom at school was old and had several rooms that were poorly ventilated. Whenever I returned to check on my prints, I'd sit in the back room and let the chemicals lull me into an even deeper haze. Sometimes I got so dizzy I'd lie down on the rough carpeting and stare at the UV bulbs burning images into my photo paper. Lying there in the dark, listening to the darkroom cacophony—the hum of the UV lights and gentle trickle of the water filters pumping their steady streams—I'd play out all the different scenarios of my mortality. I'd think about dying without ever finding love or dying the very moment I found it. I imagined dying as a very old woman, alone and childless—perhaps with a moderately successful career behind me, perhaps not. I'd envision getting married, owning a house, having children, and then feeling the need to learn how to write a will. Which brother would I leave my children to? Would I be the first to go, or would I have to suffer the lonely existence of an adult orphan?

* * *

One Friday I left work at my nanny job and headed straight to a friend's house. It was the weekend, and knowing that I had nothing to do until nine o'clock on Monday morning became ready ammunition for my reckless disposition. Though I only stopped by to pick up a few small bags of pot for myself and some friends, I was easily detained there to try whatever it was they had on the table. That day, lines of cocaine had been neatly organized on a cookie sheet and set on the kitchen counter. With bits of dried Play-Doh still stuck to my T-shirt from work, I held my hair to the side with one hand and used the other to hold a rolled-up dollar bill to my nostril. I took the lines like a champ, looked up at the ceiling a moment or two to sniff the chemicals further down into my body before grabbing my car keys and heading out the door. On the way out, I lifted my arms in the air and shouted, "This is the best I've ever felt!"

With every gulp of alcohol, every hit of marijuana, roll of Ecstasy, line of coke, and pop of a pain pill, I felt myself reaching up—my thoughts spreading outward like ferns in the morning sun, uncurling their papery fingers into the air trying to find light. It warmed me just enough to soften the edge of all that hurt.

Chapter 33

THE RELATIVITY OF SORROW

Even though it was still winter, and in Tacoma we'd had fifty-two consecutive days of rain, I found myself thumbing through seed packets at the gourmet grocery store on Proctor Street. Perhaps it was the lack of sunshine that made me think of spring so prematurely, or maybe it was something else. The seeds in the packet of grocery-store herbs shook like a muted maraca, the vibration tickling my fingers through the brightly printed paper. I didn't know the length of the growing season—or much about growing things in any season, for that matter. The quantity of packets overwhelmed me as the wire rack spun several revolutions, cooling my face with a thin breeze.

My dad used to tell me, "Never buy plants at the grocery store."

"Why?" I'd ask. "They look fine. Those ferns look pretty good, actually."

"They might have bugs you can't see and mold in the soil you can't smell. They'll hold up the first day at home, but their diseases will spread. Better to buy your plants at the nursery."

Thinking about his advice, I rested my basket full of microwaveable meals and fancy soda on the floor beside me, the plastic-covered metal handles dangling limply against each other. I remembered watching Dad delicately separate the roots of a jade plant before repotting, spritzing a miniature terrarium filled with ferns. He filled whole rooms with spider plant clippings, all shining inside water-filled glass jars until their roots began to jut out like pale

arms reaching for the sunlight. I thought about how skilled he was
with plants. How skilled with plants I was not. But it seemed good to
try, seemed somehow the *right* way to grieve. The thought of tucking
my legs beneath me in the grass and pushing my fingers down into
the ground did have its appeal. I daydreamed about sewing each row
in the rain to maximize the earth-to-hand experience.

Back home at my shared rental house, I looked around the
yard and found a corner untouched by beer cans and blackberry
bramble. I knelt in the soggy grass and started digging. I didn't have
trowels or other proper gardening tools; instead I used one glove,
a wooden salad fork from the kitchen, and the sharp end of a ski
pole. The paper packets holding the seeds soon became saturated
and torn between my fingers as I picked out each damp clump of
seeds. After my miniature garden was planted, I looked side to side
before quickly leaning down and kissing the patted mud in front of
me. Then I whispered encouragements, over and over, to my seeds.

As I walked back inside, the phone rang. On the other end,
my therapist from the Student Health Center told me that she was
starting a grief support group on campus and wanted to know if I'd
be interesting in joining. I told her it would be fine—I'd try it out. I
hung up and pressed my forehead against the rain-blurred window,
looked out at the three-by-four-foot garden patch, flat and wet under
the gentle rain.

* * *

At the group's first meeting, I looked around the room at the faces
of people I'd never seen before, which seemed remarkable given the
small size of the university. With only about 3,000 undergraduate
students, it was strange that I didn't even vaguely recollect having
walked by the four strangers sitting in plastic chairs arranged in a
circle beside me. Before the meeting began, I assumed everyone was
there because they lost a loved one the way I had. But when we

introduced ourselves, told our stories, and showed our battle wounds, I came to realize that there were varied types of loss and torment. There were four girls including myself, and one skinny boy, Doug. Lisa, a cute blonde girl I'd soon start running into at parties, was there because she'd lost her parents. Lisa's father hadn't been in the picture for a long time, and she had long since considered him gone. But recently her mother had abandoned her, told her that she didn't want to be a parent anymore, and left her to fend for herself—paying for her own college tuition and finding her way through her formative years.

I was nearly always angry with Lisa for being a part of the group, because I thought she still had a chance with her mom. My chances were all gone—I could never write a letter that my dad would read, could never call him on the phone or hug him. Although Lisa's mother was unavailable, I thought that somehow Lisa could still have a relationship with her down the road, and I resented her presence at our meetings, feeling she didn't fit the criteria to be part of our club. Still, Lisa's mom had *chosen* to leave. That was a pain I would never know or understand, something I realized after a few months of knowing her.

The tall brunette who sat to my left was Kim. She came to college and enjoyed her first few months of life there, despite a nagging ache in her hip. She had it checked out but was told she probably had growing pains. But the pain did not abate, and in her gut she knew it wasn't just growing pains. A few months later, she found a bump protruding painfully from her collarbone. Again she went to the doctor. Within two days, her condition evolved from a small bump on her chest to stage three lymphoma. She was nineteen years old, and the cancer had already metastasized to other organs in her body. Kim had multiple surgeries and several rounds of chemo, all with disappointing results; her cancer would prove to be more difficult to beat. She and her family had been on bad terms with her father since her childhood, and even throughout her illness, she did not receive so much as a phone call from him.

When her only remaining treatment option was to undergo a bone marrow transplant, her doctors struggled to find a viable match. Kim's mom managed to get in touch with Kim's paternal grandparents, who relayed the message to their son. It was quite clear that he was informed of the severity and urgency of her need to see him. He might have been the only living match for what could have been a life-changing operation for his child. Even so, he refused to see Kim. He denied her not only the love and parenting every child deserves, but he essentially resigned her to death. Although she had long since considered him absent from her life, she could not help but feel devastated by such an absolute and extreme rejection. In the end, she was lucky enough to find a close match and underwent the bone marrow transplant that sent her cancer retreating.

But before she could write her name in the "remission" category, she would suffer another loss. Through a quirk of medical fate, the surgeon removed her uterus, only to realize afterward that the procedure had been unnecessary. By the age of twenty, she had not only stood on the precipice of death and fought her way back but had also lost the ability to bear children at a tragically young age. Amid the legal implications of medical malpractice, the regrowth of her hair after the last round of chemotherapy, residual bone pain, and a permanent limp, she returned to college.

The youngest in our group, Brooke, was new to the university. Brooke's older sister had already attended the school for two years and as a returning student, she brought her younger sister to follow in her collegiate footsteps. The two girls drove the car they planned to share out to Tacoma, several hundred miles from their hometown.

"When we stopped for gas, we'd take turns driving," Brooke explained while pulling apart a damp tissue. She looked down as she spoke, making it easier for her to get the words out without crying.

"About halfway through the trip, we filled up the gas tank, but we were so tired. We forgot to switch drivers. She kept driving even though it was my turn." As they drove down the long, blank highway, they watched a car coming from the other direction as it swerved in and out of their lane. The driver of that other car, drunk and falling asleep, slammed into Brooke and her sister head-on at highway speeds. When the mangled vehicles finally slowed to a stop on the side of the road, Brooke's car was upside down and scrunched to one side. She and her sister were held in mid-air by taut, bloodied seat belts. While waiting for help to arrive, Brooke watched her sister die, their faces just inches apart the whole time. She was unable to get herself free from the seat belt, unable to move or touch her sister, unable to scream because of a jaw broken in several places. After the funeral, Brooke still came to school. Alone. The university held a memorial service, and with a wired jaw Brooke sat in the chapel pews and listened while people she'd never met eulogized her sister.

"It was my turn to drive," she told us, white crumbs of tissue littering her pants as the tears poured down into her lap. "It was supposed to be me in the driver's seat."

Doug remained quiet for a few sessions, preferring to sit back in his chair and listen to the rest of us tell our stories. One day, surprising us all by finally raising his hand to speak, he told us that he was an orphan. He said this so quietly and so plainly that no one knew how to respond, so no one did. A few weeks later, he told us the rest of his story.

His family lived in Colorado, where both parents worked as pilots for a major airline. Doug's parents often made weekend trips with Doug, his brother, and his best friend in the family's small plane. One Saturday, Doug made plans for his family and best friend to take the airplane for an evening flight over the mountains. In the process of getting his own pilot's license, it had become a family tradition to take one- or two-day trips around the state. At the last minute, Doug was called into work at his high school job to cover a friend's shift. His family went on without him, not wanting to waste a good flight plan.

Not long into the flight, the plane crashed into the mountains, killing everyone on board. Doug was seventeen years old—without a father, without a mother, without a brother, and without a best friend. They had all been killed on a trip he himself had organized.

Doug was left to deal with his family's house and estate. With his German shepherd as the only other surviving family member, he got himself through the last two years of high school, was accepted into the university of his choice, sold the home in which he grew up, and moved to Washington. Then, several weeks before our first support group meeting, Doug's beloved dog passed away from cancer.

* * *

None of these people in my group were prepared for the tragedies they endured the way I had been; I was the only one who'd had time to let my impending loss sink in before it even happened. When they cried in front of the group, I could tell how difficult their emotional vulnerability felt. But for me, I'd already been crying in public for months. Now it just felt good to finally have the appropriate audience.

After a few meetings, I expected myself to start feeling guilty for all the self-pity I'd been indulging in all that time. It occurred to me that I hadn't really been dealt such a tough hand by comparison; my childhood was privileged and carefree. I grew up with two parents, loving siblings, and an extended family to care for me. I had the benefit of a good education, the benefit of a relatively good life. Still, thinking of those who may have had it worse than I didn't do anything to diminish my pain; it just made me feel sad about the pain we were all enduring. As if loss had irreparably weakened my heart, each story of loss I heard struck me harder than the last.

My fellow grief group members had almost nothing in common with each other beyond our collective sense of loss. We came together for only one purpose: to think about and reflect on death. The glue that held us together was a morbid one, but it was effective.

For an hour each week, we didn't feel like lonely little fish flopping awkwardly out of water anymore; we felt like a homogenous school of fish, who, left to swim alone for most of our lives, could at least recognize each other in passing, recognize each other as being one of our own kind.

For so long, my brothers had been the only ones who truly understood me, but now they, too, seemed far away and out of reach. The grief group was all I had to help me feel like an equal part of something.

After the five of us told our stories and took our turns at collapsing into quivering puddles of tears, we started talking about more current frustrations. What was done was done, that which had been lost would not be returned. We began to understand this and accept it. Once I let it sink in that I would never get my dad back, I stopped yearning for it. Instead, I began to focus on how to make my life better—my grief manageable. Doug, Lisa, Kim, and Brooke wanted to do the same. But before we could truly move on, there were things we wanted to know—problems we wanted to dissect, existential questions we needed to ask. More and more, our conversations turned away from our sorrows and instead toward our inability to fall in line with the rest of our peers. I wanted so badly to fit in again, to be normal and likeable. To be happy. But none of that was a reality any more. Even if I could have managed it, it would've been a lie.

Chapter 34

INTO THIS FITFUL HEAP OF DAYS AND DEEDS

By the beginning of May, my busy schedule started catching up with me. I'd been taking extra classes each of my last three semesters in order to graduate on time, and as my last round of exams grew closer, I felt that I had less and less of myself to give with each passing day; grief, and the pressures of trying to finish this last rite of passage, had depleted me of any remaining energy.

I was spent—utterly spent. Tired of the desk in my room one sunny, mild afternoon, I ventured into the main library to finish the final essay of my undergraduate career. Though I almost never studied in the library, I felt it appropriate to spend some time there before leaving the university forever. It was usually too crowded at the library for me to get anything done; I'd always squander my time there with books splayed open on the table, untouched, while I watched people coming in and out of the tall wooden doors, the grand arches of the building's façade leading them in like unexpected guests in a one-room house. But for nostalgia's sake, I decided to try one last time and planted myself down at one of the dense oak tables lined up in rows of two, with studious-looking gold lamps neatly lined up on either side of the desks.

With a twenty-page essay on Aristotelian rhetoric, a comprehensive photography portfolio, a collection of poems, and a manuscript-length independent study to turn in, my mind, for the first time in months, was too busy for grief. It was refreshing—living those few days like a normal college student. I studied, I wrote, I researched, and I camped out in a secluded section of the library.

Exhausted and overwhelmed during one study session, I rested my head on the back of my hand and wasted a few minutes watching other students shuffle in and out of the early American literature section. A friend from the English department saw me and came over to my table. "Fancy meeting you here in this dark corner, T-bone," he said, prompting me to lift my head up from the table.

"Hey, Ryan, what's up?"

"Not much, really. I'm gonna take off in a minute. You?"

"Ugh, I wish. Professor Maley has us all doing these mock websites with lit-crit profiles," I answered through a yawn. "They're not hard—just kind of tedious. I'm going to do a sweep of the *Nick Adams Stories* and discuss issues of 'White Masculinity.'"

Ryan, laughing and leaning against the wall, said, "Should be easy, then. There's so damn much of it in there."

"Yeah," I said, looking away. "Exactly."

Thinking about Hemingway, I stopped listening to what my friend was saying. I felt myself pulled up from the chair, out of the library, away from campus, until my mind was back at camp, sitting across the kitchen table from my dad. The *Nick Adams Stories* were his favorites, and we'd often sit at the table and read bits and pieces from the collection together, then talk about the literary methods Hemingway was so well-known for.

In that instant, I became strangely aware of how much time had passed since I'd thought about my father, and I couldn't figure out why. It felt good remembering the bond Dad and I shared through our love of reading, and I was mad at myself for having gone so many days without thinking of him, for not having caught myself in the neglect of remembering. And though it did feel good to act as if I were a regular college kid, if even just for a little while, I also felt

I had somehow betrayed my grief, had let the world get the best of me by hushing the loss, dulling the sharp edges of this pain, and quieting all the anxieties that had held my reins for so long. And then it all clicked: The more stimulated I was by the outside world, the less attention I paid to my sadness and anger. I found that I didn't like this—didn't like seeing my determined, stubborn depression threatened by life carrying on the way it usually does.

Walking home from the library, I started observing the other kids walking around campus with my new, judgmental eyes. I wasn't the only one caught up in the nonsense of life; I noticed every earbud, every cell phone, every fast-paced gait. I followed a frat guy fiddling with his car keys and rearranging their order on a keychain, a flautist holding her instrument case in one hand while text-messaging with the other. No one was just simply walking. As if the lack of stimulating activity during those three minutes outside between classes were dangerous, everyone kept themselves busy in a way that I now detested. No wonder people never stopped to ask me how I was—no one seemed to stop long enough to notice anything, or anyone.

I panicked, thinking no one would ever show patience for my ongoing struggles with grief and depression, and if that were the case, who could I count on to help me find a way to keep going? I attributed this impatience, this indifference, to the fact that most of my peers hadn't yet suffered a trauma the way I had; they simply didn't know how to be compassionate toward me because they didn't know what losing a loved one felt like. I couldn't hate them for it or even blame them if they just didn't know any better.

But I started to suspect that kids my age weren't just ignoring me and my problems—they were ignoring their own issues as well. The constant binge-drinking, video-game playing, frat-house hazing, studying, texting, calling, drugging—it left no room in our minds for anything real, anything solid, anything serious. Like so many in these harried, chaotic times, we were so constantly overstimulated that when something truly extraordinary, traumatic, or life-changing happened to us, we didn't know how to slow down long enough to process and deal with it.

Though it had not been long since I was a card-carrying member of this hyper-frenetic, over-reaching generation, I was clearly becoming someone else now. I imagined myself standing on a moving walkway at an airport—listening to an iPod, writing a text message with my thumb, drinking a coffee. On all sides, people would be doing the same—not one person would just walk, just stand, or just look out the window. The walkway picks up speed and our bodies jerk with the change of pace, but no one looks up to see why. The scenery blurs past and out of nowhere, with my gaze still aimed down at my phone, Death swoops down from the ceiling and puts its thick hands on my shoulders, pushing my heels down into the rubber walkway beneath. I wiggle under the weight of it, but I am stopped literally in my tracks while the other people just keep on going.

The epiphany I felt gave me great and sudden clarity, but it did nothing to ease my mind. There was no peace in this realization, only more loneliness and disappointment. Instead of discovering this truth and feeling better for knowing it, I held my book bag in front of me and watched everyone race by. Very few people paused to say hello or even make eye contact. They all just changed their trajectory to accommodate my spot in their paths and kept on going.

* * *

What felt so disappointing and so frustrating for me, though, was that it seemed like for those of us in mourning, the rest of the world moved so quickly that everyone around us would forget what still felt so raw and sharp to us. When I showed sadness over my dad's absence, even in the smallest ways—even in the most celebratory ways—people tended to look at me, perplexed, as if to ask, *What? You're still upset about that?*

Of course I felt left behind by my peers. The world was moving too fast for me, and numbing myself with constant stresses and stimulating activities no longer worked in my favor. I felt so badly damaged by this loss that I could no longer keep pace with my peers, and they, in turn, had no clue how to slow down enough to lend me a hand. In my mind, I felt that no one asked how I was doing or actually wanted to know, and no one was able to truly reach out and make a connection with me as long as I held that belief to my heart like armor against my chest.

The only way to move forward and keep my sanity was to somehow navigate such roadblocks. My emotional baggage and I were not welcome in the college environment, but what I feared, and would soon learn, was that in our culture, emotional baggage of any kind threatens to slow us down to the point of being left behind.

Discovering this made me understand why I took such comfort in the grief group—because everyone there was standing still among the chaos, just like me. Soon, I found that I had the ability to see other people who were "stuck," as if the whole world appeared in color but mourners stayed in black and white. Knowing where to look for support, and where not to, wasn't much, but it was at least something.

* * *

I didn't want to stay at school where no one had patience, time, or compassion for my grief, but I wasn't exactly eager to jump in and join the workforce either. Other cultures seemed to pay more attention to the death of a family member—even Judaism offered me more than I was finding elsewhere, whether or not I still believed in its dogma. I needed to get out of my environment and into someplace new where I could fashion a new identity and new way of living for myself. I fantasized about my upcoming trip to Europe, imagining that I would find myself in some quaint Greek village, writing the

Great American Novel on the beach. Surely the locals would adore me and beg me to stay with them rather than traveling on to the next place, like some kind of Hemingway-esque expatriate. Never again would I have to feel so out of place. I was sure of it.

Chapter 35

WHAT IT WAS SUPPOSED TO BE

After the last meeting of our grief group, the members and I felt like we needed to celebrate in some way. Each person had reached new milestones in his or her grief, and since several of us would be graduating soon we knew we'd most likely never see each other again. The five of us ordered a pizza and sat in a booth at the on-campus pizza and ice cream spot. Doug told us that he was finally able to spread his family's ashes after putting it off for almost two years. Kim was still cancer-free and her hair was starting to grow back again. Brooke seemed to have found a good group of friends and was fitting in well at school, though I got the feeling her family life was a different story. Lisa reconciled with her mom and was working on rebuilding their relationship. Though I never understood why she kept coming to the group sessions after her reason for being there was resolved, I stopped resenting her and began to enjoy her friendship. She needed us, we'd grown to need her, and that was enough for me.

My college years were almost behind me and I couldn't wait to leave Tacoma. My tenuous grasp on relationships, my academic integrity, and my self-preservation were barely holding steady as graduation approached. I had already saved enough money to buy a computer and then do some traveling after graduation, so I let loose the last few months of the semester. I had drastically cut back on my hours working as a nanny, anticipating my permanent departure. Knowing that I would soon be gone made it difficult for me to watch the children becoming more attached. They, too, would most likely never see me again.

I gave in to the grief one last time with full force, thinking that since I'd be leaving everything behind, why the hell should I work hard or try to behave like a good girl? Though for a long time I had looked forward to getting away from school, I also knew that leaving would mean taking away a safety net. I probably wouldn't be able to sleep so many hours each day anymore, wouldn't be able to hide in my room for days at a time if the mood struck. Lying in bed the last few nights in Tacoma, I fantasized about soon having new friends, a new apartment, a new job. I could make a fresh start. I could find a place to stand where my Dad would be proud of me.

* * *

My graduation from college was one of the first big events our family had to face without my father. It was the first celebration, the first family get-together that was meant to be a happy occasion. We were all afraid of it. I didn't care very much about the actual ceremony and considered skipping it altogether; I was so eager to close the college chapter of my life and move on. I didn't need the pomp and circumstance to commemorate the moment. In fact, there was nothing that made me feel like I'd accomplished much at all. My mom kept telling me how proud she was that I'd returned to school so quickly and managed to graduate on time. But what had been the alternative—taking a year off to mope around, or skipping my final credits altogether and going straight into the workforce? None of those seemed like viable options, so in my mind I'd had no choice but to return. Still, I felt as if I'd accomplished nothing.

Of course my family simply would not allow me to let my gradu- ation pass uncelebrated, even if all I wanted was to pack my things and drive home the minute my final exams were finished. Dad's good friend Barney, Uncle Wooby, and my cousin Jeff, flew out with my family to support me, and graduation weekend ended up being much more tolerable than I'd anticipated. We ate too much, drank too much, and took far too many pictures. My father's absence was notable, was excruciating at times, but despite our grief, the event was—for the most part—what it was supposed to be.

Back at camp a few weeks later, it was time to get ready for the season to begin. Sections of the new waterfront docks were hooked up to the backs of trucks and slowly rolled into the water. The tetherballs were tied back on top of their poles, and tire swings were hung. Tennis nets, life jackets, swinging benches, painted wooden animal characters, picnic benches, trampolines, archery targets—all were brought out from their winter storage and placed in their rightful spots in preparation for the campers' arrival. All these tasks were familiar to me; the routine consisted of nothing unknown. But I had changed over the winter, had grown tired and angry, and participating in these routine procedures only made me feel worse.

There were still some things about coming home that did comfort me and, if nothing else, I was relieved to put a lid on my college self and settle in to camp life. Much as I tried to ignore it, the never- ending reel of constant reminders of my father's presence continued to play in front of me. Everywhere were flagrant reminders of his absence. Only a few days after I arrived in Minong, camp began to noticeably wear on me.

* * *

It was difficult for me to remember my dad healthy and happy—my pre-cancer Dad; instead, when I thought of him, I could usually only imagine him ill, weak, dying. Being back in my parents' house felt different than it had our first summer without him. Just when I was starting to feel like things might get better, or at least change, I was back—stuck—at the ground zero of all my most painful memories. When, just a few days before, I'd wanted to be any place other than Tacoma, now I wanted to be anywhere but camp.

I should have known right then to do something else with my summer months, cut my losses, but I felt that no matter what I might have wanted for myself, I had an obligation to show up with the rest of my family and try to keep things going as if everything were fine. No one else seemed to have the problems I was having—my mom and brothers carried on with their duties as they always had, somehow filtering through their grief and discomfort enough to function. But I didn't have the same ability to hold it in.

Every time I walked in the front door of our house, I could see into my parents' bedroom and along one wall, my father's clothes still hung in his closet. My brothers and I had each taken a few of Dad's favorite shirts, but everything he owned at camp remained, untouched, in its place. But now, a year and a half later, his smell had long since faded and disappeared. Seeing his shoes lined up with ours in the mudroom, his rain jacket still hanging by its hood on the coat rack no longer made him feel closer to me. Now it was the opposite: Every commonplace reminder that he had ever been alive was an offense—a screaming reminder of the love and security I would never feel again.

What made things worse than seeing his physical possessions, though, was sensing his influence on camp life at every turn. As Gabe took his place at the center of camp life, with Mom's guidance and support a constant anchor, I started to see just how much like our father he'd become, or perhaps always been. Gabe's voice, repeating Dad's trademark accents and intonations during announcements at daily meals, was almost identical to our father's. If I wasn't careful, I'd hear Gabe over the PA system and mistake him for my dad, letting myself get caught up in the memories of his voice, the songs he'd sung in the soundtrack of my life. I wanted to show Gabe how proud I was of him for so gracefully facilitating the transition with my mom, for giving our family and camp some of the security of knowing that Dad's legacy would hold intact, grow, and continue well into the future. But I couldn't tell him this, or even show it by fulfilling my own end of the deal. I'd come looking for an escape after leaving college and ended up at the one place in the world that could offer me no relief.

My malcontent showed clearly enough for all to see, and I did nothing to hide it. I hated working in the office and felt like it was a complete waste of my skills, having worked in that position since I was sixteen. I knew I could do so much for camp, could offer my own brand of Dad's camping philosophy and do some good work with the kids, but couldn't find the courage to try it. Though I'd eventually find my place at camp, leaving my last summer there having bettered it in some small ways, in the unceasing rawness of those first years without Dad, I couldn't get it together.

I slept in past the morning meetings and often through breakfast, only walking up to the office at the last possible moment, delaying the start of my day as long as I could. And as soon as projects let out and campers flooded the office to kill time before dinner, I'd march back home and watch TV, knowing that I was working bankers' hours in what was most certainly not a nine-to-five job. I frequently skipped meals at the crowded lodge and ate by myself in my parents' house instead, preferring the company of the television to the all-too-in-my-face happiness of the campers. I almost never participated or even made appearances at evening programs, though such events were mandatory for staff members. I had played the games and sung the songs for fifteen years; the joy amid the repetition was completely gone. I just . . . stopped caring.

Though I did continue to find solace by orchestrating the Sunday-morning services and making connections with individual campers the way Dad always had, I could see how disappointed my family members were in my behavior. My mom was too consumed by her grief and responsibilities as a newly widowed camp director to sit me down and talk about my bad attitude. My brothers, however, took advantage of every available opportunity to let me know what I was doing wrong. In turn, I gave them plenty to complain about.

With Dad gone, my brothers felt newly protective of me, as if I were their personal responsibility; in response, I bucked at the thought of being anyone's charge. They acted as though because we had lost Dad when I was still young, it was now their duty to fill in the gaps of life's lessons for me. They each began displaying behavior that felt an awful lot like parenting, and though I knew they were just trying to help steer me down a better path, as far as I was concerned they had absolutely no right telling me what to do. Now that Dad was gone, I only had one parent left, and I only wanted to be parented by that one parent.

I simply wouldn't tolerate the men in my life assuming a fatherly role over me. In fact, I felt this way about many things that my father and I used to do together. If I couldn't watch *Star Trek* with Dad, then I didn't want to watch it with anyone. If I couldn't talk about books with Dad, then I didn't want to talk about books at all. With my father dead, no one would tell me what to do. Even if I needed to hear it.

I kept thinking I'd be free and happy once I moved on to my big European adventure, unattached and beholden to nothing, no matter how realistic those expectations were. Or, in my case, weren't.

Chapter 36

DRYING UP

I did almost nothing to make the summer a successful or pleasurable one—for either my family or for myself. The less effort I put in, the longer time seemed to drag on. Every day was just another day closer to being left alone, and I did nothing to hide my feelings on the matter. What I resented most about camp was the need for my family to always keep anything stressful, problematic, or upsetting private and secret, bottled up to be dealt with away from the prying eyes of the camp community. Even while I knew we did it to protect the campers' well-being and happiness, I couldn't stop myself from resenting it. I felt I simply couldn't do it anymore and, more importantly, I didn't want to. I let all my unhappiness show without caring who saw. My family did what they could to put me back on track but eventually they, too, gave up trying and just hoped I'd get through the summer without any major incident.

I was happier than usual when August came and it was time for everyone to leave. For the campers and for many of the staff, the last few days of camp are a painfully sad, traumatic experience. Even though most campers will visit each other throughout the year and many even live in the same city, they react to being sent home as if their souls are being torn apart. They prepared for the moment of departure as all adolescent girls must: with the singing of pop songs, melodramatic cry fests, and the trading of clothes. There were special programs, special songs, and even special foods reserved for the final days of summer. When the last morning of camp finally rolled in, somehow unseasonably cold every time, the grass at the bottom of camp's long driveway morphed into a sea of mega-emotional teenagers. Most of the tears were legitimate, age-appropriate displays of emotion, but there was always at least one camper who fake-cried in order to fit in. Recognizing these glimpses of insincerity, even in such young and innocent campers, no longer amused me the way it had in the past; I only felt more jaded and bitter.

As a camper, I was always sad to see my friends and cabin-mates go home just like everyone else, but I was also ready for the place to empty out. It's an eerie kind of emptiness when all but a few old-timers have gone home. There's a silent and flat drape of calm that I'm sure most camp alumni cannot imagine. But for me, this was the best part of summer, because it meant that camp could stop being a business for a moment, could once again become my home, and nothing more. As a child, these were important times for me; sharing my family's love with the crowd—much like camp food and sleeping with sand in my bed—got pretty old by the end of summer.

Growing up, some of my favorite times with Dad were after the kids left in August. My birthday always fell two or three days after the second session ended, so when the weather was good, Dad would walk with me to the clearing where our high ropes course stood. We'd had professionals install the various sections of the course but were often equipped to handle a majority of the regular maintenance ourselves. Anytime the ropes course needed repairs, Dad and the boys would get suited up in their harnesses and climb rope ladders to the small wooden platforms encircling each of the strong red pine trees that served as sturdy pylons for the course. I'd follow Dad down there and walk around while he worked, kicking leaf piles together or looking for trash to throw away. We'd shout at each other from across the clearing, being silly and enjoying the time together. And the harder the wind blew, the more mesmerized I was by the sway of the red pines above me.

On my birthdays, Dad used to let me ride the zip line over and over until I'd had enough or until we ran out of daylight, whichever came first. He didn't have to instruct me on where to stand when I came up the ladder or how to hook on my harness, and he didn't need to encourage me or quell my fears. He just sat up in the tree, his legs kicking back and forth, looking all around at his halcyon kingdom with infectious delight.

There would be no zip-lining now that Dad was gone. I was much too old for that sort of thing anyway, and we'd taken the ropes course down the summer after Dad died. Though the trees that held it up were strong and safe, we always planned on using the course only for a decade before bringing it down. The wilderness adventure industry had grown and changed since we built this high ropes course, and a new design was long overdue. With all the ropes, cables, and logs pulled back to the earth, the clearing around the giant, slender trees began to fill with leaves. Whenever I walked by to help in the post-summer clean-up, I noticed that the lonesome trees still swayed as they had always done, naked but for the tiny wooden platforms still hugging their trunks.

* * *

I'd soon be leaving for my travels abroad, and I was completely ready to go. I used up a small chunk of my nanny-money to buy a new laptop, which would be my only companion on the trip. I had a shiny new iPod loaded with audio books and music, and a fancy new backpack to hold everything I'd need for the two-month trip.

Because my flight was booked out of Chicago, my family and I planned to leave camp a little earlier than usual. The day before we closed up the house, I decided to paddle out to Dad's ashes early in the morning. Though it wasn't yet September, the days were beginning and ending with a chill, and I woke cold beneath my summer-weight sheets. Since the window behind me was left open,

I could hear the haunting sounds of the loons already calling to each other across the water.

I stood and saw the lake behind me iced with clouded cellophane, shining and even; it called to my body in the overcast morning. It was long after dawn, but the sky was still partly dark. While the early fog softened and then gradually disappeared, I cooked oats for myself in my mom's green camp kitchen. Measuring my single serving, I squared off the top of the cup with my finger. The velvety fur on the uncooked flakes pushed gently back and forth under the heaviness of my fingertips.

My mom was still exhausted, though the kids had been gone more than a week. She and Gabe slept late into the day that time of year, hard enough that morning that I didn't bother being quiet as I closed the front door. Dad's caramel-colored solo canoe hung, and still hangs, on custom-made hooks by the side of the house. I brushed away the cobwebs and leaves before scooting off the lightweight boat and resting it on my hip and thigh to position my portage. When I lifted it up on top of my shoulders, it wobbled back and forth a few times before balancing out in the center, my arms outstretched up and in front of me, palms turned outward to grip the upside-down gunwales. I shuffled under the added weight leveraged on my shoulders, and clumps of pine needles gathered in patchwork shapes around my feet.

When I reached the water's edge, I set the boat down without minding the designated canoe landing spots only a few feet away. The docks had all been pulled out and sent away so that the only disturbance on the lake's natural shoreline was the diving-board barge, which was now pulled out of the water and onto the sand where it would tough out the winter. The diving board itself was moved to the boathouse, making the metal barge and unnaturally green Astroturf platform look incomplete and sad.

Being on the lake is a different thing in the mornings when the rest of the property is still asleep. My dad loved to paddle out at dawn or dusk, to steal away for twenty minutes of quiet amid the chaos and noise of the full-swing camp. Carrying on his time-worn tradition, I felt like a good girl. A good daughter.

My sandals squeaked against the canoe's fiberglass bottom as I pushed off the sand and deeper into the shallows. When I got past the tall grasses that stick up from the water, I turned sharply to paddle up the narrow passage, which led to a similarly narrow slit of land, and on the other side of that land, Dad's place. The gnats swarmed frenetically around my head and beneath my feet as I used my paddle to rudder the boat parallel against the makeshift shoreline, and I could feel the boat unexpectedly scraping along the murky bottom. Along the edges of the water, my paddle blade sliced foamy patches of algae, which then stuck to the smooth wood like pudding skin on a spoon. When my bow hit the slimy sticks underwater, I was able to crawl over the thwarts of the canoe and hop onto the muddy land. Once I pulled the canoe onto the thin strip of land and stood upright, I saw that the pond where my father's ashes fed the muck was drying up. The small plaque with Dad's name that we kept in place with a sunken wedge of sidewalk cement, was tilted now on its side without enough water to keep it buoyed.

The water stunk. The silt layers along the bottom were becoming exposed to the wind in several places and the smell of it reached my nose and mouth with astounding force. Under my feet, patches of mud were dry between the threads of woven twigs blanketing the dam and holding it together.

It will be swamp there before I have children. The lake has stopped feeding the pond.

I couldn't do it. The water level dropped enough that the long canoe wouldn't fit over the tiny portage without damaging the fiberglass or without me falling in. The stagnant water reeked enough from where I stood, and I had no intention of taking a closer analysis. I looked behind me at the lake and forward again to the pond, still holding the tip of the bow deck in my wet hands. Finally there was nothing else to do but turn around and paddle home, so I dropped the canoe and let it splash my knees when it hit the water. I tossed the paddle recklessly into the boat and climbed in straight-legged. If Dad were there, he'd have scolded me for abusing the expensive paddle. I settled into the cushy seat and dug the tip of the paddle into the murky solidness behind me to push off. I didn't do much but let the wind push me out to the open water after that. When the grasses thinned and the Lilliputian reach of the lake stretched out before me, I turned to face the shriveled stream one more time.

The shrunken pond's water seemed thick, viscous from this distance. I thought back to the day we took the ashes there; now the water was much lower, the gunwale of my fiberglass canoe was just as warm as my cheek when they touched. I wondered if the salt from our eyes would have fallen heavy in the fresh water. Could I have guessed all my crying would turn this place into a salt flat?

Chapter 37

THE QUIET STREET

We locked up the house at camp, packed up the dogs, and drove from Minong to Milwaukee, stopping there for a few days with the Silbermans before driving the last hour and a half to Chicago. When we first pulled into Milwaukee to make the last of my pre-trip preparations, I went out for a drive and took a long detour to our old neighborhood on Woodburn Street. I parked across from our former house and stayed in the car with my arm hanging out of the window, remembering my life there like anyone remembers the blurry image of an old babysitter. Of course the yard and garden seemed much smaller but everything was where it was supposed to be, and even though I'd probably never go inside it again I felt better knowing it was all still there. I liked the idea of keeping those halcyon memories sealed up and shut tightly, archived and preserved.

The house was originally built at the turn of the century as the tollbooth for a train depot and was later converted into a home by a local artist. He built the living quarters as if stacking the rooms, so that the house consisted of seven small levels positioned quirkily off to the sides, while a wrought-iron spiral staircase ran the center, leading off in small sections to each floor. From most any room, one could look over the railing down to the tile floors of the main level and see the open-layout library, dining room, kitchen, and foyer. The entryway came through the train depot's turret, so that from the inside, the front door was merely a sectioned rectangle amid the curve. To funk things up further, my mom had the wall surrounding the door, as well as the door itself, painted a complex, kaleidoscopic pattern. In a Willy Wonka manner, the doorknob was the only discernible evidence of how to get in, or out.

My parents loved entertaining friends and family at our cozy, unusual home throughout my childhood, and often the musicians we hosted at camp became good friends and would also come to perform private concerts for us—some impromptu, others planned engagements. I loved the way our house looked when it was filled with people; the twelve-foot-wide brick wall that stood opposite the spiral stairs seemed somehow softer, its jutting edges less jagged, when there were bodies leaning up against it with beer bottles in hand. Laughter and loud voices seemed to expand the building as if it were taking a breath, lifting up through the hollow center of the house. Because of the house's spacious core, the music would float up and over our heads, as if we were hearing it sweep through the ceilings and walls far beyond the rectangular space of the middle mezzanine's crowded living room. Before falling asleep sugar-drunk and overtired, I'd let my eyes sweep around the room one more time, catch my father bobbing his head to the music, clearly not caring how he looked while doing it.

* * *

Thinking about my upcoming travels while sitting in my car on the quiet street, I wondered what had changed inside the house. Did the new owners install their own climbing wall on the brick interior? Had they kept the red Spanish tiles on the kitchen floors? I thought for a moment about knocking on the door, but turned the keys in the ignition instead and drove off without looking in the rearview mirror.

Chapter 38

AWAY

Gabe and Dylan packed and repacked my bags several times prior to my trip, removing more items on each round. They had each traveled abroad, often together, and were gratuitously, repetitively issuing advice and travel wisdom like a pair of pull-string dolls. Sitting on the Silbermans' living room floor, I watched in annoyance as my brothers argued over the usefulness of my belongings.

The boys simply would not let me bring anything unnecessary, anything expensive, or anything overtly feminine. The two of them had traveled through Vietnam, South America, Cambodia, Africa, Mongolia, and Europe, and had witnessed some pretty seedy things. They warned me with stories of friends who got mugged in Thailand or friends of friends who were raped in Greece—my first destination. Though I would indeed be traveling by myself and had only been abroad a few times before, I knew that they were being overzealous in their warnings and travel tips. They ordered me to wear a simple, silver wedding band on my left finger, even though both agreed this was a common trick and most likely would fail to deflect any persistent men. "Couldn't hurt," they both said while shrugging their shoulders.

I let the two of them go on arguing over whether or not I should bring my own toiletries or buy them once I arrive, wear a money belt or not, and how many traveler's checks to bring. I demanded to be left alone so that I could pack what *I* felt I would need, but they ignored me and kept rearranging my luggage.

Still, I was starting to get pretty nervous about the trip, and for the first time in a while, I felt warmed by my big brothers' joint efforts to keep me safe. Again I felt pulled by some unspoken obligation to follow in my brothers' footsteps just as I had before my NOLS course in Alaska, though no one ever told me to do so in either situation. It wasn't enough to see Europe; most college kids will make their way abroad as part of some requisite American rite of passage. For me, the only way to achieve that much-glorified "Chernov status" was to take this trip all by myself. I don't remember if people questioned my reasons for this, or if I minded being asked.

At the airport in Chicago, I had everything I needed and was feeling pretty excited. I could do this. All I had to do was get on that plane and the rest would fall into place. When I went to buy a few magazines for the flight, Gabe and Dylan followed me into the door-less airport newsstand and bought a handful of Snickers bars. They then tucked them into my backpack and Gabe said in his father-voice with one hand on his hip, "Now, Snickers are always good to have on hand if you're in some strange place. You can almost always find them, they store easily, and you know what's in 'em." I was less than amused.

"Um, okay," I said with a sharp edge of attitude.

"Seriously, Tan—he's right," Dylan interjected. "Sometimes you can't find anything safe to eat so you should always keep them around. They're pre-packaged."

At the gate, as my mom squeezed me and rocked her feet side to side so that our torsos swayed with the movement, I didn't feel so brave and excited. Before I could do anything to stop it, tears started rolling down my face. I tried to wipe them away quickly and hold the jerky urges to sob inside me, but my emotions betrayed me. I didn't want anyone to see, but it was no use. As soon as they noticed my crying, Mom hugged me again and squashed me against her chest even harder this time. Dylan put his hand on my back and rubbed it roughly a few times.

"Oh-o," he said, his voice dropping down half an octave over the two syllables. "You're gonna be fine," he said, removing his hand and putting it back on his hip. "You'll feel better once you get to London and then you breathe a big sigh of relief when you get to the hotel in Athens, okay? Just don't forget to keep your bags with you in the cabs. Don't let the driver put them in the trunk—he could easily just drive off with it that way." I nodded a few times and wiped my nose on a crumpled tissue from my mom's purse.

All year—all my life—I had wanted my family to see me as an adult and trust that I could take care of myself no matter what, and here I was crying like a little girl. I'd been itching to get away from the three of them all summer and was now suddenly terrified to leave them. What if something happened while I was away? What if I couldn't get to a phone card or Internet access? What if something bad happened to me—how would they ever know?

Gabe glanced over at Dylan before taking a small, faded-green book out of his pocket. He handed it to me, and I rubbed my fingers over the gold lettering that read, *Travels Abroad,* and below it, a swirling plane cutting through squiggly clouds. The leather binding was split all the way up its side, revealing jagged nubs of paper so worn and soft they felt like cloth under my fingertips.

"This was Dad's," Gabe said to me, his eyes fixed on the weathered journal. "It's his diary from his Europe trip after college. We thought about giving it to you earlier, but decided it would be a nice surprise and might help calm your nerves." I didn't even know the book existed; I was simultaneously pissed at the two of them for keeping this precious piece of Dad a secret all this time and elated to now be in on that secret. I held the book in my hands as I made one last round of hugs, then walked to the gate. Dylan's last words of advice as I waved goodbye and walked away rang through the air: "And remember! No cleavage!"

Waiting for the plane to take off, I began to feel nervous about the flight. I had always been a good flyer and never suffered the fears or anxieties so many people seem to have about air travel. But this flight was different. I was *really* alone. Flipping open the small six-ring journal, I saw on the first page in my father's messy cursive handwriting the following list:

Tina—Black gloves #6 Paris
Mom—Umbrella Eng.
Pop—Pipe

Apparently he hadn't started writing in all capitals—a habit I also adopted—until he became a lawyer. When I traveled to Israel a few years before, I had written out the same format for my souvenir-gift list. Another trait I inherited from Dad: elaborate list-making. I remembered Dad sometimes referencing this woman named Tina; she was Dad's only other serious girlfriend before he met my mother. I continued reading:

Date: 6/12/67
Place: Chicago
Took the Northwestern to Steve's—ride was hot and long, more from anticipation than physical elements. Steve's family is very warm and friendly. Early bedtime—big day tomorrow . . .

1967: Fourteen years before I was even born. That made him twenty-two years old when he traveled—the same age as me. How funny that he'd left from Chicago too. It was strange to read his own account of the life he had before creating our family, and to see how many parallels existed between his adventurous endeavor and my own.

Poring over his entries felt somehow like cheating or stealing; I felt like I was getting something no other fatherless child could possess. I read on, not noticing the flip in my stomach as the plane lifted up off the tarmac and into the bumpy air shafts above the runway.

New York:
Caught a flight on American to Newark—bussed to Kennedy to get our
luggage and meet Steve Lewis. Saw a profusion of nature's beauties—
most of them in mini-skirts.

Gross. I know he was only twenty-two, but . . . gross.

Eyes now bloodshot and tired. Sat next to a pot-smoking Russian on
the plane. A very interesting cynic.

Lux:
Arrived late at 9:30 pm, got through customs in ½ hr. Found hotel
for $3 then went bar-hopping until 1 AM. Double shot of bourbon on
plane cost 25 cents!

I closed the book and put it securely inside the pack at my feet. I
wanted to save it for later, knowing that there would be plenty of time
I'd want to fill, and knowing already that letting my mind wander was
a dangerous business. Besides, there were decent movies to watch on
the plane, and I had an Ambien in my pocket.

* * *

Arriving at the Athens International Airport sixteen hours later, I
found a currency exchange booth and got some cash. I kept checking
and rechecking my traveler's checks and passport as I walked
through the terminal, paranoid about them getting stolen or lost. The
heavy packs, one on my back and the smaller in front, pushed my
feet down into the vinyl floor as I followed the English signs pointing
to the exits. Even after Gabe and Dylan had removed so many items,
the luggage was too heavy for me. I decided that I'd have to leave
behind some books to lighten the load.

I waited in line for a cab and tried to take both of my bags in the car to keep them next to me on the seat, but the cab driver was confused and insisted on putting them in the trunk for me. Throughout the ride into the city, I kept imagining the cab driver kicking me to the curb before speeding off into the distance with all my clothes and new computer, the open passenger door still flapping wildly in the distance. Instead, he very kindly delivered me to the right address and carried my bags to the hotel's lobby. I dropped my bags inside my room and left to begin my first evening alone in Greece.

The next steps of my arrival instructions were to buy a phone card and call home to let everyone know I'd safely made it to my hotel. Downtown Athens was scary in the dark, but shops and grocery stores seemed to remain open no matter how late the hour or how empty the city. The wet streets shifted between patches of asphalt and dull-edged cobblestone beneath my feet, casting dwarfed shadows around the buildings. I walked around trying to decide where I should purchase a phone card, the warm air ruffling my brown linen shirt. I pulled my baseball hat down over my eyes and paid for a phone card and bottle of water, surprised at how easy it was to complete the transaction without exchanging a single word with the shopkeeper. I walked back to the hotel feeling tough and capable. Relieved, even. After calling to tell Mom that I'd made it safely, I turned the TV on, popped the other half of my Ambien, and crawled in bed, the air conditioner vibrating the metal curtain-pulls at each side of the sealed-shut window.

Chapter 39

HOOKERS IN THE WOODS

I spent a few days in Athens sightseeing and preparing for my longer residency in the Greek islands. I planned to stay on Santorini for a whole month at a small hotel in Karterados, near the town of Fira.

Before I left Athens, I saw the historic sights highlighted in all the travel guides and enjoyed walking around the bustling city. When I spoke to waiters or shopkeepers, or anyone else who spoke English, I loved seeing their surprise when I told them I was traveling solo. They all seemed so impressed that I was brave enough to travel alone, and this made me feel like I was doing the right thing, was on the right track.

The night before my ferry to Santorini, I sat down for one more big-city meal at a sidewalk café not far from my hotel. From my single seat at a large round table, I could see the Acropolis, its dusted ivory stone punctuating the dusted ivory air. I watched its sharpness jet from the hills through the rat-maze intersections and through the creamy chalk air. I ate spongy, wet moussaka and greased dolmas so brined that grape-leaf crumbs stuck to my teeth and gums throughout the week. Between the traffic sounds I heard Beyoncé's latest pop anthems pumping out over the ashy sidewalks, past shaded storefronts, crawling along brittle shrubbery before reaching the dried walls of the Acropolis. Nearby, a street girl lay sleeping off a drug, her arms dangled off the low cement wall holding her. She looked about the same age as I, was even dressed similarly. Toward her came a shadowman: a Greek priest who moved swiftly, smoothly as if with wings, though not angelic as he left her right where she was. The priest walked past the café, past my table, and, caught by the breeze, his long robes lifted and curled around him like a floating black bell, split in the center.

That night, I took another sleeping pill thinking I'd be lucky enough to avoid jet lag. But even as drowsy from the narcotic medication as I was, I still could not sleep. I woke early, packed up my things, and caught the eight-hour ferry to Santorini. I arrived around one in the morning and had to wake the pension's owner to get into my room. Though he had promised to pick me up from the ferry port, he failed to show up at the appointed time and then seemed annoyed and confused by my arrival. I dropped to sleep on the low bed without washing my face or even brushing my teeth, and slept solidly despite the previous night's insomnia.

In the harsh light of the following morning, I found that the room had no shower curtain, no toilet seat, and no blankets. It was decidedly less comfortable than I'd expected, but I shrugged it off and set to work making a little home for myself in the sparsely furnished room. Unpacking my things, I realized that I'd already lost the little blue Leatherman my summer boyfriend had given me at the end of the season when we parted ways. Though these were trivial matters and fairly easy to fix, I started feeling anxious and homesick.

I toured the surrounding towns and found that the local folk, much to my surprise and dismay, did not want to be my friends. The tourist season had just ended, and everyone behaved as if they had tired of foreigners for the year. I tried to be as polite as possible, to engage in conversations and speak as much Greek as I could, but it made no difference. I was an outsider, and I would remain that way no matter how charming I tried to be. Anytime I went to the beach or pool, the only other people around were in pairs, mostly honeymooning twenty-somethings and aging Europeans on holiday.

I quickly learned that this island was not meant to be best enjoyed by solo travelers.

As the homesickness continued to incubate, I decided to explore the big town of Fira, about a twenty-five-minute walk from my austere room in Karterados. I easily found the row of museums, the alleys with cheap jewelry, and the boat-tour stands. But where were the friendly villagers to welcome me to the island? Where were the gorgeous, cheap hotels on sun-bleached cliff sides with the quintessential Greek white and blue paint? Where were the other people my age who I was supposed to run into at every turn? Gabe and Dylan kept telling me that I would meet people all over the place, but everyone here was with family or spouses; nobody cared to even look in my direction let alone strike up friendly conversation. I found myself experiencing the same feelings of loneliness I had hoped to escape by leaving college.

In just one day I covered all the attractions of the island I was supposed to spend a month exploring. During my next trip into town a few days later, I bought a few groceries and disappointingly killed much of the day walking around and sending emails. I wrote newsy mass emails just like my brothers had done on all their trips, trying to sound convincingly cheerful. Then I promptly wrote a separate one to my family and told them the truth—that I was damn miserable and already wanted to go home. I was lonely, bored, and scared. No one spoke English or gave any hint that they cared to. With no one to talk to for days on end, I had nothing to do but live inside my head, and being stuck in there was not somewhere I wanted to be.

With nothing much to do with my time, I split my days swimming and reading at the beach or pool, then messing around on my computer or sleeping the rest of the day. I decided to write a post-modern retelling of Kate Chopin's *The Awakening*; it would be my first novel. I'd fallen in love with the book during a women's lit class in college, and this novel-writing idea fit in well with my grandiose, Hemingway-esque expectations. I expected everything to fall into place just as I'd imagined it, feeling that I deserved at least this much after everything I'd been through. And I suppose I thought writing a novel would be easy if I had all the time in the world to devote to the task.

But when I sat with the blank page in front of me, I could only write journal entries. I made several attempts at starting the novel but couldn't stop writing my own problems and personality into the characters over and over again. After a few hours of this futile practice each day, I'd give up and instead watch a DVD on my computer. The people of Karterados continued to not notice what I was or was not doing in my little room.

Because I slept so much during the day, I'd lie awake each night, torturing myself with thoughts of pity and self-loathing. I already regretted my decision to travel, and though I'd felt so displaced back in the States, I felt even more unwelcome and uncomfortable in my foreign surroundings. After a particularly lonely and sleepless night, I dumped out my bottle of sleeping pills onto the bed and counted the little white ovals to figure out how I would need to ration the bottle for the rest of the trip at the rate I was taking them.

All year, I'd anticipated this trip with excitement; what I'd wanted more than anything was to find a place where I could be by myself—without the watchful eyes of those who knew me. And here I was, with all the time and privacy in the world to look inward, and what I saw I didn't like. Though my self-destructive urges had grown and festered since Dad's death, they now expanded with reckless abandon once I removed myself from the distractions that had insulated me from the true darkness of my own thoughts.

Finally, I couldn't stand the overwhelming gloom any longer and called home. From a pay phone in the middle of the busiest part of town, I deciphered the Greek instructions on my phone card and dialed. I broke down crying as soon as Gabe answered. He tried to console me by telling me that the first week was always the worst and that I would snap out of it soon. Mom picked up another phone in the house and told me it would be okay, that I would start to enjoy myself if I just got out and explored more. But when I couldn't stop crying, Dylan got on the phone sounding worried.

"The beauty of traveling alone," he said, "is that you can leave and go somewhere else whenever you want. If you hate it there, leave the island." When I still could not be calmed, he and Gabe agreed to look into flying out and meeting me at some point so we could try traveling together. They each wanted to explore Europe a second time and had nothing on their schedules prohibiting them from making a week-long trip. We hung up and though I kept crying all the way back to my room, I got through the night by reminding myself that I had new plans and only needed to hang on by myself a little longer. I was also grateful to have such caring brothers—brothers who had the time, the means, and the urge to come save me from myself. The next day, I cancelled my reservations and booked a ferry to Mykonos.

I enjoyed being on Mykonos more than I'd expected and started to gain a little confidence after getting myself to and from each destination without speaking or understanding the local language. There were incredible restaurants and shops around my hotel, and walking the narrow alleyways to find new, tucked-away places easily filled my days.

I still spent each night feeling sorry for myself as I lay awake in the dark unable to sleep. Every time I let my mind drift into idle thought, I obsessed over all the things I'd done wrong since Dad died. I remembered all the stupid boys I'd slept with, all the drugs I'd done, all the behavior I suddenly wasn't very proud of. The days would start on a positive note at the beach, where I listened to music and read while tanning. But if my iPod's battery died or I finished my book early, I'd start thinking about why I'd come on this trip, who I thought I was impressing.

I became obsessed with the idea of being alone; every time I closed my eyes I saw visions of my family members being taken away from me by car crashes or illness. I felt sick to my stomach all the time, worry consuming my every thought. My long hair started falling out in tangled clumps after I showered, and my skin broke out all over.

A week later, I flew to Munich to meet Dylan for a few days. On an inclement day, I decided that since Dylan had already visited a concentration camp, I should visit one before he arrived. On my journey to Dachau, the first thing I noticed was how short the bus ride was to the site where so much horrific death occurred; how could the people living only fifteen minutes away not know what was going on? And then, of course, how could they stand by and do nothing to stop it? I'd taken a teen-tour trip to Israel when I was fourteen years old and had experienced Jerusalem's famous Holocaust History Museum, Yad Vashem. Even at that young age, the horror struck me with intensity and permanence. When I visited the Dachau Concentration Camp Memorial Site, I felt the same sense of frustration I'd experienced at Yad Vashem years before, the same embarrassment to be a human being, if this was what human beings were capable of.

But I was older now and had experienced loss for myself. Among all the atrocities, I was haunted by the unshakable notion that all over the world, people have proven themselves capable of ignoring horror even when it stares them in the face. My father's death connected me back to my Jewish heritage not just in the religious sense but also in a secular, humanistic way. I understood what loss meant now and seeing a place where so many lives were taken struck me differently than I'd expected.

I searched through my dad's journal on the bus ride back to the city, hoping to find something about his feelings on being a mostly secular Jew in post–World War II Germany. Like me, Dad never took his Jewish heritage very seriously, and I wondered what he thought about visiting a country where many of our own relatives were killed. What were his thoughts on mortality as a young man, what kind of loss had he experienced by my age?

8/25

The people here still wear World War II uniforms [he wrote of Hamburg]. *I can't help wondering how many of the middle-aged men were soldiers and how many of them killed Jews. It still feels strange to be in this country.*

By the time Dylan arrived at the Munich airport, I considered myself rescued from the torment of solo traveling. The two of us rented a car at the airport and drove east through Germany, Austria, Hungary, the Slovak and Czech Republics, Poland, and then back to Germany. From there we took a few trains to Amsterdam to finish up the last days of Dylan's trip. While we traveled, I saw that Dylan's idea of adventure was a little bolder than my own. He liked ordering from non-English menus and exploring the post-Communist ruins in Bratislava; he even liked searching for hotels in the seedy parts of Wrotslav, Poland.

When we stopped in Vienna, Dylan and I talked about what a cad our father seemed to have been in his youth; many of his journal entries talked about meeting girls and partying the night away. It was nice to talk about Dad the way we imagined him to be as a young man. So removed from his years of illness and dying, I hung on every word of his travel journal and never let myself read more than one entry per night, savoring every page like rationed sustenance.

During our stay in Budapest one night, tucked away up high in the raised loft of an ancient hostel, I fell asleep easily while Dylan was still awake reading a book. After what felt like just a few seconds later, Dylan nudged me awake.

"Hey—roll over or something. You're snoring," he said flatly.

"Really?" I said, resting my face back down on the pillow. "I *never* snore."

"Well, it sure sounded like you know what you're doing."

When I drifted back to sleep, I dreamed about being at the Tucson house with Dad. In the dream, we were trying to plant a garden in the rocks next to the veranda but kept cutting our hands and burning our feet on the hot brick patio. I woke up feeling disoriented, and tried in earnest to fall back to sleep so I could finish the dream.

Throughout my travels, I frequently had dreams about my father, some of which were clearly the wild meanderings of my subconscious. Others, though, were too vivid and too powerful to possibly be anything other than visits from my father. I didn't try to explain it or understand it, but I usually woke from those "visit" dreams knowing that my father had reached out to me and that we'd managed to find each other somewhere in the subconscious ether. But as wonderful as those dreams were, they often left me feeling a bit empty and unsatisfied. What I wanted most was to see him again, to hear his voice—even if only for one brief second, even if he would only leave again afterward.

* * *

Driving through the chaste countryside in the Slovak Republic, Dylan and I were stunned by its beauty, so sharp in contrast to the Communist-style housing projects in Bratislava. Making our way down the rustic expanse of the Carpathian highway, we were surprised to find the golden-tipped wheat fields and sun-baked rock faces suddenly punctuated by ladies in hot pants and mesh tops, dancing roadside to the Neil Diamond music we could hear through our cracked-open windows, pumping from some haphazardly hung speakers dangling from weathered poles behind the prostitutes. The barely clothed women were positioned about twenty feet apart from one another, all standing in a jagged line right in the middle of the highway. Truckers had pulled over on each side of the road, and were talking to the women, touching their arms and lighting their cigarettes.

"So, um, Dyl . . ." I asked quizzically as we drove slowly, giving the women a wide berth.

"Yeah, Tan?" Dylan replied, an amused smile stretching wryly across his face.

"Those are hookers, right?"

"Oh, I'm pretty sure they are. Strange place to be soliciting, huh?"

"Uh, yeah," I said, turning to Dylan and laughing as I rolled up my window. "I mean, they must be cold out there." This got a hearty chuckle out of Dylan, which I was proud of, and I continued, eager to make him think I was funny: "And where in the Carpathian forest do you think the business transaction takes place?"

"Hmmm . . . that's a good question," Dylan replied. We surmised that the constant shaking of fish-netted asses and leather-gloved waving at passersby must have been enough to ward off any cold the winter was offering that day. As we continued a little way down the Tatran highway, we saw simple wooden shacks that offered space for the exchange. There were no shades in the windows of these "efficiencies," only red-laced curtains and strings of hosiery to obstruct the view from the road. Business on the Slovak highway appeared to be thriving, and the forest prostitutes seemed genuinely happy. Though they sang along with Neil Diamond's suddenly ironic lyrics: *Everywhere around the world, they're coming to America . . . today!*, the hookers in the woods seemed damn content with their location.

I leaned my forehead against the rental car's window as we passed the last of the women. Dylan was smiling as he navigated the winding roads, and I was so relieved that the two of us were having fun together; though of course I knew my brother loved me, I wasn't convinced that he liked me enough to enjoy traveling with me, confined to a small car and shared hotel rooms. I wanted to relax and enjoy the time with him, but I felt displaced.

I watched the women's slender figures grow smaller in the side-view mirror, jealous of their good humor, whether genuine or—more likely—feigned for the sake of closing a sale.

It occurred to me that jealousy was a peculiar response to seeing prostitutes selling their bodies in the Carpathian wilderness, but I let the thought pass and instead said to Dylan, "This is one of those things, you know?"

"One of what things?" he asked, keeping his eyes forward as he steered our compact Fiat smoothly around a bend in the road.

"One of those things that I want to call Dad and tell him about. If he were here, I mean."

"Oh." He exhaled and moved his left arm from the steering wheel to the window beside him in an "L," his elbow resting on the door frame and two fingers wedged into the gummy rubber seal where the glass rose to the top of the frame. Finally, he tilted his head back and let out a single puff of a laugh, as if imagining to himself what Dad would have said about what we'd just seen. "Sure is."

Chapter 40

SPIRAL STAIRCASES

On the day before Dylan left, we took a train to Leiden to get a break from the seedy red-light district where we were staying in Amsterdam and after an uneventful attempt at sightseeing, we were back on the train platform, waiting to return to Amsterdam. Dylan noticed my change in attitude and asked what was wrong.

"I don't know. It's just—it's kinda weird reading Dad's journal, like all of us felt like this was something we *had* to do. Like every other American schmo, we plan this post-college, bullshit journey of supposed self-discovery. Like a middle-class societal rite of passage or something. And I just don't think that it's really what it's cracked up to be. I've just been thinking about it a lot. I mean, because even in the sixties, Dad expected the same shit I did before coming here. And we both had kind of horrible experiences while looking for . . . whatever it is we were looking for."

Then, as if he'd been waiting to say it since the moment he arrived in Munich nearly a week earlier, Dylan casually said, "You know, you could easily come back with me tomorrow if you wanted."

My throat clenched up, heart pumping with the thought of being able to quit and go home just like that. "If it's seriously that awful, then there's no need to put yourself through it any longer," he said. I didn't even look at him while I let the idea register in my mind.

"What are you talking about?" I finally asked, drawing the words out slowly so I could process the idea. "Gabe's already paid for his flights—he'll be here in less than two weeks—how would that even work?"

"Don't worry about it," he said with cool indifference in his voice. He shrugged and put his hands in his pockets. "We could figure that all out, but it's silly for you to stay when you could so easily just come home with me tomorrow."

I wanted to slap him or scream at him for even putting the thought of canceling my trip early into my head, but quickly the tears were coming and I knew if I opened my mouth to talk, all that crying would rush out and I'd make a fool of myself. I desperately wanted to put him in his place but couldn't do it while I was crying like a little kid. Of course I'd fantasized about leaving early, but I didn't want to let myself take such an easy way out. Just like I gave myself no choice but to return to school after Dad died, I had given myself only one option in this situation and that was to stick it out. Be a champ. I was damn lucky to have the opportunity to be there in the first place. I couldn't live with myself if everyone knew that I'd failed.

Our train arrived and we took our seats. I wanted to hide my tears and tried to inconspicuously wipe my cheeks with the sleeve of my jacket. Dylan could see how upset I was, but mercifully left me alone until I could compose myself. We rode most of the way without speaking, until finally I was calm again.

"No," I said, breaking the long silence.

"No, what?"

"No, I don't want to go home with you tomorrow. I want to stay and tough it out. Even if I keep hating it, I wanna stay." Even as I spoke the words, I longed to take them back and deal with the consequences of my decision. I was so unsure of myself, so unsteady in my determination to be independent.

"Good, that's what I was hoping you'd say." Dylan leaned forward and rested his elbows on his thighs, looking straight at me. "I knew if I presented you with the option, you'd make the right choice."

"Wait, what?" I asked, stunned. He'd been testing me all along. "You know something? You're being a total prick right now."

"What? Whoa!" He was laughing to dispel the tension, to try to calm me down, but I was fuming, seething-mad—as much at myself as at him. I felt foolish for having gotten so upset over a phony offer. So I lashed back at him. "You are not my psychologist, you are not my father. In fact, right now, you're not even being my friend. You're being a dick—that was a dick move you just did." I was taking it too far, letting my emotions run wild, but I couldn't stop myself.

"I'm not a child, and I don't need your help," I said. I couldn't escape the thought, though, as we sat there in silence, that I'd asked him to come rescue me, and I realized that I could no longer be mad at him for treating me like a kid—I had absolutely been acting like one.

The next morning, Dylan left on a train to the airport, carrying my small backpack with my beloved laptop computer. I knew the novel-writing idea was toast—I'd never be able to write it there, and the computer was weighing me down. Though I was still mad at him for messing with my emotions the day before, I was shaky as I waved goodbye to the only person on the continent who knew me.

* * *

Next I traveled to snowy Lucerne, where I did some exploring before checking into a hostel. There were thick, opaque layers of ice on the stone bridge curving around the town square, and I stepped carefully around the snow banks, trying to keep the bottoms of my jeans dry. I walked down the road, past the overpriced retail shops and empty morning cafés, all looking unfriendly to my eyes in the off-season's cold. I scanned the storefronts and road signs, settling my gaze on a bright blue door at the end of the row. This thin, tall building had one plain, modest sign that had PICASSO chiseled in its stone door frame.

I entered the doorway and was forced up a set of scrubbed-adamantine spiral stairs enclosed in dirty-white brick walls with no railing. Walking up the staircase brought my thoughts back to our old house on Woodburn Street. Its own spiral stairs filled the center of its space, just like this one. Our stairs—made from wrought iron and narrow, wooden steps—carried us each to our rooms like bohemian royalty, peeking at each other through its railing slats. Along the wall we hung photos and art, a perfectly non-linear chronology of our family's history. At the top of those stairs, my father's favorite print hung, filling the space above the landing outside my parents' bedroom in Milwaukee for so many years. The picture, now hanging in the camp house, shows a grand, wood-floored room cast auburn by a lit fireplace. A single chair by the fire is the only furnishing, and a man sits with his back to the camera.

Wishing I'd taken more than one art history class at school, I knew I wouldn't understand Picasso's abstractions and amalgamations in a museum full of his paintings. But there were no paintings in this Musée Picasso, or any of his famous sketches. Instead, photographs of the legendary artist and his family hugged the curve of the staircase a very long way up. Pictures showed the children playing nude through the Italian villa, their father lounging in his studio, dressed in his sailor-stripe shirt and espadrilles. I lingered a while at each picture, until the whites and blacks and grays of the scene softened into a dullness the color of newspaper edges. Climbing the curvature of the building, I found I was the only patron, and lost time in the quiet.

Best were the frames showing Picasso as he sketched his children, naked, playing in the garden behind. His last love, Jacqueline, as she sat at the kitchen table peeling tomatoes.

Nearing the top of the museum, I realized that I was sad to be at the end of the small ascent and considered beginning again from the bottom. The very last picture, reigning at the top of all those stairs was my dad's favorite—the old man sitting fireside, alone in his chair. And the caption below it read: "Picasso, near the end."

At that moment, the young man I'd been reading about in the travel journal merged into the man I'd known as my father. Since his death, I could only remember him as he was when he was sick and dying. Whenever I conjured his face in my mind, it was always the thin, jaundiced face of his cancer. This terrified me, and I wondered if I would ever again be able to remember him as the healthy, vibrant man who'd been the center of my universe for the majority of my life. But now I could picture him at all the stages of his life, could imagine him as a young man just returning from his travels, entering law school, meeting my mother, and getting married.

In a flash-forward rush of images, I called back to my mind the memories of looking at my parents' wedding album—my mom with her high-necked dress and white eye shadow, and my dad sporting a Fu Manchu. In that instant, as if willing it into being had been all that was necessary this whole time, the happy memories of my father came flooding into my mind. I remembered the big, jiggly belly he'd always had when I was a little girl, his strong arms that would lift me up by the back of my overalls and spin me around, flying like Superman. I could see him hanging the Picasso picture in our dining room at the Tucson house—a memory I'd long since cast aside as insignificant. He was there—clapping wildly in the audience at my choir concerts, waking me up with smiley-face pancakes, bouncing in the Jeep with music blaring, feet hanging out the door-less side. It was back—his happy, smiling, healthy face had come back to me, pushing aside those sad memories of his illness to make room for the good stuff.

Chapter 41

Someone Else's Wet Styrofoam

In Lucerne, I shared a large, well-lit room with a few nice girls from my hostel and finally felt like I'd made some friends. It was nice to go for dinner together and share travel stories, since most of the other girls were also traveling alone. Though we promised to keep in touch with each other, I was sad to say goodbye to them when I left the hostel.

Walking everywhere was much easier with just one pack now, and I was happier without my laptop. Without my computer to watch a DVD or play games on, I found it easier to force myself outside to explore. With this newfound zeal for my upcoming destinations, I bought a ticket to Venice and boarded the overcrowded train.

I practiced flirting on the Italian train leaving Switzerland with a European boy camped out across from me. I liked him when he sat down, liked his messy hair and his loose sweater, his weathered pants that hung on him the way pants ought to hang on a boy. I pretended not to notice him, tried to catch his attention and look my prettiest, staring out the window a few seats over. He tried, too, not to give himself away but we each caught the other staring more than once. I made a little smile, wet my lips, and looked away. I watched like a child while he rolled cigarettes, smoked them between sips of coffee, and glanced out the window, then back to me. I wanted him to speak English. I wanted him to ask my name. When he fell asleep against his backpack, I imagined myself moving like a thief across the tops of the seats, to kiss his eyelids without even a word of hello.

But it wasn't for me to wake him up, and the men who did were far less sweet than I fantasized I would be. Nine sweating Italian police hurried toward us, looking more like commandos than civil servants, covered in green from head to toe and carrying weapons too large for such a confining space. Swinging their rifles around to their backs, they flipped through my passport as their eyes examined my body. The dogs watching me at their knees were not like the dogs I knew from home, but thin and poised, dutifully at work. Turning to the boy when they'd finished with me, who was still sleeping in his seat, they slapped his forehead a few times then began unpacking all his things. His embarrassment was wracking for us both. The Polizia Ferroviaria, yelling and laughing and smacking the boy on the head, didn't mind my watching. I could tell, though I spoke no Italian, that they were talking about it. Laughing at me.

When they pulled my would-be love out of his seat and threw his things on the floor, he looked at me again and asked for a *sigaretta*. I knew enough Italian to understand cigarettes, but couldn't lift my arm to give him one. I watched from behind the window as he was taken away. The train jerked forward one, two, three sputtering lurches before picking up speed and continuing down the tracks. When he was out of my sight, I took a sip from his cold cup of coffee and smoked that cigarette myself.

Suffering the loss of my father made me so sensitive to the world that every loss of a relationship, idea, dream, or object became exaggerated. As Italy unfolded itself from the north, through the mountains and toward the great cityscapes, I looked at the empty seats all around me and though I didn't even know the boy I'd been watching, I found myself strangely missing him.

* * *

After the frightening experience in Italy, I thought again about going home. But Gabe would be meeting me soon, and I knew I could hang on until then. I made friends with two sisters from Albany at an all-female hostel that was part of a convent in Venice. The sisters and I snuck out after our 9:00 PM curfew and walked the streets of the waterlogged city, finding late-night cafés and glass-blowing studios. After a few pleasant days in Venice I headed to Florence, where I struck up an immediate friendship with an Australian guy named Reed, whom I'd met on the train. Spending the day with another traveler took the pressure off making all the decisions, discerning confusing directions, and remembering how to get back to my room.

Reed and I found that we had much in common for two people who came from opposite sides of the world. Reed was also Jewish and had worked for many years at a summer camp in Australia much like my own. He'd just lost his grandfather a few months before and understood my grief if not for his own reasons, at least for his mom, who had descended into a depression he'd never seen in her before. He and I cultivated an instant, easy friendship, and we had fun touring Florence together. This was my first platonic male friendship in a while, and it was refreshing.

Over meals and on bus rides, we talked about life at home, the toils of traveling, and grief. I told him about the worries I was starting to have about how my mom was handling my father's death; she still refused to start looking for a house in Milwaukee, saying that she preferred to continue living in isolation at camp. I thought the lack of human contact couldn't be good for her. She talked to the dogs a little too much and left the boundaries of camp very rarely. Sharing a plate of pasta Bolognese, Reed and I confided in each other about watching our mothers fall apart after experiencing loss.

"I keep waiting for her to just wake up one day and be her old self again, you know what I mean?" Reed asked me.

"Yeah, but that's the thing—" I said, gulping the last of my wine. "I don't feel like it's possible for me to return to who I was before my dad died—like that person just doesn't exist anymore. So for sure now, my mom must be someone new too. I think you shouldn't expect that kind of outcome from your mom. That other person is gone."

"That's hard to do, because in a way it's like I've lost her, and no one warns you about that," he said, nearly speaking my exact thoughts. It felt so good being understood, being validated by someone who didn't need me to explain all my feelings from scratch.

"I feel exactly the same," I said quietly, sadness sweeping in, "like in some ways I've lost both of my parents now. She's still my mom, but she's a different kind of mom." After that, we ate in silence until it was time to pay our check and leave.

* * *

For a long time after my father died, I only wanted to talk to other people who knew loss. Being able to freely discuss the ever-changing challenges of grief with someone who understood those challenges was invigorating; I couldn't yet find in myself any compassion or tolerance for people who didn't understand what I was going through. Perhaps because Reed never knew the pre-grief version of me, we had an easy time discussing such weighty matters. When it was time for us to go our separate ways, Reed and I made sure to exchange emails and phone numbers, promising to keep in touch once we each returned home from our travels.

* * *

My first day in Rome was cold and rainy, so I spent most of my time at a cozy, corner Internet café, writing to friends and family, biding my time until Gabe arrived in Rome. There, I had time to think back over the past year and how I'd treated, and often mistreated, many of the people in my life. Awash with the overbearing memories of every painful and embarrassing moment I'd had in the past year, I started to hate myself with renewed fury. I was proud of nothing I'd done, regretted who I was becoming. Loss was supposed to enlighten me, make me more mature and more resilient, or so I'd been told. But instead, it stirred up inside me things that made me turn into a bitter, manipulative, and selfish girl. I so badly wanted to be the kind of girl my dad would have been proud of but couldn't imagine ever pulling myself out of the mess I'd created. I sat with my head in my hands, elbows resting on either side of the keyboard, determined to finally *do* something to fix myself.

I eventually dried my face and looked up at the screen's "Message Sent" box. After a few more minutes of staring at the keyboard and contemplating how to begin, I started writing another email, then another. From there I just kept going, sending messages to all the men I'd wronged, friends I'd neglected, and people I'd hurt in the recklessness of my grief.

I'd come on this trip to face my demons and evolve into someone better, but I'd gone and spent the entire time feeling sorry for myself, obsessing over every bad thing I'd ever done but not letting go of any of it. I wrote long, earnest, pleading letters, not expecting anyone to respond, but I knew the apologies needed to be written, no matter how they were received.

When I left the café, I walked home feeling that with each letter of apology, I'd shed a little bit of my former self—the parts I didn't like. I would only be traveling for a few more weeks and walking back to the boisterous hostel in the warm rain, I decided I'd honestly try to make the best of those remaining weeks.

I was tired of feeling sad all the time. It'd been almost two years since I'd allowed myself to be happy. Feeling good always seemed like some kind of betrayal against the loss, an insult to Dad's memory. As long as I was miserable, he was missed—there was logic in this for me. I couldn't predict what would happen to my grief once

I started living my life in a healthier way and was terrified to find out. Would I learn how to honor my father without sacrificing my own happiness? Though I figured I wouldn't really know the answers to those questions until I got home, I was eager to start finding out what kind of person I wanted to be; to decide for myself what it meant to grow up.

* * *

The next morning, I met Gabe at the airport, where we rented a speedy little Alfa Romeo car. I was elated to have Gabe with me and felt ready to have an adventure that would forever be just ours. Both of my brothers had moved mountains to come to my side halfway across the world, and I was beginning to get back to a place where I could show my appreciation to them. Like I had with Dylan a few weeks earlier, I felt safe in my big brother's care and looked forward to our grand Italian journey.

Fumbling with the map, I started scratching at my calves absentmindedly.

"What are you doing?" Gabe asked while pulling into a gas station.

"Nothing—I've just got the *schpilkes* today."

"No—I've seen you antsy before. What's the matter? You got scabies or something?" he said jokingly. But then it hit me: There were whispers of a bedbug problem at the hostel back in Rome. Inside the gas station's bathroom, I pulled down my pants to find hundreds of tiny red dots all over my legs and belly. The more I scratched the more I itched, and on top of the unrelenting discomfort, I was completely disgusted.

I couldn't help but notice the timing of this inconvenience. As if the moment I'd forgiven myself for all my depression and bad behavior, the bedbugs swarmed in like some kind of immediate karmic retribution.

After quarantining and sanitizing all of my belongings, Gabe and I drove to Orvieto, Assisi, Gubbio, San Gimignano, Sienna,

Cinque Terre, Bologna, and Milan. We ate our way through each city, splitting bottles of wine at every turn, though I usually got drunk so quickly that it was left to Gabe to finish off the bottle on his own. Most nights we stumbled back to our room stuffed and happy. Then I'd take my Ambien and crawl into bed.

Traveling with Gabe was easy and we talked constantly about everything from our favorite entries in Dad's travel journal to the last few episodes of *ER* that I missed while I'd been away. We ended our trip by touring the Ducati factory and museum in Bologna, both of us drooling over the gorgeous machinery and thinking about how much Dad would have loved all the motorcycle memorabilia.

Gabe succeeded in building up my confidence for the last leg of my trip, so I wasn't as sad or scared when it was time for him to go. After Gabe left, I bought myself a leather jacket in Milan, ate my last Italian meal, and took a train to Paris, where I would stay at a friend-of-a-friend's apartment. When I got to the elegantly ancient building, I was exhausted and sweaty inside my brand-new leather jacket. The flat was tiny, almost smaller than my dorm room at school, but was situated only a few minutes from the heart of the city. Other than being amazed to learn that the French had discovered a way to fit a shower into a closet-like space the size of an airport bathroom, I was thrilled to settle into the crowded, cozy home. It made a big difference to have the place to myself and be done with hostels for the duration of the trip.

Exploring Paris, I found the Louvre to be just as enormous and overwhelming as my Dad said it was in his journal, but in the thirty-six years between our visits it had visibly changed and improved. Though I couldn't get close enough to the *Mona Lisa* to decide if Dad had been right about her image looking better in reprints, I spent four hours at the museum and came back again the next day, still not feeling that I'd seen enough.

I took the Chunnel to London and followed directions to the flat I'd be staying at in West Hampstead. It was well into autumn there and as I walked through the residential streets to the address written on my hand, I felt strangely at home. It was comforting to hear English being spoken, and I felt relatively safe walking around by myself. The apartment in London was much bigger and much fancier than the one in Paris, and though the owner was out of town, he left me Post-its all around the flat to help me figure out the lights, the shower, TV, computer, and so forth.

I stretched out, cooked some dinner in the pristine kitchen, and relaxed. Though everything was significantly more expensive in London than anywhere else I'd been, I ate well, shopped for gifts, and saw a few shows. I loved walking around the massive city and felt good about myself for finally and thoroughly enjoying the traveling experience. I wished that I'd spent more time in England, or began the journey there as a better introduction to international travel; perhaps things would have turned out differently that way.

Soon enough, it was time for my flight home. At Heathrow Airport, I took out the two journals I'd carried with me throughout the trip one last time, flipping through their pages to reflect on how my father and I had filled them. I intended to add my final traveling thoughts into my own leather-bound book but could find surprisingly few words to describe my feelings about coming home two long months after I'd started out.

I took out Dad's journal, which I'd stuffed away for the last week or so. I was surprised to learn that my dad felt much the same way when he went home—humbled and eager to start again. His entry represented a man I never knew—a young man who was unsure of himself and his place in the world. Knowing that my father could transform into the caring, thoughtful, intelligent, and trustworthy man he became after such unsteadiness in his youth gave me a newfound hope and motivation for my own place in the world. The narrator of those journal entries didn't even come close to matching up with the memories I held of my father, but I felt warmed by the company of his words nonetheless. Following in his footsteps, no matter where they led, felt like an anchor, pulling me back down to earth.

8/28

I feel no compulsion to talk for the sake of talking—to strike up a conversation. I have things I would like to say, but very few people to say them to. There are things I should do that won't get done, things I should say that won't get said. I don't want to carry this to the point of distraction, but I'm really none too pleased with myself. I just don't have the guts to try to be what I would like to think of myself as being.

Of my European trip, the preceding pages are filled with some good, a lot so-so, and some bad. All of it was worthwhile, and nothing small enough to be forgotten. But we are all filled with the same "nada." The very fact that makes us human destroys us. Que es la vida!

Chapter 42

Winter's Proxy
Welcomes Me Home

Clearing my bags through customs, I could barely contain my anxiousness at seeing Mom. Above everything else I'd experienced on the trip, what haunted me most of all as I walked to the airport exit was the fear of being without her, a fear I'd held onto the entire time I was away. Having only one parent left made that one parent so much more important, and being across the world from her made me more uncomfortable than I could bear. When I saw her standing at the international terminal's waiting area, I half-ran, half-walked over to her, dropped my things, wrapped my arms around her, and let my face disappear inside her puffy winter coat. Back in the safety of my mother's arms, I let my emotions pour out of me as I cried into her sleeve. I realized with this mixed purge of relief and sadness just how ready I was to be home.

After spending a few days catching up in Milwaukee, Mom and I headed back up to camp. Midway through the six-hour drive, a misty curtain of snow began to fall. The flurries turned to thick, heavy wafers and began to drop down, the flakes clumping together in large clusters that seemed to darken the sky above the bare trees on either side of us. We'd been busy enough in Milwaukee to avoid talking too attentively about my trip. But with nothing on NPR and a long drive ahead of us, I started telling Mom about the things I liked about traveling—the museums I enjoyed and all the different foods I tried. I was especially pleased to report my new ability to dine alone without needing a reason for doing so. I did feel more independent, more capable, and a little older now that I was on the other side of the whole experience.

"So do you feel good about it all now that you're home?" Mom asked.

I considered for a moment letting my mom think things hadn't been as bad as they really were, if for no other reason than to save her the burden of knowing how much pain I'd been in, all alone on the other side of the world. But she knew me too well to believe anything other than the truth, and I knew it.

"Not at all," I finally answered. "I tried to do this big thing, and I completely failed. I had to have the boys come save me. Of course you know I'm glad they did come, and I'm glad I stayed past the first week, but no—I do not, on the whole, feel good about it."

"Oh, but honey." Mom's voice was low and soft, weighed down into sadness, and already I questioned my decision to share my unpleasant experiences with her. But she continued on, sweetly and confidently: "Don't you see that it was all your grand expectations that got you into trouble? I think if you hadn't placed so much pressure, so much of your self-worth on the outcome of this trip, things might have been different. Of course it wasn't going to live up to all of that stuff you wanted. It couldn't possibly have."

"I know," I said, and I did know. I had to recognize the way in which I'd sabotaged my chances of having a good trip before I'd even set foot out my door. "I know that part—I do it to myself, but . . . I don't know why."

I thought about it further, tried to sort out the pathology behind what I'd just come back from. "I wanted to be Hemingway," I blurted out. "Obviously, that wasn't going to happen. I guess I just felt like

I wasn't making it here, so maybe I could make it there, but then I found out it didn't matter where I was if I was determined to be totally miserable."

Even as the words came out of my mouth, I was surprised to hear them. I suppose this *was* what I'd gone through, but the way I'd phrased it made me sound so fragile, even to myself. But the new truth was that I didn't actually feel very fragile anymore. I'd attempted something colossal, had worked my way through it when I wanted to give up. I could eat dinner at a restaurant alone, could get myself from one place to another in foreign countries even when I had no help and didn't speak the language. There was a power in those experiences—the power of being a capable person.

"I mean, listen, I get it, honey," Mom said as we continued on the highway a few minutes later, having turned what I'd said inside her mind as she drove. "It's like we have to go someplace else, someplace away in order to do our grieving. And if we don't—if we stuff it down and refuse to walk through it, it'll come back to bite us. Harder than before."

"What do you mean?" I asked. "Like we have to get away from civilization?"

"Exactly. Well—no. Not civilization, but society. Because our society doesn't make it easy for us to do what we need to do in order to get healthy. To hurt until we are finished hurting, however long it takes."

I wasn't entirely sure what my motives had originally been in going to Europe. Even though I didn't think I found what I had been searching for, what I *had* gained was the opportunity to confront my grief in a concentrated state. Without the escapes I had previously surrounded myself with at school and camp, I'd had no choice but to cross a great and terrible distance in order to reform my identity.

I also came home from the trip with a much more comprehensive knowledge of my father as a young man. Reading Dad's accounts of the same places I visited was a bizarre sort of reverse déjà vu, but above everything else it helped me to rediscover how my father was in life, not just in death.

The next morning at camp, I woke up to a world full of white. Long after we pulled into the front driveway, the winter continued to let itself in. I was ecstatic to see it—nothing made me feel more at home than fresh snowfall. I slipped into my old pair of Sorel boots and tied the laces twice around each leg, the leather-and-nylon boot bunching up my flannel pajama pants. I wound a scarf around my neck, put gloves on each hand, and wrapped myself in one of my dad's old fleece jackets. Zipping it up over my chin, I searched for the smell of his skin around the collar, but couldn't be certain that anything was there. I zipped it back down again, and tied the scarf tighter around my face. Stuffed the ends inside the jacket.

I walked up to the office expecting to see my mom working at her desk upstairs but everything was dark inside, the heaters all turned off and unplugged. The dogs followed me as I took a quick circle around the office, lodge, and kitchen. I didn't see footprints anywhere and the car tracks we made in the road the night before were still half-covered. The tire's imprint was just barely visible under the surface of the drifted dustings of yesterday's snowfall, as if it had been gently covered with tracing paper, pressed down and left to stay covered. I stomped back to the house, trying to knock all the snow from my boots before walking back inside. I found my mom still in her room, awake but lying down. I'd slept until almost eleven o'clock, and was surprised to see her doing the same. She'd always been an early riser, usually coming in to my room to wake me long before I was ready.

We made breakfast together and ate at the big table in our pajamas, the scarf still around my neck.

"So what are you going to do today?" my mom chirped. Both of us were excited by the prospect of my big, empty future, ripe for the planning.

"Well, I don't know. I want to catch up on phone calls and maybe run into Hayward for some new books. I don't know—just relax today, I guess. Maybe I'll go skiing tomorrow if they groom the trails at Totagatic."

"Mmm-hmm. That sounds good. Would you mind shoveling the car out before all that—I need to go to the pharmacy in Spooner."

"'Course," I answered, happy to be able to do something to help.

In the driveway, I jabbed the side of the shovel against the house to knock off bits of ice that had formed around the metal overnight, then pushed it down at an angle into the fresh snow. It was a dry batch, light and airy, and this made it easier for me to lift each load off to the side. I moved quickly, efficiently. I didn't look around to notice the flatness of the lake, now coated in several feet of ice and snow. I didn't turn around to look in the windows of the house. I didn't stop to catch my breath. Reaching the end of the divided snow, I turned and made another pass.

When I finished, I stood up and arched my back to stretch. Camp was beautiful again. Empty and quiet, it was my home once more, and I found solace in returning to take my rightful place there. All the ghosts of the summer and years before had gone away. It was just home again. As if it knew of my homecoming, winter's proxy had dropped a fresh drape of snow like a clean piece of paper all around our house.

Chapter 43

DEAR SUSAN

I spent a few weeks cross-country skiing and relaxing at the camp house before boredom set in. Now that I was back home, I no longer wanted to move to New York City, as I'd once planned. I was afraid of working my butt off to just barely make ends meet and wasn't fond of the idea of going to a city where again I would be all alone and need a roommate. I entertained the idea of moving to Chicago, where I had a lot of friends and family, but deemed it just a little *too* close to Milwaukee and camp.

Every day, I'd wake up just after the winter sun started warming the surface of the snow and would set out to navigate a network of one of the nearby trail systems. I usually wasn't too adventurous about finding new trails, and instead preferred the same two or three spots within a range of thirty miles, where rather than stress over staying on the right loop I could just settle into my rhythm for a few hours, let my mind rest and my body take command.

The flats of the Totagatic trails were the finest for this purpose; the pale sky punctuated by muted yellow grasses and naked, brown trees melting around me in a soft dullness just right for letting thoughts wander. The Pacific Northwest kept coming back into my mind while I skied, and eventually I decided that just because I'd had some bad times in Tacoma didn't mean that the rest of the state was unavailable to me. Some of my friends had moved to Olympia or Seattle after graduating, and I liked thinking of living in Seattle.

I could envision myself being happy there, could already conjure up images of favorite restaurants and stores, yet the move still seemed an intimidating and brave undertaking. It was a big city, though not nearly as daunting as New York. Finally I'd made up my mind: One way or another, I was going to get myself back there and start over.

I preferred to have a job in place before moving to Seattle but in the end I didn't let that postpone or sway my decision to leave. I couldn't stay in Minong forever, and in fact didn't want to stay there much longer at all. I spent hours on the computer in the office each day, ravenously searching for apartments and jobs, setting up possible moving dates and working out realistic timeframes for making it happen.

On the rare, warmer days that winter, I'd take Dad's car-washing bucket filled with a well-worn scrubby-mitt, Armor-All, and wheel-shine, and walk to the Church of the Foaming Brush. Under a large car port near our house that Dad had named "That Building," I set to work on his car. Moving under the cover of the open-air structure, I could hear my father's voice booming over the lodge's PA system: "Yoga will meet in That Building this afternoon at four-seventeen and forty-two seconds." Then the entire camp would shout in unison while my dad waited and smiled. "What building?" they'd ask.

"*That* Building," he'd say back, throwing a thumb over his shoulder in the tin-roofed space's direction.

"Oh, *Thaaaaaat* Building."

Wrapped in winter sweaters and fingerless gloves, I tried to remember the order in which Dad used to do things. I pictured him whistling under the Arizona sun in our driveway, standing in sandals to wash his Jeep's shiny hood. My mind moved next to the way he looked when he was sick, hunched over his Subaru with one hand bent against the hood for support.

I was devastated to think that I never had the opportunity to watch my dad become an old man, never saw his hair and beard naturally grow in gray, or notice the wrinkles deepen beside his eyes; never saw him slow and gradually detach from the banalities of daily events. When I finished drying the last streak of moisture from the car's flanks, I sat on the little cement curb to admire the result of my efforts, knowing that although there was no reason for it, the car would seem to drive better because of the shine. When the sun warmed my hose-water-chilled hands, and the breeze settled into an afternoon calm, I felt my dad's presence, felt him sitting next to me so strongly that I turned my head, expecting to see him there.

* * *

The more I moved toward living happily and peacefully again, the more deeply my mom seemed intent on slipping into her grief. Still unable to sleep, she continued taking sleeping pills even though the boys and I had mostly been weaned off the medication. I didn't like the way the sleeping pills made me feel when I woke up in the morning or the hallucinations I'd sometimes experience. Apart from those side effects, however, the pills were—to me—a symbol of the darkness I'd gotten lost inside. I was just starting to climb out of that hole and taking the pills seemed like a giant step backward into it. I suggested to Mom that maybe she should try to get back on her own sleeping schedule without the medication, but she didn't think she could do it. She told me that she'd tried several times over the last two years but never got any sleep without the pills and ended up feeling worse for the effort; as exhausted as she still was from losing her father and then her husband in less than two years, we could all see how badly she needed proper rest, and I felt guilty for pushing her.

I thought perhaps it was the pills, or the isolation, which was palpable and at times oppressive, but something was different about my mom; it was as if she had sent a piece of herself along with my father like an offering of some kind of spiritual Viking bride, to keep him company for the journey when he died. She knew it, knew she would never be the same. It was the rest of us who still had to learn this. Looking back at it now, I'm not sure who had it worse: my mom, for knowing grief and knowing at least in some part what she would have to endure to walk through the pain; or my brothers and I, who were still so new to the business of grief and were still learning what we would endure and how we'd change in order to endure it.

Mom wasn't taking a very large dose of sleeping aid but did take it every night, sometimes staying awake until after two or three in the morning, then lying in bed, drowsy but awake, for hours the next day. When we talked about our grief, it was clear how incomplete my mom felt without my father and how drastically her life and daily routine had been altered since his death. They shared their lives and their love for thirty-five years, and now he was gone.

*   *   *

I tried to fill my time as productively as I could at camp while waiting for confirmation on a retail job I applied to in downtown Seattle. I worked on sewing projects and wood-burned a four-by-six-foot map to be placed at the trail-head of the single-track trails Dylan and I had built while Dad was sick. I sat in front of the TV with the heavy wood on my lap, keeping me warm under its sturdy weight, and centimeter by centimeter, I dragged the soldering tool across the grains, shading and outlining the curves and dips of our trails. The repetition was meditative and hypnotic, the hours blurring together.

My mom went to Milwaukee to visit friends, leaving me alone at camp for the last two weeks of January. Most days, I was the only person for miles and unlike my travels, this kind of being alone felt right. I didn't mind the quiet, didn't mind the time to think and plan.

Then the freeze came. The temperature dropped almost forty degrees in one night and didn't rise above -10 for almost two weeks. Mom was unable to make the drive back up with most of the main roads closed, many sections overcome with black ice and rendered impassable. I was stuck. The tires of my truck squared off, a Nalgene water bottle froze and cracked. The two older dogs peed in the house rather than be forced to go outside in the cruel cold.

Alone for 500 acres, big girl in a little town. I washed my hands in freezing water to toughen them up against the cold—my favorite Arctic trick. Allowing the simple, country life to wash my psyche clean once again, I started to see the blessings my father always spoke about toward the end of his life. He loved this place, and knowing how much joy it had given him was enough to keep me happy there too, despite the conditions. Every time I went outside and around the house to get more wood, I braved the frigid air with just a sweater on—testing myself against the cold. At night I'd set my alarm every two hours, wake to the orange glow of the wood-burning stove filtering into my room, dogs piled together on the bed with me. Lowering logs into their places, squatting boyishly in long underwear, my face illuminated and hot, I scanned the house around me, the house we'd fitted for winter with our own bare hands. The plastic covering stretched flat around the windows, the woodstove snapping and smoking in front of me, the glow of the snow coming in through the cracks of the house. It was never meant to hold a family year-round, but it held me then, tied me tight inside the frost.

* * *

Since my mom was held up in Milwaukee longer than planned, I spent a week redecorating the back bedroom as a surprise for her. Part of a recent addition to the house, we'd never had enough time to make that room a welcoming guest bedroom for all the visitors who stayed with us during the summers. I knew she would never have the time to do it herself so I sewed matching curtains and blankets and built a cushy, upholstered headboard to decorate the room. The project kept me busy, kept me warm, and made me feel good for doing something to cheer her up. I finished just in time for her arrival, blindfolding her and leading her by the hand to the back room for the "big reveal." She was completely taken by surprise and cried proudly as she looked around the room, seeing how much work I'd put in while she was away. The moment held still in time just perfectly—it felt so good to see her smile, to catch her off-guard with something so innocuously simple.

But that same night, Mom dozed off on the couch and stayed there for hours, a book nestled against her leg. I finally kissed her goodnight and went to bed around eleven. I woke at four in the morning to get some water, and when I walked into the kitchen I saw that the lights were still on in the living room and my mom was sitting exactly where I had left her.

"Mom. Hey, Mom. What are you doing?"

"Hmm? Oh. I'm just catching up on some reading," she said, slurring her speech. I was fairly certain she'd just been asleep that whole time, the book still open on her lap, but I couldn't be sure. She was acting just like I did when I stayed awake after taking Ambien and drinking wine in Italy. She didn't even turn her head to look at me—she just kept her glassy eyes fixed on the page, her body curled up with both knees against her chest under a blanket.

"Come on, Mom. This is crazy—it's, like, four in the morning." Fuzzy and sleep-fogged, she finally stood up and walked into her bedroom.

The next morning when I asked my mom how often she stayed awake all night reading like that, she didn't know what I was talking about. She couldn't remember anything after taking her pill. I relayed to her the details of our exchange but got the feeling that she didn't believe me or thought I was exaggerating. This same routine began to repeat itself several nights each week, and I was worried about her— wanted to rescue her from the pain that was keeping her so depleted and so profoundly affected. Whenever I tried to discuss these events with my mom, she brushed me off. I suppose she thought I was trying to make a big deal out of nothing, but I was starting to really fear for her safety at night.

I decided to leave for Seattle on February 10, job or no job. My big moving day was rapidly approaching, and I worried how much more intensely my mom would grieve without me there. Even though she was clear and intent on purposely staying at camp so that she could do her emotional work in private, I was nervous and felt guilty for leaving.

Eventually I phoned my brothers, who had by then begun to pick up the pieces of their own lives and were becoming, with every passing day, more like our father. For the first time in my adult life, I was the one bringing *them* into the situation. Though I had mixed feelings about our changing sibling relationships, I needed their help with Mom and knew they'd want to be filled in on what was going on at camp. The three of us promised to stick together; we would keep trying to convince her that Minong wasn't the best place for her anymore and that the sleeping pills were doing more harm than good.

The three of us realized as we came together to help our mother that we'd come such a very long way since the winter we'd spent together when Dad was dying. We were each finding solid footing in our respective career paths and could finally respect one another's accomplishments, no matter how divergent they were from our own. The sense of connectedness between us slowly began to pervade our conversations and interactions, and I found myself resting easy in that shared feeling. My brothers and I, at long last, broke new ground that would prove to be the foundation for our adult sibling relationship in the years to come.

The weather stayed nasty that winter, threatening in its fierceness, and one evening while Mom and I ate dinner and watched a movie, we heard a loud *pop* from beneath the house. Since another cold snap had blown in that week, we knew the pipes were at risk. Sure enough, we found Mom's bathroom counter flooded with water that was now flowing in a steady deluge across the floor. We quickly bundled ourselves from head to toe and grabbed a flashlight to search out the source of the explosion we'd heard. We tried calling both of camp's caretakers—two brothers named Rich and Russ, close family friends of ours, who oversaw all of camp's maintenance and construction matters—with no luck. It was late at night, and in our vampire hours, Mom and I were alone. There was no one we could call to help us—no twenty-four-hour plumbing service, and no friendly handyman neighbor; we'd need to take care of the problem ourselves.

In order to get under the house and look at the pipes, we had to first lift a heavy wooden door that covered the three-by-three-foot square entrance to the crawl space. We then needed a ladder to climb down. The walk from the front of the house to the sub-basement's entrance was difficult while carrying the freezing cold aluminum ladder, and with each step I grew more pissed off. I was bitter from the cold and mad at my mom for wanting to live there during the hard-knock winters. I was sick of living in such a remote place; it was time for me to get back out into the world. I was sure of it.

I handed the flashlight to my mom and dropped down into the damp darkness. I took the flashlight back from her and squatted wordlessly under the doorway. Over my constant stream of expletives in response to the situation, I listened to Mom's instructions and found the broken section of pipe. There wasn't much to do but shut off the water line leading to the affected areas, so after twisting the cold spigot with bare and rigid hands, I turned around and crawled back. As I pulled the ladder up and pushed the cover back on, my mom seemed too cheerful for the situation, her defiantly good humor only angering me more.

"Good job, honey," she said while rubbing my shoulder with a mittened hand, smiling the adoring smile of a proud mother.

"What're you so damn happy about?" I snapped. "This sucks. Normal people don't have to do this stuff."

"Yeah, that's what is so great about it—makes us tougher women."

"Really?" I asked sarcastically. "I'm glad you're so pleased with the good old country livin' since you're so determined to stay here."

"I like living here," she said, quickly turning serious. "I like this simple life, being close to Dad." Hearing the resoluteness in her voice stunned me silent. "I can walk into my grief here in peace. I'm better here."

We walked the rest of the way to the front door in silence, both missing Dad and thinking about how different the night would have been if he were still alive.

After we cleaned up the mess in the bathroom and thawed our hands in front of the fire, we changed into pajamas and went to bed. When I woke up the next morning and went to check my email on the computer in the kitchen, I saw that mom had started writing an email to Susan after I'd gone to sleep. Obviously too sleepy on her pills to think clearly, she'd typed out disjointed and desperate thoughts in a sprawling note, and even held the keys down too long in her haze so that repetitions of letters flowed across the screen.

She didn't get far enough to have pressed "send" yet, so I left it up on the monitor for her to see. When she woke up, I asked her to come over and read the email. I wanted her to believe what I'd been telling her all winter—that her grief would continue to eat her alive as long as she took the sleeping pills, no matter how badly she needed them. She'd never be able to find her way out of this dark spell if she kept taking medication that I now knew with total certainty to be potentially dangerous, and I finally had something tangible to prove my warnings true. I sat in the corner behind my mom as she read over the email, her hand slowly rising to her mouth as she read on:

Dear Susan—

I can't take it this not sleeping never rested alone in my bed.

Iiiiiiiiiiiiiiiiiiiiiiiiiiiiiiiiiiiiiiiiiiiiiiiiiiiiiiiiiiiiiiiiiiiiiiiiiiiiiiiiiiiiiiiiiiii don't know how you sleep with a person almost forty years and then don't. I never sleep. I know you don't either.

When Alan first died did you feel like this? The kids are always rearranging my pantry and throwing things away. Don't you miss him? Iiiiiiiiiiiiiiiiiiiiiiiiiiiiiiiiiiiiiiiiiiiiiiiiiiiiiiiiiiiiiiiiiiiiiiii miss him worst at night. Does your medicine take as long to work?

Thhhhhhhhhose sunglasses of yours are still broken on top of the pizza oven, you left them here last winter. You know you can't walk around it, Susan. You have to walk right through it or it'lllllllllllllllllllllllllllll llllllllllllllllllllllll come back and hit you harder, laterrrrrrrr it always does.

Do you get anything done? Do your coworkers ask how you're holding up? Isn't that a funny way to say it—holding up, what should we be holding up? I say yes, I'm here, aren't I?

When Alan first died and then Richard, I thhhhhought, now we're so far away and there's so much wood to chop here, the winters get so long.

I cried while watching her read the unsent email. I had been so quick to judge the way she was handling Dad's death but I had no idea what kind of pain she was actually facing. The grief had long since stopped being so complicated for her and now it boiled down to one simple and pure truth: She just plain missed him. We all did. The stress of taking on many of Dad's responsibilities both at camp and in parenting was clearly wearing her down, and I couldn't blame her for putting off the enormous task of setting up a new house for herself. When she would eventually buy a house, she'd have to unpack all the boxes from Tucson, still in storage all these years, and sort through all of Dad's things along with her own. She would need to sift through thirty-five years' worth of reminders of their life together and of how terribly it had all been derailed. No wonder she wanted to prolong her time at camp, because as long as she stayed in Minong, her life was still aligned with Dad. A new house would be hers alone and that prospect offered an overwhelming array of things to feel sad about.

Above the pangs of my own grief, I was heartbroken for my mom. Having lived over twenty years of her life without her own mother, the sorrow of loss was no stranger to her. She'd lost her father and her husband in less than two years and was grieving for both of them. Seeing the Ambien-tainted email was a huge shock for her because she didn't remember writing it or even sitting at the computer the night before, and was horrified at the thought of having come so close to actually sending it. Finally, she believed all the stories I'd been telling her about her bizarre nighttime behavior. She promised to slowly wean herself off the pills, and I promised to stay up with her at night while she made the transition off the medication.

In the last few weeks at camp before Mom and I drove my Subaru back to Washington, I was once again afraid to leave her side. I worried about her being all alone up there. I'd had a taste of life in a Northwoods winter and though it taught me some valuable skills, it was a lonely way to exist.

Still, I understood why she was so drawn there: to walk through her grief without the prying eyes of society watching her. I'd gotten myself around Europe alone, and I could do the same here in the middle of nowhere or anywhere else for that matter. I could build my own fires, could chop my own wood, fix the pipes if they should happen to freeze and burst beneath my house. I did feel tougher and stronger for having lasted a winter there just the two of us, but I could easily notice the effects of the isolation on us both. Mom seemed incomplete, stuck in time. She became someone new the day Dad died and then stayed that way, while the rest of us were working hard to find our way back. She was different now—still my mom but in a different way. She wasn't able to bring herself out of the darkness of her grief and didn't seem to want to yet.

I thought back to the conversation she and I had in the car coming back from Milwaukee after my vacation. I went halfway around the world to do my grieving away from the judgmental eyes of my peers and pressures of my life. Dylan had traveled even farther, skiing deep into the landlocked heart of Mongolia, where he could scream his emotions into the vast winter landscape in private. Gabe pushed himself deeply into camp business, where he could process his grief through the work that so desperately needed to be done and that he so clearly had a passion for. And finally, Mom came back to camp to busy herself in confronting the loss. None of us felt comfortable dealing with our sadness in front of society, and this pattern disturbed me. Because our culture at large is so uncomfortable with death and dying, the four of us felt unwelcome in our grief, unwelcome because of it.

I was so terrified of losing my mom in part because I already *had* lost her—to the grief, to the depression, to the unbearable absence of my father. The lonesomeness that swallowed her up in its dark, giant jaws changed our relationship irrevocably. She would always be my mother and would forever take care of me, but it was time for me to start taking care of her in return.

I urged her to rethink her living situation and start looking for houses in Milwaukee. In Minong there was no one to keep her company. No one urging her to get fresh air or eat well. At least in Milwaukee she'd be near family and friends and could drive up to camp whenever she wanted. After Gabe and Dylan joined me in constantly nagging her to reconsider, she eventually agreed to start looking at houses the following fall. I didn't like the idea of her spending another six months alone at camp, but I also knew that she would only leave her well-crafted, safe, Dad-approved grief nest when she was good and ready. She knew she'd need more time to establish new bearings for herself, and my brothers and I trusted her instincts enough to give her the space she needed.

Chapter 44

THE QUEENSBOROUGH

It was time to go. My bags were packed and loaded into the car. I'd spent a few days cleaning everything out of my room in the camp house and putting the things I couldn't take with me to Seattle in storage. Though the harshness of winter had done some of the work for me in changing the way the house felt, I wanted to make sure that when I came home again, things would look different than it did while Dad was sick and dying. I would have to make peace with the house at some point—I knew that much at least—and wanted to do what I could to make that easier for myself the next time I came home. Boxing up my extra ski clothes, old books, and stack of pictures, I felt as clean in my mind as the room was beginning to look. The happiness that cleanness gave me was nothing short of therapeutic.

After securing my skis to the car rack and checking the tire pressure with the gauge Dad had given me on my sixteenth birthday, we set out on highway 2 across the northern states. Our departure was well-timed, and Mom and I looked forward to starting our road trip with clear weather. My best friend, Rachel, now living in Olympia, would meet us in the city and help me find an apartment close to my new job. I couldn't wait to start life in the big city and felt very grown-up, having appointments scheduled to view downtown-area apartments as soon as we arrived.

The road trip wasn't that different from the one I'd taken with Dad a few years earlier; Mom and I sang songs and talked about my future, showing enthusiasm about my life on the West Coast. Though I was older now, I again took to the passenger seat when the weather turned nasty and the roads were scary, letting my mom handle the sketchier driving conditions. The trip was good medicine for us both after being cooped up at camp for so long. I could see the change in her as we headed farther west; although camp was a safe and comforting place, there was no denying that it was impossible for the four of us to be there without feeling weighed down by our painful memories. I was excited for her to visit Seattle again too, because it had always been a favorite city of hers as well as mine.

Arriving in Seattle was like entering a city I'd never seen before. Though I'd visited Seattle countless times during my four years in Tacoma, I'd forgotten how beautiful it was. The great Olympic and Cascade Mountain ranges bordered the city to the west and to the east, with fresh snow shining across the water of Puget Sound, positively glistening with wind and sunshine.

My mom, Rachel, and I spent a few days looking at apartments, eating at fun restaurants, and shopping for furniture to fill my new home. Valentine's Day came, and with the three of us exhausted from a day of walking and shopping, we decided to take in a movie as our Valentine's Day celebration. Not knowing its premise, we settled in to watch the film *Big Fish*. By the end of the movie, in which a son finally learns how to love and understand his father right before he dies, the three of us were crying hysterically, sharing tissues and not bothering to quiet our sobs for the benefit of those sitting near to us. Long after the credits finished rolling, after the lights came up in the theater, and after the cleaning crew moved in, the three of us fatherless daughters sat in our seats and sniffled.

* * *

My large apartment building, decorated with the regal-sounding title "The Queensborough" elaborately painted in green cursive lettering on one side, was situated on a hill near one of Seattle's infamously confusing intersections. Mom and I missed the turn five times before figuring out how to arrive at the building we could always see but not reach. And each time we made another pass on the one-way street, I kept staring into the large windows of a Thai restaurant a few blocks away. Finally on the last circle, I remembered why the restaurant looked so familiar to me: Dad and I had eaten there together during my West Coast, college-hunting trip. We ate the best pad thai we'd ever had there, and I took this as a good omen—deciding before I even saw the apartment that this must surely be my new home. The coincidence was too profound to be ignored. Though I viewed several spacious apartments on the outskirts of the city, I signed a lease for that tiny studio in Seattle's Lower Queen Anne neighborhood, about one mile from downtown and just a few blocks from some pretty good Thai food.

Fortunately the apartment was clean, cute, and safe—perfect for my first study in the art of living alone. I wanted to stay right in the middle of things, where it would be harder for me to hide out and isolate myself. I also thought it was more practical to live in a place I knew I would be able to afford, with easy access to transportation. For the first time in my life, I was proud of myself for not only thinking pragmatically but acting that way as well. My bed may have been just a few feet from the refrigerator, and my dresser stuffed in the bathroom, but I was happy there in the space that was all my own.

Dropping Mom off at the airport, I knew we'd have an easier time saying goodbye than we'd had in several years. I worried less about her now that she was looking at houses in Milwaukee and beginning to wean herself off the safety and seclusion of camp life. I could already see her beginning to climb her way out of the deepest parts of her grief, making steady, forward momentum. She, too, felt comforted leaving me, knowing that I'd be okay in this big city. And though I wouldn't be working at camp anymore now that I had a grown-up job, we understood with absolute clarity that the four of us would continue to gather together more frequently than the average family. When we hugged, I thanked her for driving through the bad weather for me, and she laughed as she waved one hand behind her while walking into the airport.

* * *

Driving away from the airport, I wondered if I would be scared or lonely my first night in the new apartment. I worried that the depression and loneliness that had so plagued me on my travels would follow me to Seattle. But my first night passed with the opposite result; it felt incredible to be alone. I put on some good music and began decorating the place any damn way I wanted. I danced all around those 400 square feet of mine and ate two dinners, knowing that no one could see me or judge my actions. Until, of course, I realized that my large, curtain-free windows were letting the hundred or so people in neighboring apartment buildings see absolutely everything I did. It didn't take me long to drive down to IKEA to buy myself a very worthwhile set of blackout drapes.

I spent so much time enjoying the extreme privacy and seclusion of winter life at camp that being back in a city setting was jarring at first. And though I did miss my daily ski runs and walks along the frozen waterfront, I felt invigorated as I walked among crowds of people. As it turned out, a little bit of anonymity suited me well. Walking out of the woods and back into a life full of culture, friends, work, and hobbies made me feel more like my father than I'd felt in years. Though I could sense his presence so strong and clear at camp, I was certain that getting myself back out into the open was the best way to honor his memory.

All of my creative juices—whether they were for craft projects, organizing, or writing—seemed to truly come to a boil in the dark, winter months in Seattle. I did my best work when there was little reason to go outside, little reason to venture out of my newly decorated, cozy home.

While sewing some new curtains to pretty up my blackout drapes, I watched a show about ghosts. A man told a story about how, after his father died, he started noticing strange occurrences around the home his father lived in and how, eventually, he even saw his father's image standing before him, giving him a very important message. While most ghost stories tend to scare me—so much so that I feel a need to turn on every light and check inside every closet before going to bed—this particular story was, to me anyway, more sad and beautiful than anything else. I sat there on the floor in front of my sewing machine, layers of blue fabric bunched in my lap, crying hysterically. Maybe my reaction to this story *should* have been fear, but instead I felt jealous. Though I did feel my father's presence around me from time to time, I'd never had any kind of real-life visit from him since his death.

Perhaps what made me feel most jealous was that this sighting came when the man was feeling really lost in his life—in need of the kind of reassurance and advice that only a father can give. Certainly by then I'd had more than my fair share of times when I felt lost and in need of my father's reassurance. And indeed, throughout my grief there had been many times where I called out to my father through a fit of tears or a moment of real fear, wishing more than anything for some kind of sign from him. But it never happened. He never appeared.

I called my mom after the show ended, and she told me that whenever I felt like I needed my dad's advice or opinion on something I should just remember who he was and that I would know, somewhere inside, what he would tell me. I'm lucky to have had my father in my life long enough to know what kind of man he was and to know with absolute confidence how he felt about me.

"Don't be so jealous of those people who receive real-life visits from their dead loved ones, honey," Mom said, "because it usually implies that there was some unfinished business—things unsaid or unresolved in that relationship."

In my relationship with my father, we were blessed with the time and courage to have said all that we needed to; my father and I knew how much we loved each other. And when I did find myself in those moments when I wished my father were there to help me find my way out of something painful, chances were that I did know—somehow— what he would say to me. His impact on my life was solid enough to get me through most things. And what he didn't instill in me, I was managing to instill in myself.

My mother reminded me then of something Uncle Wooby said during his eulogy at Dad's memorial service. He turned to my brothers and me with sheer adoration in his eyes and said, "When people ask the three of you what kind of man your father was, all you will need to say is that he was the kind of man who raised a person like me." I realized then that I didn't need to see Dad's face, as much happiness and peace as it would bring me, because he'd given me enough love to last me the rest of my life.

*　*　*

While I waited to start my new job selling shoes in the illustrious Salon shoe department at Nordstrom's flagship store downtown, I had no trouble busying myself by getting settled into my new place, exploring the neighborhood, and looking at writing classes at the Richard Hugo House, a well-established local writing center.

On my way to meet with my new boss for the first time, I was so nervous about saying the right things, wearing the right outfit, and getting there on time that I parked in the first parking garage I could find and then rushed off to find the block-long Nordstrom building. The meeting went well, and I left feeling excited and confident. But back on the rapidly darkening city streets, I realized that I had no idea which garage I'd parked in. In a panic, I called Gabe, hoping he'd tell me what to do.

"Well, I hate to say it, Tan," he said gently, "but you're just going to have to go in every parking garage until you see something familiar." I could hear him trying to mask his amusement.

"Seriously? Couldn't I call the police or something?" I asked. I couldn't imagine walking the whole downtown area in my brand-new high heels, which were already starting to hurt. It was raining, to boot, and I'd left my umbrella at home in the interest of looking like a well-seasoned Seattle native, who just about never carries an umbrella.

"What do you think the police are going to do for you? They'll laugh in your face, Tanya. They've got bigger fish to fry. If I were you, I'd just start walkin'."

Luckily, I only had to explore six parking garages until I found the one in which I'd parked the Subaru. To this day, I always write down the garage and level of anyplace I leave my car. Lesson learned.

Chapter 45

As Suddenly, Sunshine

Living in Seattle suited me. I loved being on my own and quickly found that I almost never got lonely. I was good at my job and made plenty of money to support myself. Working in retail was a refreshing change after spending so much time living inside my head and not really liking it there. I dressed to the nines every day and quickly built up an impressive collection of designer shoes, indulging in the shallow pleasures of life after so many years spent under the weight of pain and darkness. In this new life, I went to work during the day, spent my nights at home or out with friends, and had very few responsibilities beyond basic daily tasks. It was a simple time for me, and I loved being able to enjoy my friends and the culture in Seattle and get back to the business of being a young person.

I enjoyed working downtown and often walked from my apartment to the Nordstrom building; taking in both the beautiful and the gritty parts of the city made me feel authentic and city-savvy. I felt tough, strong, and more at peace than I'd been in a long time. One night on my way in from work, I picked up a package from my mailbox. Mom had sent me a care package just like the ones Dad used to put together, and I couldn't wait to get upstairs to open it. It was filled with candy, gag gifts, and goodies, but I was surprised to find a real gift waiting at the bottom of the box. Mom framed one of my favorite pictures of Dad and me so that I could hang it in my new apartment. Though she had helped me buy a bed, couch, plants, and kitchenware, this picture was the one thing that truly made it feel like home.

I've seen pictures of myself and my brothers as babies in my father's arms. He's always dressed in his bathrobe, hair matted to one side from sleeping. My favorite picture shows him with his arms crossed at his chest, my three-month-old body nestled in the crook of his bent knee resting on the other leg. My arms are crossed too, in the mock pose of a stubborn moment. We stare at each other against a background of large-print floral wallpaper. In the next photograph, he has scooped me up close to his face and his mouth is wide open, laughing. My mom tells me that early mornings were his favorite time of day with us. She'd wake with us in the middle of the night to nurse us back to sleep, so he would get us out of our cribs when we woke in the mornings and let my mother sleep in late. He'd change our diapers, get a bottle ready, and sit with us at the kitchen table. With no one else around, he would sing silly songs to get us giggling or play games of peek-a-boo and "Sooooooo Big!" He loved speaking in funny accents, although I'm not sure we appreciated the humor at three or four months old.

Dad especially loved to take us outside when the weather was nice. He'd carry us out in our little chairs or lay us down on a blanket beside him. He told me once I was older how much he loved to watch our eyes follow the leaves and clouds as we looked up into the tree canopies, to the sky beyond.

As we grew older, we played a favorite game we'd made up, called "Lazy." Reserved for lazy Sunday mornings, my dad would lie on his side on the living room rug, and we'd climb on top of his big belly, saying, "Lay-zeeeeeee, lay-zeeeeeee," over and over again. We couldn't get enough of it.

In another photo, the one that Mom sent me, my dad sits on the floor playing a guitar while I lean my head on his shoulder, mouth open in song and knees bent in dance, my head tilted to touch my father's bearded cheek. I am two years old, dressed for the winter chill that blew through our aging house. Dad has much more hair in this picture than I remember him ever having, and he holds the guitar at an angle on his leg in the classical form. I look up at the camera, but he looks at me.

While I looked at the picture on my wall, I couldn't take my eyes away from Dad's sweet, smiling face. For the first time since his death, I could look at my father's face in photographs and feel happiness instead of devastation and despair. I'd been continuing to grieve even in my new life in Seattle, only now the complications grief brought had faded away. I wasn't feeling angry, or cheated, or bitter any longer. I just plain missed him.

Also in the box was a small black album, filled with a few photos and copies of all the things Dad said to us toward the very end of his life. I sat down on the floor with the album in my lap and read hungrily, tears rushing down my cheeks in fast drips.

I could hear him speaking the words inside my head, re-membered him talking this way at the end of his life. As if he were some great chief or tribal elder, the words flowed effortlessly from him—as if by divine order. And now, looking back on the challenges I had faced since that time, I could pinpoint exactly when he said each of these things. That day on the boat when we were just entering the period of waiting for Dad to go, I asked him how I would know what to do without him, and he answered me beautifully: *It begins with filling your heart with love. If you fill your heart with love, everything looks different. It's easier to accept other people and their paths. Make some physical contact with everyone every day—a high-five, a hug, a kiss on the forehead—to let them know "I see you." It doesn't matter to be right. If you move from that loving place everything you do will be right—everything. It's important for people to feel loved and safe and free here. The things we do are vehicles for that—to be able to face a challenge, overcome a fear of failure. That's my vision for camp and my vision of parenting. Just look at the three of you—I know it all works. We did more right than wrong and you will do the same.*

As I read through Dad's final insight on life, I thought about how far my brothers and I had indeed come since the death of our father. Though we were all living in different cities now, we talked and visited often, and finally understood how to communicate with one another in a way in which we all felt respected and heard. Camp was thriving under Gabe's diligent care, and I knew Dad was proud of us for keeping it going even though it had been such a painful process at the start. And finally, I read something that absolutely shook me enough to abruptly stop my crying: *I want more years, but it's selfish, because what I want is to spend time with Mom and watch you kids live as adults and take more pride in the things you each do. But that would be trying to control the outcome of my life and the outcome is already done. So the quantity of time doesn't matter.*

It was simple: I wanted my dad to live, and certainly he fought like hell to stay with us. But what we wanted and asked for so vehemently and so desperately did not come. I don't know whose hands fate is in, but it definitely wasn't in ours. I had this knowledge all along but had let it reach inside me and turn me sour. Now I realized that it could do the opposite.

All the time and energy I'd spent searching and waiting for the big epiphany I felt I deserved had been wasted. It was right there, in Dad's words all along. It had been there, staring me in the face every day that I woke, rose, and went out into the world. I kept expecting some kind of grand wisdom to shower me in glory, wholly filling me with the light of the universe. But instead, the epiphany was waiting for me to get over myself enough to see it. It wasn't about becoming enlightened or special; the true gift of loss is learning to enjoy life for what it is—to love fully and not waste time being unnecessarily angry or sad. My father knew this to be true, and I was lucky to witness what that knowledge did for him. Now it was my turn.

My day will come, too, and I have no control over that decision or the landscape of that journey. What I do control is my own interior landscape—my life is mine and mine alone, mine to make happy or mine to destroy. I watched my father choose happiness, and I knew it could be done. All I needed to do was find what made me happy and follow it. To be nice to the people around me—cherish my friends and be kind to strangers. To always have dogs in the family. To laugh every day, to laugh at myself, to laugh when all else fails. To be silly. To be sincere. Giving. Loving in everything I do. He'd done it all. And he died happy.

Chapter 46

BRIDGE

A man lies down to sleep.
Hawks and crows gather around his bed.
Grass shoots up between the hawks' toes.
Each blade of grass is a voice.
The sword by his side breaks into flame.
—ROBERT BLY

When I came back to camp one February for a visit during a break from grad school, winter was still hanging heavily in the air, allowing the cold to find a way to crawl inside my lungs and rob a part of each breath. Though springtime was on its way in Seattle, stepping off the plane in Duluth reminded me that spring was still a long way off in this part of the country. Back home at camp, I saw that Mom brought some of my things from her new house in Milwaukee and had redecorated my room a little, hanging different pictures on the wall and adding a few favorite throw pillows to the bed. In the corner, above my dresser, hung a beautifully framed picture I'd taken of my dad several winters earlier.

On the day the photo was taken, Dad and I walked down the long road through camp to check out some cabin construction he was overseeing. As we walked through the unplowed snow, Dad wore his favorite winter outfit: tall hiking boots, warm Gramicci pants, and a woollen, candy-striped Hudson Bay blanket that Mom had made into a coat for his birthday one year. Dylan's dog, Jimmy, trotted along behind us, and I snapped pictures with my new camera while Dad called out aperture settings as he walked on ahead of me, reminding me to bracket my shots to accommodate for the flat winter light. As I knelt down to get a close shot of an ice-topped tree stump, Dad snuck up behind me and just as I pushed my finger down to capture the image, he dropped a snowball down the back of my coat. When I turned around to yell at him, he was already running backward away from me, laughing, his hands tucked inside the pockets of his rough wool coat.

When we reached the cabin where the construction was just barely underway, we walked around the foundation of the new building. Standing behind him, I noticed that the horizontal stripes on his coat were lining up with the horizontally laid floor joists. The white space between the colors of his coat matched the curved white coating of snow atop the wood. Under Dad's tutelage, I recognized a beautiful image when I saw one. I quickly removed the lens cap, set the focus just right, and took the picture, standing back to secure the sight in my mind as well as on the film in my camera.

* * *

As I walked out the front door of the camp house, I silently wished it weren't winter; I hadn't been out to Dad's favorite spot since my failed post-summer attempt years before, and now the lake was frozen. The opportunity was lost for the season. When my mom and I drove to Hayward to watch Dylan race in the famous annual cross-country skiing event, the Birkebeiner, I voiced my hesitation to leave without saying goodbye to Dad.

"I wish I could've gone out to see the pond one more time. I don't know if I'll make it out here this summer between work and writing; I'm gonna be busier than ever," I said to Mom while we moved through the crowded streets of Hayward.

"Well, it's kind of cold, but we can walk out there later if you want," she said nonchalantly.

"What are you talking about—you want me to walk on the ice? It's been warm the last few days—I think it'd be kind of dangerous?"

"No, silly. You don't have to walk on the ice. Just use the boardwalk."

"What boardwalk?" I asked, sensing that I'd been left out of some very important development.

"Oh, that's right. You weren't here last summer. I'm so sorry, honey. I can't believe we didn't tell you."

"Tell me what? I'm always the last to find out everything in this family. Case in point *right* here."

"Well, I thought the boys already told you, but I honestly just forgot. After you tried to portage there and couldn't make it that one time, the boys tried themselves and had to turn around just like you did."

"What—they didn't believe me that it's not passable anymore? Figures."

"No, no, no—I think they just wanted to see how bad it was. Anyway, Dylan and Mark built this gorgeous, long boardwalk that's kind of elevated and it leads right to the pond. It's still pretty well-hidden, but now we can get there from the other side without the canoes."

* * *

Dressed in fleece-lined pants and warm boots, I threw on a wool hat and walked toward the north end of the lake. I cut through the Trip House parking lot where the spot reserved for my mom's car still had a sign that read "Richard and Barbara," past the staff housing quarters Dad named for *Star Trek*'s "Worf," "The Enterprise," and

"Zulu Longhouse." I walked the trails Dad used to take to see the eagles' nest, the ground now solid and unforgiving beneath my feet. When I reached the end of the trail, I followed my mom's directions and looked for the frozen remains of a tree some beavers felled years earlier. The gnawed-off edges of the trunk pointed me down the slope of the hill and there I saw the beginning of the boardwalk.

I was impressed with Dylan and Mark; their craftsmanship represented well their urge to pay homage to our fathers. The wide planks of this wooden aisle emerged from the shoreline and formed a "T" at the edge of the drying pond. Walking toward the edge of the boardwalk offered a different view of the lake than I'd seen in the eighteen years I lived there. When I reached the pond, I couldn't believe how beautiful it looked from this side. The water was frozen over, with delicate filigrees of ice lacing the surface. The pond and surrounding marsh had changed, were evolving into something else as the lake cut itself off from the pond.

Before we drizzled the ashes there, I fantasized about a casket and a cemetery plot. Someplace traditional, someplace I could go. But sitting on the cold wooden bench at the edge of the boardwalk, I knew that it would always be better there in Dad's place at camp than a graveyard next to I-94 West could have been. I felt against my back the hard coldness of the bench's plaque that read IN MEMORY OF TWO BEST FRIENDS, RICHARD AND ALAN. I remembered paddling that October day—the colors of the sunset, peak leaves twisting in the trees. The varied shades of green filling the space around the water in layers. The inverted reflection of the trees, shrubs, and grasses, darkened by the tint of the lake water.

The trees were bare now, the sky mild with a late-afternoon winter sun. I folded my arms in front of me and tucked my cold hands into the folds of my jacket. Looking up past the naked trees and snow-patched swamp overtaking the pond, the eagles' nest stuck out of the brambles in the tallest pine tree, easy to see even without binoculars. When the sun began to dip down past the tips of the treetops, I stood to walk back toward the car. My hands tucked into my pockets, I looked down at the horizontal gaps between the planks of the boardwalk, some filled with patches of ice and some not. The faster I walked, the more quickly each plank blurred into the next, every piece of lumber showing a different design of cracks and stains.

As if I were a spool of thread growing fuller with every turn, each step I took made my heart feel bigger and warmer inside my chest. Unlike the other times I'd visited his ashes, I could feel my father's presence growing stronger alongside me the farther I walked away. While my feet passed over the last section of wood and then onto the frozen soil, I lifted my face toward the whitewashed sky and let the cold sunshine kiss my cheek.

Acknowledgments

This story owes infinite gratitude to many who gave so generously of their love, care, and attention.

Heartfelt thanks go to my partner in crime, Kelly Davio: Thank you for your friendship, your unceasing creative insight and encouragement, and your willingness to read those same four or forty or 400 pages just one more time. You guided me through the labyrinth of this book when all I could see before me were dead ends. This book is nearly as much yours as it is mine.

And to the rest of my literary family—my precious network of geniuses and artists—thank you all for your guidance over the years. Warm thanks go to Stefanie Freele, Carolyne Wright, David Wagoner, Caleb Barber, Bruce Holland Rogers, Mark Cull, Kate Gale, and Jennie Shortridge. Professors Ann Putnam and Hans Ostrom, who were there at the very beginning as my literary godparents, know just how very much I owe them for steering me in the right direction when I could scarcely see which end was up.

Gordon, you have championed me through every up and down of this long process, and I have been so lucky to have you on my side. You believed in *Girl* even when I couldn't. You're the best agent and friend a gal could hope for. Thanks also to Andrea, who saw the spark of something wonderful in this little story and fanned the flames. My brilliant editor, Julie—thank you a million times over for getting me to the finish line.

Thanks to the divine Miss Anastasia Lake, and Misters Tom Santay, Scott Walker, and Perry Holzchnecht (or something like that), for their many artistic, technical, and emotional contributions. And, of course, for the daily kvetching. Gracious thanks to Whitney Haas for your incredible patience and support, and for bringing me into the family. To my wonderful friends Rachel Alm, Beth Friedman, Victoria Simmonds, Jenna Brody, Cindy Stern, Jennifer Reiner, Rachel Kruse, the Silberman family, Peter Davio, David Swernoff, Ginny Morey, Scott Allison, and Kristian Unvericht for having my back. Barney and Uncle Wooby—I am so lucky to have you as surrogate fathers.

I'd like to express my fond appreciation to the greater camp community—a better bunch of people simply can't be found in this world. A warm thank-you goes to the Huse family for sharing your life and story with us; it has always been, and ever shall be, the utmost honor.

Most importantly of all, the deepest thanks go to my family: Gabe, Dylan, Erin, Maura, and Mom. The warmth of your love buoys me every single day. Mom, I am so proud to be your daughter and to carry on Dad's legacy—thank you for being our constant beacon of strength. My big brothers, Gabe and Dylan, thank you for taking the many tearful, late-night phone calls over the ten years it took me to complete this book. Without your memories and support, this book would not exist. None of this would mean anything without you.